Namo Guru Vajradhara
Vakindra Samati Shasanadhara
Samudra Shri Bhadra Ye Soaha

Homage to you, guru Vajradhara,
supreme lord of speech, mind of sublime clarity,
master of the exalted Teachings,
ocean of merit and wisdom,
glorious benevolence!

Tibet:
Treasures from the Roof of the World

བོད། འཛམ་གླིང་ཡང་རྩེའི་པོན་ཆེན་དངོས་རིགས།

TIBET:
TREASURES FROM THE ROOF OF THE WORLD

The Bowers Museum of Cultural Art,
Santa Ana, California

in collaboration with

The Bureau of Cultural Relics, Tibet Autonomous Region;

The Potala Palace; The Tibet Museum; and The Norbulingka

© 2003 Bowers Museum of Cultural Art, All rights reserved

ISBN: 0-9679612-4-6

Library of Congress: 2003107427

Exhibition organized by:
The Bowers Museum of Cultural Art,
Santa Ana, California in collaboration with
The Bureau of Cultural Relics, Tibet Autonomous Region;
The Potala Palace; The Tibet Museum; and The Norbulingka

This catalogue was made possible in part by grants from

The Giles W. & Elise G. Mead Foundation

Choice Lithographers

The Institute of Museum and Library Services by an Act of Congress

Guest Curators:

Terese Tse Bartholomew, guest curator and catalog author, M.A. History of Chinese Art, University California, Los Angeles, is Curator of Himalayan Art and Chinese Decorative Art at the Asian Art Museum of San Francisco, where she has served in the curatorial department since 1968. She was curator-in-charge of *Mongolia: The Legacy of Chinggis Khan* (1995) and wrote the catalog with Patricia Berger.

Patricia Berger, guest curator and catalog author, Ph.D. Chinese Art, University of California, Berkeley, is Associate Professor of the History of Art at the university. Previously, Berger served as Curator of Chinese Art at the Asian Art Museum of San Francisco. Her research interests are Chinese tomb art, Buddhist art, the art of Mongolia, and Himalayan art. Representative of her publications are *Tomb Treasures from Ancient China: The Buried Art of Xi'an* (1994) and *Mongolia: The Legacy of Chinggis Khan,* with Terese Bartholomew (1995).

Robert Warren Clark, guest curator and catalog author, Ph.D. Tibetan Studies, University of Virginia, is an independent scholar and consultant to the Himalayan Department at the Asian Art Museum of San Francisco, and Curator of the Bernard-Murray Collection of Tibetan Art and Artifacts at the University of California, Berkeley. Clark has lectured widely on Tibetan studies, and has translated over fifty-five Tibetan texts. He worked as an engineer at the private offices of His Holiness, the Dalai Lama, in Dharmasala, India, and is a Tibetan language interpreter for Tibetan Lamas teaching in the U.S.

Editors (Bowers Museum):
Vickie C. Byrd, M.A.
Kathy A. Hamilton
Nancy R. Johnson

Printed and bound in Taiwan by Choice Lithographers.

Design and composition: ThinkDesign, Buellton, California

Jacket, Front Cover Image:
Gateway to Lhasa, 1937
Photo: Theos Bernard
The Theos Bernard Collection,
Gift of the Eleanor Murray Estate.
Phoebe A. Hearst Museum of Anthropology,
University of California Berkeley,
(R XXIII-13).

Title Page Image:
Potala Court, 1937
Photo: Theos Bernard
The Theos Bernard Collection,
Gift of the Eleanor Murray Estate.
Phoebe A. Hearst Museum of Anthropology,
University of California, Berkeley
(RXXII-34).

DEDICATED TO

GILES W. MEAD

Teacher

Mentor

Environmentalist

Scientist

Museum Director

and

Friend

ACKNOWLEDGEMENTS

We wish to thank everyone who contributed to the success of:
Tibet: Treasures from the Roof of the World.
Unfortunately, there are far too many to acknowledge individually.

One person, however, stands out
Above all, and has touched the hearts
Of virtually everyone involved on both continents.

A *very special Thanks* goes to:

ANNE SHIH

Without whose perseverance, passion, and diplomacy
This exhibition would not have been possible.

MESSAGES

The Board of Trustees and staff of the Houston Museum of Natural Science are honored to host *Tibet: Treasures from the Roof of the World*. This remarkable exhibition is comprised of masterworks, many of which are central to the history and culture of Tibetan Buddhism. The priceless objects in this landmark exhibition have been generously loaned by the Potala Palace, the Tibet Museum and The Norbulingka in Lhasa, and have never before been seen in North America.

The influence of Buddhism on all aspects of Tibetan life can be seen in the many devotional and secular objects included in the exhibition. The exhibit explores the unique historical, religious and cultural achievements of this region, and we are honored to be able to share this rich cultural legacy with the people of Houston.

We wish to express our profound thanks and gratitude to the honorable Qiangba Gesang, Director, Potala Palace; Dan Zeng Lang Jie, Director, Tibet Museum; Rinchin Tsereng, Director, Administrative Bureau of Cultural Relics of Tibet Autonomous Region; and the State Administration of Cultural Heritage, People's Republic of China.

We would also like to recognize Dr. Peter C. Keller, President of the Bowers Museum of Cultural Art in Santa Ana, California, who, working with the officials in Lhasa and Beijing, gathered together a collection of unparalleled historic importance and graciously included the Houston Museum of Natural Science in the exclusive North American tour of this important exhibition.

Appreciation is also extended to the many supporters of *Tibet: Treasures from the Roof of the World*. Their generosity has ensured that countless visitors to the Houston Museum of Natural Science will have the opportunity to obtain a better understanding of the significance and beauty of the arts and culture of Tibet.

Rebecca A. McDonald
PRESIDENT, HOUSTON MUSEUM OF NATURAL SCIENCE

It is with great pleasure that the Rubin Museum of Art (RMA) welcomes *Tibet: Treasures from the Roof of the World* to its galleries. RMA, which opens spring 2004, is dedicated to the exhibition and conservation of Himalayan art. RMA collections consist of over 1,500 paintings, sculpture and ritual objects representing most major schools of Himalayan art since the 12th century. Himalayan art came relatively late to the notice of Western art critics and historians, although its beauty, craftsmanship and complex intellectual tradition rivals that of any culture. The Museum's intention is to make this art accessible to a wider public, and present it in such a manner as to promote further inquiry. Exhibitions from museums worldwide can be viewed on the website of the Himalayan Art Project (www.himalayanart.org), along with images from the RMA collections and thousands of other examples of Himalayan art.

The Board of Trustees and staff of RMA offer their thanks to Dr. Peter Keller for his vision and tenacity in bringing this significant exhibition to the United States. We also gratefully acknowledge our colleagues, Qiangba Gesang, Director, Potala Palace and Dan Zeng Lang Jie, Director, Tibet Museum, for their willingness to allow these treasures to be shared by American audiences.

RMA extends its respect and admiration to the curators, Terese Tse Bartholomew, Dr. Robert Clark and Professor Patricia Berger, whose collaborative efforts produced this fine exhibition and catalogue.

RMA is delighted to be the New York venue for *Tibet: Treasures from the Roof of the World*.

Donald Rubin
CHAIRMAN, RUBIN MUSEUM OF ART

The Asian Art Museum of San Francisco manifested its interest in Tibetan art in 1991, with the execution of the important exhibition, *Wisdom and Compassion, the Sacred Art of Tibet*, which attempted to define for the lay person the function of Tibetan religious art in its sacred context. Subsequent to that exhibition, the Museum also produced the landmark 1995 exhibition, *Mongolia, the Legacy of Chinggis Khan,* which, like *Wisdom and Compassion*, also featured the arts of esoteric or Tantric Buddhism, a form of the faith which gained acceptance and popularity in the regions of the Himalayas and Mongolia. Therefore, it is with great enthusiasm that we participate in this unique presentation, *Tibet: Treasures from the Roof of the World*, which is comprised of objects drawn entirely from the Potala Palace, the Tibet Museum and The Norbulingka in Lhasa. These wonderful works demonstrate the independent imagination and rich artistic quality that distinguishes the extraordinary tradition of sacred art in Tibet.

The Asian Art Museum extends its deep appreciation to Qiangba Gesang, Director, Potala Palace and Dan Zeng Lang Jie, Director, Tibet Museum for their courtesy and faith in assisting the exhibition of these important treasures for American audiences. The support of the State Administration of Cultural Heritage, People's Republic of China, and Rinchin Tsereng, Director, Administrative Bureau of Cultural Relics of Tibet Autonomous Region were also essential to the success of the show, and we are pleased to acknowledge their efforts with our thanks.

Dr. Peter C. Keller, President of the Bowers Museum of Cultural Art, and his Trustee, Mrs. Anne Shih, worked tirelessly to accomplish their mission to gather the best loans for the exhibition. We are indebted to them for their hard work and vision. The Asian Art Museum is also proud to recognize the contributions of the guest curators and catalogue authors, Terese Tse Bartholomew, Curator of Himalayan Art and Chinese Decorative Arts, Asian Art Museum of San Francisco; Professor Patricia Berger, Department of Art History, University of California, Berkeley; and independent scholar, Dr. Robert Clark, to this project. These seasoned professionals bring to the project the considerable scholarship and expertise an exhibition of this magnitude demands.

The Asian Art Museum is honored to host a San Francisco venue for the exhibition, and we are pleased to congratulate all who where involved in a job well done.

Emily J. Sano
DIRECTOR, ASIAN ART MUSEUM OF SAN FRANCISCO

PREFACE

Country of beauty, land of splendor, plateau covered with snow, mountains and rivers filled with wonder, this is the land known as Tibet. From time immemorial, the prehistoric forefathers who lived on the wonderland of the Tibetan plateau developed a unique highland culture. The excavated Neolithic sites of Ka Ruo in Chang Du, Qu Gong in Lhasa, Chang Guo in Shan Nan and many other places uncovered the mysterious veil of the legend of "Luo Sha", the origin of the Tibetan race.

Blessed by abundant natural endowments and pivotal geographic location bridging the East and the West, our ancestors created plentiful religious and historical heritages characterized by their simplicity, delicacy, profundity and grandeur. This cultural achievement was not only nourished by the Han culture from the central plains of China, it also absorbed the essence of surrounding ethnic cultures. This is indeed the pride of Tibetan culture and a treasure of human civilization.

The long-pursued mission of the Administrative Bureau of Cultural Relics of the Tibet Autonomous Region is to promote the world's appreciation of Tibetan culture and understanding of China as a whole. It is highly significant that, as human history stepped into 21st century, the Bowers Museum of Cultural Art, out of their fondness and caring for culture and art, invited us to hold this exhibition in the United States. Here we would like to celebrate the opening of this exhibition as scheduled, and deem it as a great event in the bilateral cultural exchanges between China and the United States.

It is my privilege to acknowledge and thank all related departments and people in China that have helped to make this exhibition possible. I wish to applaud Dr. Peter Keller, Mrs. Anne Shih and Mr. Edward Roski for their tireless efforts and many trips to Tibet. Their foresight and persistence have made this exhibition possible. We also admire the staff of the Bowers Museum for their hard work and dedication, and we wish to express our sincere appreciation to all of the visitors who will come to see these priceless objects.

There is no superiority or inferiority among cultures; no national boundaries or limits separating art. The best reward to all the pushing-hands of this exhibition is to offer an opportunity for the American people to gain an understanding and appreciation of Tibetan culture, history and art.

We truly wish peace and stability to the world and prosperity and happiness to all people. Tashi Deleg!

Rinchin Tsereng
DIRECTOR, ADMINISTRATIVE BUREAU OF CULTURAL RELICS,
TIBET AUTONOMOUS REGION, CHINA

FOREWORD

Over the past ten years or more, the Bowers Museum has focused its efforts on bringing important exhibitions from around the world to the people of California and beyond. Our mission is to "bridge world cultures through art." While we have brought a host of important exhibitions to southern California, none is more important than *Tibet: Treasures from the Roof of the World*. This exhibition consists of almost 200 masterworks, drawn almost entirely from the rich collections of the Potala Palace the recently opened Tibet Museum and The Norbulingka in Lhasa. The material is breathtaking; particularly when one considers that none of it has ever before been seen in the Western World. Interest in Tibet has been extremely high for westerners. Explorers since the mid-19th century have endured extreme hardships in their mostly failed attempts to reach the Holy City of Lhasa. There have been scores of important exhibitions on Tibetan culture, art, and religion, but none were able to draw upon these premier collections.

Tibet: Treasures from the Roof of the World focuses on the Potala Palace, built over a period of 50 years by the Fifth Dalai Lama and one of the largest such structures in the world, with 1,000 chambers. Through life in the Potala, the exhibition explores all aspects of Tibetan history and culture in a way beyond the popular notion of Tibet as a mythical Shangri-La. *Tibet: Treasures from the Roof of the World* is divided into four distinct sections. The first and most basic is the introduction, which focuses on the history of Tibet from the 7th - 19th century. The exhibit then explores Tibetan Buddhism through the use of its incredible ritual objects, Tibetan art, which is again related largely to the practice of Buddhism through its thangka paintings; stone, wooden, and metal sculptures and its incredibly detailed embroidery and other textiles. Finally, the exhibition focuses on the daily life of a Tibetan nobleman. Much can be learned through their clothing, jewelry, and daily utensils.

Two people deserve very special thanks; Ed Roski and Anne Shih. Ed accompanied me, as our Tibet Committee chair, along with Board member Anne Shih, on our initial trip to Tibet in May of 2001. His support, enthusiasm and encouragement led to five more trips to Tibet to negotiate contracts, select objects, and gather background information on the exhibition. But, as in all important projects in life, it is the personal relationships that make things happen. If it were not for the hours and hours of negotiations by Anne, as well as her charm and sensitivity to protocol, this historic exhibition would never have become a reality. Because this exhibition is so important, the Bowers Museum was fortunate to invite three leading scholars in the field, Terese Tse Bartholomew, Patricia Berger, and Robert W. Clark, Ph.D. to provide essays and organize the exhibition as our guest curators. The Tibetans have worked very hard on the exhibition as well, and I am very pleased to have the opportunity to acknowledge Qiangba Gesang, Director, Potala Palace; Dan Zeng Lang Jie, Director, Tibet Museum; Ni Ma, Director, Norbulingka Administration Office; State Administration of Cultural Heritage, People's Republic of China; Rinchin Tsereng, Director, Administrative Bureau of Cultural Relics of Tibet Autonomous Region and staff; Wang Mingxing, Deputy Party Secretary, Chiang Yang, Director General, and Ma Rulong, Party Secretary, Tibet Cultural Department; Zhong Jianhua, Consul General of People's Republic of China in Los Angeles; Wang Qingzheng, Director, Chen Xiejun, Director, and Chen Kelun, Deputy Director, Shanghai Museum. They were incredibly cooperative, yet very mindful of the importance of the objects and the risks involved in letting them travel to the West for the first time. I also would like to thank Congresswoman Loretta Sanchez for her enthusiastic support of this exhibition.

An exhibition of this magnitude and complexity cannot become a reality without significant financial support. Ed Roski not only offered his advice and personal support as Chairman of our Tibet Committee, but brought important financial support as well, by hosting all of our Tibetan curators and dignitaries while in southern California. We are also deeply grateful to our many other sponsors, including Donald Murray of Resources Connection; The Leo Freedman Foundation; The Giles W. & Elise G. Mead Foundation; D. Diane Anderson and David Poiry; Tiffany & Co; John and Mary Tu; and many others who provided major financial support for this historic exhibition.

The Bowers Museum has been forging friendships with museums throughout China and all of Asia for many years. In doing so, we believe that we are providing an important bridge between our vastly different cultures. *Tibet: Treasures from the Roof of the World* is hopefully providing a new understanding of Tibet's great history, art, and culture to the people of the western world. The sacred arts of Tibet are comparable to any of the great religious centers of the world. For the first time, westerners have the opportunity to experience these arts on the very highest level. The Bowers Museum is very proud to have been able to make this a reality.

Peter C. Keller, Ph.D.
President, The Bowers Museum of Cultural Art

Front View of the Potala, 1937
Photo: Theos Bernard
The Theos Bernard Collection, Gift of the
Eleanor Murray Estate.
Phoebe A. Hearst Museum of Anthropology,
University of California, Berkeley (XXII-27).

CONTENTS

INTRODUCTION
PATRICIA BERGER
17

TIBET: ITS LAND AND HISTORY
ROBERT W. CLARK
21

TIBET: ITS RELIGION AND RITUAL
ROBERT W. CLARK
57

SACRED ARTS OF TIBET
TERESE TSE BARTHOLOMEW
125

DIPLOMATIC GIFTS
PATRICIA BERGER
128

LIFE IN LHASA, THE HOLY CITY
TERESE TSE BARTHOLOMEW
201

END NOTES
252

BIBLIOGRAPHY
254

INTRODUCTION

PATRICIA BERGER

Lhasa-The Potala Palace

My pulse quickened as we rode through the Pargo Kaling—the Western Gate—an archway cut through an imposing *chorten*, and found ourselves directly under the Potala. That fabulous and monumental building dominates the whole landscape around Lhasa and always presents another fascinating perspective, no matter from what part of the city or nearby countryside it is viewed. With the gold-roofed Potala, the monasteries and temples glistening in the sun, the crowds of people in their gay, picturesque costumes, Lhasa seemed to me like a rich illustration from a medieval manuscript, magically brought to life.

Lowell Thomas, Jr., *Out of This World: Across the Himalayas to Forbidden Tibet* (1950)

The Potala Palace (Figure 1), commanding the view over the Tibetan capital of Lhasa, has stirred the imagination of Buddhist pilgrims and foreign adventurers for centuries. The Potala is, without doubt, one of the most powerful symbols of Tibet, a magnificent structure consciously designed to evoke awe and reverence in those who approach it. The soaring red and white masonry walls protect a complex series of interlocked structures that are said to contain a thousand rooms. Built upon the remains of a 7th century royal palace, the site was completely transformed in the 17th century to accommodate the religious and administrative functions of the Dalai Lamas and has been frequently renovated ever since.

The Potala has particularly profound meaning for Tibetan Buddhists, because it contains stupas (Tibetan: *chorten*, reliquaries) that house the remains of eight of the Dalai Lamas. Dozens of elaborately furnished Buddhist temples and shrines, each dedicated to a different deity, occupy half of its floor space, and grand audience halls designed for the entertainment of Tibetan and foreign dignitaries, as well as a warren of administrative offices and storerooms, fill the rest. The Potala's double function as sacred and worldly space, distinguished so clearly in its red and white walls, corresponds to the complex religious and political role that the Dalai Lamas played, beginning with the ascendancy of Ngawang Losang Gyatso (1617-1682), who is universally honored with the epithet "Great Fifth."

The name "Potala" refers to "Potalaka," the Bodhisattva of Compassion, Avalokiteshvara's (Tibetan: Chenrezig) mountain home, which Buddhist tradition locates in southern India. The royal and monastic masters of the Potala site, including the early Religious King Songtsen Gampo and all the Dalai Lamas, have been considered emanations of Avalokiteshvara at least since the time of the Fifth Dalai Lama. Tradition also holds that the Fifth Dalai Lama's choice of Red Hill (Tibetan: Marpo Ri) from a number of other possible sites around Lhasa was sanctified by the discovery of an ancient image of Arya Avalokiteshvara in a cave beneath the original 7th century palace.

The choice of Lhasa as Tibet's capital was made during an epoch of Tibetan history when the early Yarlung kings had consolidated their power and had begun to build a major empire in Central Asia. In 631, King Songtsen Gampo, who was just fifteen years old at the time, moved his government from the ancient home of the Tibetan kings, the Yarlung Valley south of the Tsangpo River, northwest to Lhasa, where he built a large, multi-roomed palace on the site of the Potala, Red Hill. This early palace was immense, said to measure thirty "planks" in height. Tradition has it that there were three rings of walls and a total of nine hundred and ninety-nine rooms even in Songtsen Gampo's time. But warfare, natural calamities, and a devastating fire at the end of the 7th century all took their toll and the original palace was severely damaged. What remains of Songtsen Gampo's building on the Red Hill are the Phagpa Lhakhang, which contains the Arya Avalokiteshvara, considered the most sacred image in the Potala; and the Chogyal Drubphuk, a cave that houses extraordinarily vivid sculptural images of Songtsen Gampo and his retinue.

Figure 1
Gateway to Lhasa, 1937
Photo: Theos Bernard
The Theos Bernard Collection,
Gift of the Eleanor Murray Estate.
Phoebe A. Hearst Museum of
Anthropology, University of California
Berkeley, (R XXIII-13).

In 1645, the Great Fifth Dalai Lama, Ngawang Losang Gyatso (1617-1682)—the first of the lineage actually to rule Tibet—decided to move his administration from Ganden Podrang, a residence within Drepung Monastery, to a more advantageous site. Ganden Podrang did not fulfill the Dalai Lama's newly felt needs for a large, imposing, prestigious building. Following the model of Jangchub Gyaltsen (1302-1372), who had changed the Tibetan political landscape by dividing the country into districts, each one dominated by a large fortress, the Dalai Lama planned a new palace that would be designed like a castle and placed in a strategic position overlooking Lhasa.

Also in 1645, the Dalai Lama commissioned his very able secretary and treasurer, Sangye Gyatso (1653-1705), to begin work on the first major portion of the Potala, the so-called White Palace (Tibetan: Podrang Karpo) (Figure 2). The site for the palace came down to two choices: Lhasa and Gongkar Dzong. Gongkar Dzong offered a number of advantages; it was close to some of the most important monasteries of the Dalai Lama's Gelug order, including Sera, Drepung, and Ganden. But Lhasa's Red Hill was also still vividly remembered as the site of King Songtsen Gampo's palace and Lhasa was emerging as an important pilgrimage site for Tibetan Buddhists, particularly during the Great Prayer ceremony (Monlam), held at the New Year, which Tsongkhapa, the founder of the Gelug order, instituted in 1408 at the Jokhang. So Red Hill was selected for its historical associations, its relevance to Tibetan religious life, and its auspicious, protected location between mountains that rise five thousand meters above a swampy marshland. The decision was validated with the discovery of the Arya Avalokiteshvara image, just as the first foundations were laid. Red Hill came to be identified with Avalokiteshvara, just as Chakpo Ri (Iron Hill) is Vajrapani, and Bhama Ri with Manjushri. Lhasa's topography was thus redefined as a sacred landscape, under the benign protection of the great Bodhisattvas.

Figure 2
White Palace of the Potala
Photo: Peter C. Keller, Ph.D.

The Dalai Lama did not occupy the nine-story White Palace until 1649, after the extensive murals in the eastern section of the palace were completed and several major shrines installed. With his move, this part of the palace became the administrative center of the Gelug order and of the whole of Tibet. Records, some of them contradictory, suggest that it was not until 1690, eight years after the Fifth Dalai Lama's death in 1682 (an event Sangye Gyatso, now Regent of Tibet, concealed for a total of twelve years), that work began on the Red Palace (Podrang Marpo), the second major part of the Potala. The Red Palace, with its great Western Audience Chamber surrounded by four two-story chapels, placed at each of the hall's corners, was the heart of Buddhist Tibet. The Fifth Dalai Lama initially conceived the Red Palace as a site to house his own stupa. It presently holds the remains of seven of his successors as well (excluding the poetic Sixth, whose decidedly unmonastic life ended in his violent and mysterious death in 1706).

Work on the exterior structure of the Red Palace, which the Regent placed under the direction of the engineer Bokgong Monpa Lodro Gyaltsen, was finished in 1693. However, it took four more years to complete the elaborate and labyrinthine interior. Seven thousand workers toiled on the vast structure, along with one thousand five hundred artists and craftsmen. Foreign craftsmen participated as well; nearly two hundred Nepalese artists worked side-by-side with their Tibetan colleagues (giving the murals of the Potala a particularly Nepalese flavor), and the Manchu Kangxi Emperor of the Qing Dynasty (reigned 1662-1722) sent seven Chinese and ten Manchu craftsmen to assist in the complex project. Studies of the structure of the Potala suggest that its present exterior contours evolved over a long period of continual renovation (part of the White Palace, for example, was demolished to accommodate the construction of the Red Palace). A drawing based on the first-hand observations of the German Jesuit Johann Grueber, who arrived in Lhasa from Beijing in 1661, already shows the Potala's familiar and imposing face, with encircling walls in place and the entire east-west span (three hundred sixty meters in length) clearly laid out.

The Regent may well have purposefully stalled construction on the Red Palace to help conceal the death of the Fifth Dalai Lama from foreign powers, and thus curtail Mongolian and Manchu meddling into the choice of the next incarnation (who would be the irreverent Sixth) and interference during his childhood and youth. When the Fifth Dalai Lama's stupa was completed in 1692 and his remains and reincarnation both safely installed, the Regent broke the news of his death.

The Potala stands as a monument to the wide-ranging religious and political genius of the Great Fifth Dalai Lama. The Fifth Dalai Lama was an active player in the spiritual debates of his day and, moreover, he was also a political strategist who literally transformed the face of east and central Asia, from the Manchu Qing Empire in China to Mongolia, Siberia, and the farthest reaches of western Tibet and southwestern Russia. The Potala became a hub of diplomatic activity during his lifetime, when extraordinary gifts, some of them important historical objects, already antique when they were presented to the Dalai Lama, poured into its coffers from all sides. As Heinrich Harrer recalled from his experience filming the whitewashing of the Potala's walls, when he was granted extraordinary access to its hidden chambers:

> I was allowed to enter any room in the palace. Many of them were pitch-dark with their windows blocked by piles of lumber accumulated during the centuries, through which I had to fight my way to the light. The effort was worthwhile. I found old, forgotten statues of the Buddha before which no butter lamps now burned and, hidden beneath thick layers of dust, numbers of splendid tankas.
>
> (*Seven Years in Tibet*, 1953)

The immense riches held in the Potala even today more than fulfill the expectations raised by the Chinese name for much of Tibet: Xizang, which might be translated as "Western Treasury." The inventory of its collections still records a total of some twenty thousand statues and stupas, twenty-five thousand Tibetan historical documents in Tibetan script, five hundred Indian palm leaf sutras brought back by Tibetan monks, two thousand five hundred square meters of murals, untold thousands of thangkas of various sizes and materials, and thousands of ritual implements, some from China and elsewhere. These objects demonstrate the importance of the Potala as a major center of Buddhist ritual, practice, and scholarship, where religious activity had important political ramifications.

Beginning in the middle of the 18th century, the Norbulingka (Jewel Park) (Figure 3), more than a hundred acres of pavilions, palaces, ponds, native and exotic animals, flowering plants, and trees on the western outskirts of Lhasa, served as the official summer residence of the Dalai Lamas. The habit of leaving the Potala during the warm summer months evolved under the Seventh Dalai Lama (Kelsang Gyatso, 1708-1757), who went there to bathe in a medicinal spring each summer. He eventually had a formal pavilion built at the spring and, in 1755, ordered the construction of a palace nearby (Kelsang Podrang, named after him). All of his successors moved to the Norbulingka on the eighteenth day of the third lunar month (late spring), returning to the Potala in autumn. The Eighth Dalai Lama especially enjoyed Norbulingka and spent a great deal of time there in meditation. He also supervised one of the largest expansions of the site and its gardens. Many of the buildings in the Norbulingka's park were completed in the late 19th and 20th centuries, during the lifetimes of the Thirteenth and Fourteenth Dalai Lamas.

The Fourteenth Dalai Lama's new palace, Takten Migyur Podrang, was the last major construction at Norbulingka. The garden-like setting of the palace was a place where the Dalai Lamas could retreat from political life and pursue Buddhist goals through extended meditation. Its halls were thus equipped with all manner of Buddhist sculpture, painting, and ritual implements. Many of these objects eventually came into the collection of the Tibet Museum, which opened in October 1999.

This exhibition, organized by the Bowers Museum of Cultural Art in association with the Potala Palace and the Tibet Museum, is the first ever to present to American audiences objects from collections in Lhasa, including the Potala Palace, the Norbulingka, and the Tibet Museum. This event has only a few precedents: the 1991 exhibition, "A Well-Selected Collection of Tibetan Cultural Relics," held at the Palace Museum, Beijing, which was shown simultaneously with "Cultural Relics of Tibetan Buddhism Collected in the Qing Palace," a show that brought together a group of Tibeto-Chinese objects from the 18th century Manchu court, drawn from the Palace Museum's own collection. Most recently, in 2000, the exhibition "Treasures from Snow Mountains" opened at the Shanghai Museum with many of the same objects included here.

The uniquely Tibetan Potala Palace, gazing out over the landscape of the roof of the world, has been a memorable symbol in the minds of many of Tibet's inaccessibility and aloofness from its neighbors. However, its extraordinary contents, which have survived political turmoil and natural disasters, provide a clear record of the Tibetans' long history of creative interaction with peoples along its borders. As visitors to this exhibition will see, Tibet was never really a sealed "hermit kingdom" and, from earliest times, its Buddhist traditions were strikingly cosmopolitan, closely interwoven with those of its neighbors in India, Mongolia, Nepal, and China. Yet Tibetan culture and Tibetan Buddhism have their own particular brilliance. This exceptional cultural flowering, which survives in the objects presented here, is undeniably an invaluable part of the world's common heritage.

Figure 3
A view of the gardens at the Norbulingka (Jewel Park)
Photo: Peter C. Keller, Ph.D.

Tibet: Its Land and History

Robert W. Clark

The highest land mass in the world, the Tibetan plateau and its associated Tibetan ethnic areas encompass over a million square miles. That is over five times the size of the state of Texas. Tibet is a country of geographical extremes. In the south is the highest point on earth, Mt. Everest (*Jo mo gangs dkar,* Lady of the White Glacier). In the north, the land falls precipitously from the high peaks of the Kunlun and Altyn Tagh mountain ranges on Tibet's border, down to the lowest spot on earth in the Tarim Basin of Eastern Turkestan.

Tibet is in South Asia, with the southeastern tip lying further south than Miami, about two hundred forty miles north of the borders of Laos and Vietnam. The southern slopes of the Tibetan plateau are covered with steaming jungles where rice, cinnamon, and spices are grown and giant leeches plague the traveler.[1] The Chumbi Valley in the Pari region of the south has semi-tropical rain forests where oranges and bananas are cultivated and fabulous orchids grow wild. The bamboo jungles of East Tibet are the home of one of Tibet's most beloved native species, the panda.

From these lower elevations on the edges of the Tibetan plateau, the land rises suddenly to dizzying heights; the high valleys on top support thriving agricultural areas. The vast grasslands and alpine meadows of Tibet provide some of the best pastureland in the world. With fertile soil, and an abundance of bright sunlight and seasonal rains, a large variety of nutritious grasses and broadleaf plants support great herds of goat, horse, donkey, sheep, cattle, yak, and *dzo* (a yak/cattle hybrid). The female of the yak, known as the *dri*, provides milk, butter, and cheese.

Over two hundred species of mammals are native to Tibet, including varieties of the sheep, bear, squirrel, deer, bat, leopard, wolf, rabbit, badger, dog, cat, kogar (a small mountain cat), horse, jackal, civet, monkey, marmot, porcupine, gazelle, pig, otter, fox, skunk, hyena, antelope, donkey, tiger, weasel, and, of course, the yak and its huge cousin, the wild *drong* (*'brong*). Tibet has over five hundred species of birds, nearly one hundred species of reptiles and amphibians, and thousands of distinctive insects. With its many climate zones, there is a wide variety of plants in the southern and lower valleys of Tibet including asparagus, bamboo, betel nut palm, cherry, blueberry, breadfruit, camphor, cardamom, dandelion, delphinium, edelweiss, fig, fir, ginseng, gooseberry, grape, hemlock, holly, honeysuckle, mahogany, maple, mint, oak, orchid, plum, poplar, rhododendron, rhubarb, spruce, sycamore, almond, willow, lemon, and orange.[2]

Tibet is known for its extensive mineral wealth, including borax, cesium, copper, gold, gypsum, iron, lead, magnesium, rock salt, silver, tin, and uranium. Tibet has far more mountain glaciers than anywhere in the world. With over twenty thousand square miles under glaciers, Tibet earns its ancient name "*Gangchen*" (land of glaciers). The most common high altitude crop is a variety of barley that can be grown even in valleys over fifteen thousand feet. In lower elevations in the south, corn, wheat, and rice are cultivated. Other common crops, especially in the south of Tibet, include varieties of apples, apricots, bananas, berries, cabbage, cauliflower, celery, garlic, grapes, onions, oranges, pears, radishes, tea, and turnips.[3]

In the regions of central and southern Tibet that lie at lower elevations, the Tibetan diet takes full advantage of many varieties of meat, grain, vegetables, and fruit. In the north and at higher elevations, the diet is based mostly on barley, the meat of the yak and sheep, and dairy products from the *dri*. A common high-altitude meal would be a soup made from yak meat with salt, onion, and ginger for flavor, and perhaps some turnip or wild greens. Hot peppers may be added. Barley grains are roasted and then ground into a powder called *tsampa*. This may be moistened with the yak meat broth and formed into balls to be enjoyed with the soup. As an alternative to *tsampa,* wheat flour is used to make noodles for the soup. Yogurt made from the milk of the *dri* is a favorite desert. Tea churned with *dri* milk and a small amount of butter and salt is the national drink of Tibet.

Entrance to Lhasa, 1937
Photo: Theos Bernard
The Theos Bernard Collection,
Gift of the Eleanor Murray Estate.
Phoebe A. Hearst Museum of Anthropology,
University of California Berkeley (XXII-39).

From the highlands of Tibet come the greatest rivers of Asia. In the west are the headwaters of the Indus, Sutlej, Jamuna, and Ganges. From the south of Tibet comes the Brahmaputra, and from the east, the Yellow River, the Yangzi, Mekong, and Salween. Tibet has an abundance of vast, deep lakes, including Koko Nor (Tibetan: mTsho sngon) that is over sixty miles across, and deeper than any of the Great Lakes in North America.

The borders of Tibet, as with most countries, have shifted with changes in regimes, political fortunes, and military power. Since the Chinese takeover in 1959, Tibet has been divided into sections, so that parts are now included in the Chinese regions of Xizang, Qinghai, Sichuan, Gansu, and Yunnan. Other areas that are historically and ethnically Tibetan are Sikkhim and Bhutan, and neighboring parts of India and Nepal. The people of these lands share a common culture, religion, and language, as well as racial and ethnic characteristics dating back to their Paleolithic ancestors. The Tibetan language has over two hundred major dialects, all sharing a common written and literary language, but not necessarily a mutually intelligible spoken form. Tibetan is related to Burmese, being part of the Tibetan-Burmese language group.[4] It is not related to any Chinese, Indian, or other known language.

Tibet is situated between the two most populous countries on earth, India and China. However, its vast land is home to only a small population of Tibetans, around five million in 1950. This is less than four people per square mile, as compared to over thirteen thousand people per square mile in Hong Kong. The sparse population is at least partly a function of the high altitude. The highest peaks are nearly thirty thousand feet above sea level. Much of the plateau is above sixteen thousand feet, with vast areas covered by glaciers. Most of the population lives in the lower valleys of the south, where the average elevation is around twelve thousand feet. This is low enough to support sustained agriculture, but not enough for a large population. Before 1959, Tibet never suffered from famine, as the population was kept in balance with the environment. The Buddhist culture of Tibet has imparted a profound sense of respect for nature that seeks harmony with the environment rather than mastery over it.

The geological record tells us that the plateau of Tibet began to rise from a primordial sea some two hundred million years ago. Evidence shows that a land mass collided with the southern coast of Asia and formed the area now known as northern Tibet, Laos, Cambodia and Vietnam. A few million years later, another land mass joined to form central Tibet, Burma, Thailand, and Malaysia. Finally, about forty million years ago, the land mass of India and southern Tibet collided with South Asia and began pushing up the Himalayan range.[5] It is still growing today, four to eight-tenths of an inch per year.[6] Being the highest land mass in the world, Tibet is a natural fortress. It is surrounded by high mountain ranges that prevented any large-scale sustained invasion from foreign lands, until the second half of the 20th century, when modern mechanized armies, with aircraft and tanks, were finally able to breach its boundaries.

Tibetan legend speaks of a time in the remote past when the land had just risen out of the ocean and no humans lived in Tibet. The Bodhisattva Avalokiteshvara, seeking to benefit the beings of this world, decided to create the Tibetan race. He manifested a monkey-like form who took up his abode in the high snow mountains, entering a meditation on universal compassion. At length, he heard the distant cries of a lonely demoness. Wild and lustful by nature, she wandered the vast empty plateau in search of a companion. Monkey, moved by compassion, invited her into his cave, and satisfied her desire. From their union were born six ape-like children who lacked tails and walked upright. These were the first Tibetans. In this manner, Tibetans account for their remote origins, as well as a unique combination of a wise and compassionate heart, and a wild, colorful, and indomitable spirit (see no.1).[7]

Archaeological evidence establishes the existence of early humans on the Tibetan plateau in the Paleolithic age, as early as thirty-three thousand years ago.[8] The Tibetan people who developed from these early ancestors are some of the hardiest people in the world, famous for their longevity and physical vigor. Before the establishment of Buddhism, Tibetans were known throughout Asia as fierce and powerful warriors.

In the reign of the thirty-second King of Tibet, Songtsen Gampo (ca. 618-650 C.E., see nos. 2, 3 & 5), Tibet was the master of much of Asia. He was the first of the Dharmarajas (great religious kings). His armies descended from the high plateau and dominated Central Asia and its Silk Road in the north, Nepal and parts of northern India in the south and west, and much of China in the east. Songtsen Gampo sent his chief minister, Gar Tongtsen (mGar stong rtsan) to the powerful kingdom of Nepal to receive the tribute of King Amshuvarman (see no. 4). He asked the king to send the Royal Princess, Bhrikuti, and an extensive dowry, as gifts for the Tibetan king. Before their wedding, she presented Songtsen Gampo with a fabulous gilded bronze image of Shakyamuni Buddha, appearing in the form of an eight-year old Akshobhyavajra (a tantric form of Buddha), as well as an opulent image of Buddha Maitreya, and a precious sandalwood image of the Goddess Tara.[9] These became the precious national treasures of Tibet, and were honored in the temples of Lhasa for over one thousand three hundred years, until they were destroyed by the Chinese Cultural Revolution in the 1960s.

Gar Tongtsen was then sent, with a military expedition, to the capital of China, Chang-an (Xi'an). There, the Tang Emperor Taizong (reigned 627-649), offered his daughter, Princess Wencheng (Tibetan: Chu'i nang gi Padma, Water Lotus), and a fabulous dowry, hoping the Tibetans would allow him to keep his throne. Her dowry included a choice selection of the imperial treasures of China: thousands of the finest silks and brocades, precious jewels and delicate ivory carvings, powerful weapons, and ingenious devices for utility and pleasure. She brought an extensive library of all the arts and sciences of China, as well as treasures of Buddhist literature transmitted from India. However, the greatest of her gifts was a golden statue of Lord Buddha at the age of twelve called the Jowo Rinpoche. According to Buddhist texts, this image was made by the heavenly artist Vishvakarman in the presence of Shakyamuni Buddha himself. It had been sent to China many generations earlier by an Indian Buddhist King to convert the Chinese. Jowo Rinpoche is known to possess the personal powers and blessings of Shakyamuni, such that anyone who looks upon him with the eyes of faith will be released from the miseries of the cycles of birth and death. Jowo Rinpoche was installed in the great temple of Lhasa, which then took his name, the Jokhang (house of the Jowo). It is still there today and is the chief object of worship for pilgrims in Tibet. Princess Wencheng did much to advance the cause of Buddhism in Tibet, including building the great temple of Ramoche in Lhasa. She is considered by Buddhists to be an emanation of the Goddess Tara.[10]

At that time, the Tibetan language had no standard written form. King Songtsen Gampo sent his minister Thomi Sambhota to India to study its system of orthography and grammar.[11]

After years of study; he returned and created the Tibetan alphabet with its thirty consonants and five vowels. He composed eight volumes on grammar and literary arts. Songtsen Gampo also invited many great Buddhist scholars from India and Nepal to help him establish Buddhism in Tibet. These included the Acharyas (professors) Kumara, Brahmanashangkara, and Shilamanju. They worked with Tibetan scholars to translate a large number of sutra and tantra texts (i.e., the general and the mystical teachings of Buddha). Songtsen Gampo also sent an army of artisans to China and built a number of shrines and temples on Wutaishan (Five Peak Mountain), abode of Bodhisattva Manjushri.[12]

In this manner, Buddhism was established in Tibet. It had first come to Tibet in the year 433 C.E., when King Lhatho Thori received sets of Buddhist texts from India. However, linguistic obstacles prevented reading these texts. He also received the Six Syllable Mantra ("Om Mani Padme Hum") and a golden stupa. Though he honored and preserved these sacred objects, they were not really understood until the time of Songtsen Gampo, five generations later.

The next great king (Dharmaraja) after Songtsen Gampo was the thirty-seventh King of Tibet, Trisong Detsen (ca. 740-798). Realizing that Buddhism had a tenuous hold in Tibet as it was limited to the elite circles of central Tibet, King Trisong Detsen was determined that it be available to everyone throughout the vast realm of Tibet. He was also concerned with establishing the pristine, original form of Buddhism, as taught by the Buddha himself. To this end, he invited the most famous and venerated Buddhist scholar in India, Shantarakshita. At this time, there was much opposition to Buddhism from the powerful priestly class of the indigenous religions and spirit cults of Tibet, as well as from the gods and demons they propitiated.

Shantarakshita, a master of the sutras and tantras, found none who could stand up to him in the academies of India when it came to debates on logic, philosophy, or epistemology. However, he was at a loss to deal with the wild demons of Tibet and their human partisans. He therefore prevailed on King Trisong Detsen to invite the Buddhist yogin and mystic, Padma Sambhava (see no. 6). Padma Sambhava had a reputation of converting non-Buddhists through his miraculous deeds, and converting demons through his mystic powers. Legend says he refused the royal escort sent to bring him to Tibet and, instead, mounted a tiger and crossed the high Himalayas in a few days.

Meanwhile, back in Tibet, opposition to Buddhism had reached a point of crisis. Opponents and their demonic forces were poised to destroy Buddhism and its supporters. Tibetan religious histories record epic battles between Padma Sambhava and the demons and local gods of Tibet. One by one, Padma Sambhava won over the opponents. He forced the gods to accept his logic and the demons to acknowledge his power. All of them, together with their human followers, swore perpetual allegiance to the Buddha. Among these early non-Buddhist traditions were the predecessors of the Bon religion of Tibet. Since the time of Padma Sambhava, they gradually took on much of the philosophies and disciplines of Buddhism. In modern times, the Bon religion is very similar to Buddhism, distinguished more by its myths and history than its religious views and practices.

Padma Sambhava joined King Trisong Detsen and Shantarakshita in building the first great Buddhist monastery in Tibet, Samye. They were joined by other distinguished Buddhist teachers of Tibet, including the translators Vairochana, Nyag Jyanakumara, Kawa Paltseg and Chogro Lu Gyaltsen. Together, they founded monasteries and monastic schools throughout Tibet and its neighboring lands. They translated a tremendous body of Buddhist literature, including large parts of the Buddhist canon (*Tripitaka*). Trisong Detsen, Padma Sambhava, and Shantarakshita together overcame forces that threatened to extinguish Buddhism in

Tibet, and established it in many lands where it had never appeared before. In these ways, they were probably more effective than anyone in history until the present-day figure of the Fourteenth Dalai Lama.

The forty-first King of Tibet, Tri Ralpachen (reigned 814-836, see no. 5), was the third of the three Dharmarajas of Tibet. He used the power of his throne and his tireless efforts to consolidate Buddhism throughout Tibetan lands. He built over one thousand buildings for the study and practice of Buddhism. He established legal and economic structures for the support of monastic Buddhists. Ralpachen is also honored for the many important Buddhist teachers he brought from India, including Jinamitra, Surendrabodhi, Silendrabodhi, and Danashila. He sponsored new translations of Sanskrit Buddhist texts, such as the sixteen volume Prajnaparamita text of one hundred thousand quatrains (see no. 38). He promoted the revision of texts translated in earlier times, to clarify obscure passages and to develop new standards of accuracy and exegesis. A layman himself, Ralpachen is remembered for his humble reverence for monks who upheld the monastic rules (*Vinaya*) given by the Buddha.[13]

After the time of these three Dharmarajas, Tibet faced a period of upheaval with the brief reign of the forty-second King, Lang Darma (reigned 836-842). Lang Darma and his partisans disliked Buddhism. Where Tibet was once the most powerful force in Asia, conquering lands near and far, it was now tamed and subdued. Buddhism had turned Tibetans inward. Rejecting the ephemeral pleasures of the material world, they meditated and prayed for the transcendent states of Buddhas and Bodhisattvas. Great warriors were thus turned to quiescent and scholarly monks. Lang Darma violently repressed Buddhism, destroying monasteries, libraries, and senior teachers. Soon he met his own violent end, but not before he caused great harm to Buddhist institutions. Over the next century, Tibetans struggled to restore Buddhism. However there was much confusion and loss of direction.[14]

Surviving Buddhist masters (Lamas) established themselves in East Tibet (Kham) and gradually, Buddhism was reestablished there. Others invited distinguished teachers from India or went there themselves to learn the authentic Buddhist traditions in the great universities of their homeland. From this period, the 10th and 11th centuries, come some of the major figures that shaped Buddhism for the next thousand years. These include Atisha (Dipankara Shrijnana), Drom Tonba, Rinchen Zangbo, Pa Dampa Sangye, Machig Labdron, and Marpa the Translator.

In the next several centuries, four great traditions differentiated themselves. The first, which traced itself back to the arrival of Padma Sambhava in Tibet (810 C.E.), was the Nyingma (Old School). The Nyingma emphasize the tantric traditions brought to Tibet by Padma Sambhava, and known as the Dzogchen (Great Perfection). It was Longchenpa (1308-1363) and Jigme Lingba (1729-1798) who gave the Nyingma system a philosophical basis and dynamic structure that integrates the tantric treasures (*terma*) of Padma Sambhava[15] with the mainstream of traditional Buddhism.

The Kagyu (Oral Lineage) was brought to Tibet by Marpa the Translator (b. 1012) and taught to his disciple Milarepa the Translator (see no. 7). Milarepa's principle disciple was Gampopa. He had several distinguished disciples who founded different lines of the Kagyu tradition. One of these was Dusum Khyenpa, the first Karmapa. After he died, a young boy, Karma Pakshi, was recognized as his rebirth. He was followed by the third Karmapa, Rangjung Dorje (see no. 8). In this way, the tradition of recognizing reborn Lamas (*tulku*) began in Tibet. The present Karmapa is the seventeenth in this line.

Founder of the Sakya tradition in Tibet, Khon Konchog Gyalpo (1034-1102) followed the *Lam Dre* and *Hevajratantra* teachings of the great Indian Buddhist master Virupa as translated and taught in Tibet by Drogmi (992-1072), Atisha, and others. He and his successors such as Sakya Pandita Kunga Gyaltsen, Phagpa (1235-1280), Kunga Nyingpo (1092-1158), and Drakpa Gyaltsen (1147-1216) established the Sakya as the preeminent power in Tibet for several centuries. Their success was due to their profound knowledge of Buddhist lore, and their skill in establishing alliances with the Mongols (see no. 85).[16]

The latest of the four traditions is the Gelug, founded by Je Tsongkhapa (1357-1419), which incorporated the Kadampa teachings of Atisha (Dipankara Shrijnana, arrived in Tibet in 1039) and his disciple, the translator Drom Tonba (1004-1064 a.k.a., Gyalwei Jungne). Together with his disciples, principally, Khedrub Je and Gyaltsab Je, Je Tsongkhapa gathered the vast Buddhist canon with its commentaries, and presented them in concise, practical texts known as Lam Rim (Stages of the Path). This organized the entirety of the Buddhist tradition into one body of precepts for practice and resolved any appearance of contradiction between the various aspects of the Buddha's teaching (e.g., Hinayana, Mahayana, and Vajrayana). Je Tsongkhapa founded Ganden Monastery, and is known as the great reformer of Buddhism in Tibet. He restored the strict monastic discipline given by Buddha Shakyamuni as the foundation of monastic life.[17] Other close disciples of Je Tsongkhapa's were Shakya Yeshe and Gendun Drubpa. Shakya Yeshe (1354-1435 a.k.a., Byams chen chos rje, see nos. 9 & 10), founded Sera Monasteries near Lhasa. He was Je Tsongkhapa's ambassador to the Ming court, where the Yongle and Xuande Emperors honored him with lavish gifts and titles. Gendun Drubpa (1391-1474) was both disciple and attendant to Je Tsongkhapa. He is known for his devotional poetry, for founding Tashi Lhunpo Monastery, and for being the First Dalai Lama. The present Dalai Lama, whose sacred treasures are presented in this catalog, is the fourteenth.

When asked to characterize the differences between these four traditions of Buddhism in Tibet, the Dalai Lama compares them to airliners. Like airliners built by four different companies, they are similar in concept, function, and purpose. They differ in superficial details such as color and style, but not in substance. Any of them will get you to your destination with similar speed and efficiency. They are equally based on the insights and designs of the same person (the Buddha), but were produced in different places by different individuals.[18]

Tibet: Its Land and History

In the centuries since these four traditions developed, Buddhism prospered in Tibet. These were difficult times in India, which suffered waves of Moslem invasions in the 11th - 13th centuries that destroyed the ancient monasteries, temples, universities, and libraries that sustained Buddhism in its homeland. By that time, however, India and Tibet had been closely connected for nearly one thousand years. Unlike remote Buddhist cultures, such as Japan and China, Tibet benefited from direct and constant contact with India over the millennium. The Buddhist canon, some seven thousand four hundred texts, had been translated and often retranslated several times into Tibetan from its original Sanskrit. With its eclipse in India, the sun of Buddhism remained bright in Tibet.

Tibet became the center of Buddhist culture from the 13th century until the second half of the 20th century. Rather than sending armies to conquer China, Nepal, and Central Asia as in former times, Tibet now sent teachers who converted first the powerful Mongol Khans, then the Manchus, and many other Asia peoples. The Mongols conquered most of Asia and much of Europe and the Middle East. However, in the end, they were conquered by Buddhism and from their ranks came some of the greatest Buddhist scholars and artists. The Manchus conquered China and then began to enter Tibet. However, they quickly formed alliances and took the Lamas of Tibet as their teachers and advisors. Until the end of their Qing Dynasty in 1912, the Manchus were great patrons of Buddhism, and especially of Tibetan religion and arts.

For the first half of the 20th century, Tibet remained what it had been since the dawn of history: a unique civilization in a high, remote land largely untouched by the conflicts of the outside world, possessing its own distinctive language, culture, and religious government.[19] In 1950, the People's Republic of China invaded from the east, using newly developed engines of war: aircraft, bombs, and tanks, which allowed it to overcome the natural barriers of the high mountains. In 1951, China declared its annexation of Tibet. Over the next eight years, China moved vast armies of soldiers, bureaucrats, and workers into Tibet to remake it into a Chinese province. A popular uprising in March of 1959 was crushed with tremendous loss of life among Tibetan civilians. Over the next ten years, over one million two hundred thousand Tibetans, one fifth of the population, would die at the hands of the invader. Only thirteen of the six thousand two hundred and fifty-four Buddhist monasteries of Tibet would escape systematic destruction.[20]

The Dalai Lama fled to India in March of 1959, leaving the objects seen in this catalog behind, but taking with him the hopes and prayers of all Tibetans and Buddhists worldwide. From his new home in Dharamsala, India, he has reestablished the ancient traditions of monastic Buddhism in its original homeland of India, built great institutions to maintain and strengthen Tibetan cultural, literary, artistic, and religious traditions, and spread these spiritual and sacred treasures to an ever growing audience of new Buddhists in virtually every part of the world (see no. 12).

1
The Origin of the Human Race
Color Painting on Cloth
Tibet, 18th century
H: 81.5 cm; L: 62.5 cm
Tibet Museum, Lhasa
Published: *Tibet Museum Catalog*, p. 68, no. 3; *Xizang tangka*, no. 7

[1] A basic sourcebook for early Tibetan history and religious lore, attributed to King Songtsen Gampo.

[2] John Powers, *Introduction to Tibetan Buddhism* (New York: Snow Lion, 1995), pp. 122-123.

This thangka, originally from the Potala Palace, is the first among a series of paintings illustrating the early history of Tibet. Pictured here are scenes from traditional accounts of the origins of the Tibetan people. According to the *Mani Kabum* (*Mani bka' 'bum*) Avalokiteshvara was asked by Buddha Shakyamuni to go to Tibet and establish Buddhism.[1] Accordingly, he manifested as a handsome monkey king in the plateau of Tibet that had recently arisen out of the waters.[2] (This ancient account is consistent with modern scientific theory that says the arising of the Tibetan plateau and the Himalayas began some millions of years ago, with the collision of the Indian subcontinent and South Asia).

The handsome Monkey King established himself in a mountain cave and entered into profound states of meditation on compassion and emptiness. The high land of Tibet was empty and uninhabited at that time, except for a beautiful Demoness of the Rocks (*brag gi srin mo*) who haunted the mountains of the Himalaya in lonely pursuit of a companion. Just as the Monkey King was motivated by compassion and rooted in wisdom, the Demoness was moved by avarice and driven by lust. When they met, the Demoness immediately fell in love with the handsome Monkey King and from their union came six children. The texts say that they walked upright, had no tails, and shared the natures of both parents. In this way, Tibetans credit both their peaceful, contemplative nature, and their wild, mischievous ways. Having established the Tibetan race, Avalokiteshvara continued to guide the Tibetan people through the ages, emanating as various influential figures such as the first King of Religion (Dharmaraja) Songtsen Gampo (ca. 618-650 CE) and the line of the Dalai Lamas to the present day.

The castle located at bottom center of this painting is Yumbu Lakhang (Yum bu bla sgang); believed to be the home of early kings, it is the oldest surviving dwelling in Tibet.

Songtsen Gampo (ca. 618-650), the first unifier of Tibet, was also the first of the great religious kings. He married two Buddhist wives, one from Nepal and the other from China, and was the first king to actively promote Buddhism. Here, he appears seated on a bolster, wearing a robe in the style of his time (the 7th century), with crossed lapels, tightly belted torso, and loose sleeves. Yan Liben's famous 7th century painting of the Tang Dynasty Emperor Taizong (reigned 627-649), greeting Gar Tongtsen, Songtsen Gampo's minister, shows him wearing a similar robe (see Figure 1, p. 130).

In this figure, the king's hair is dressed in three braids and he wears the tilted turban characteristic of images of early kings. The head of the Buddha Amitabha crowns the turban, indicating that the king is an emanation of Amitabha's spiritual son, Avalokiteshvara, the Bodhisattva of Compassion. The textile that covers his shoulders is decorated with dragon roundels surrounded by pearls, a style popular throughout Asia in the 7th and 8th centuries.

Images of Songtsen Gampo are usually made of clay and show him accompanied by his wives and two ministers. Examples of these images can be seen inside a cave in the Potala Palace and in the Jokhang Temple. A metal image such as this is rare.

2
King Songtsen Gampo
Gilt copper
Tibet, ca. 13th century
H: 47 cm; W: 30 cm
Potala Palace Collection
Published: *Precious Deposits*, vol. 1, pp. 193-195, no. 114

This three-quarter view of Songtsen Gampo (ca. 618-650) depicts him seated on an elaborate throne, holding a lotus in his right hand and a Dharma wheel in his left, indicating his double role as an emanation of Avalokiteshvara and a Dharma king. His two principal wives, the Nepalese princess and the Chinese princess, and his two ministers, Thomi Sambhota, holding a book, and Gar Tongtsen, holding a staff, accompany him. In front of him is Palden Lhamo in her peaceful form as the white Sri Devi. She holds an arrow and is attended by her lion-headed and *makara*-headed acolytes. In Songtsen Gampo's turban is the head of his lineage Lord, the Buddha Amitabha. An eleven-headed form of Avalokiteshvara appears in the upper right. In the upper left is the king's root lama (guru). The Jokhang, which still contains the Jo Rinpoche, the now gilt-encrusted sculptural image of Shakyamuni Buddha brought to Tibet by the Tang Dynasty Chinese Princess Wencheng, appears in the background as a golden-roofed building surrounded by the city of Lhasa. The Jokhang is the most important focal point of pilgrimages by Tibetan Buddhists.

This thangka is based on a series of woodcuts of the Dalai Lamas and their former incarnations carved at Narthang Monastery in eastern Tibet during the 18th century. Songtsen Gampo, who, like the Dalai Lamas, was an emanation of Avalokiteshvara, is therefore included in this series.

3
King Songtsen Gampo
Thankga, colors on cotton
Tibet, 18th century
H: 47 cm; L: 29.5 cm
Tibet Museum, Lhasa
Published: *Tibet Museum Catalog*, p. 162, no. 3

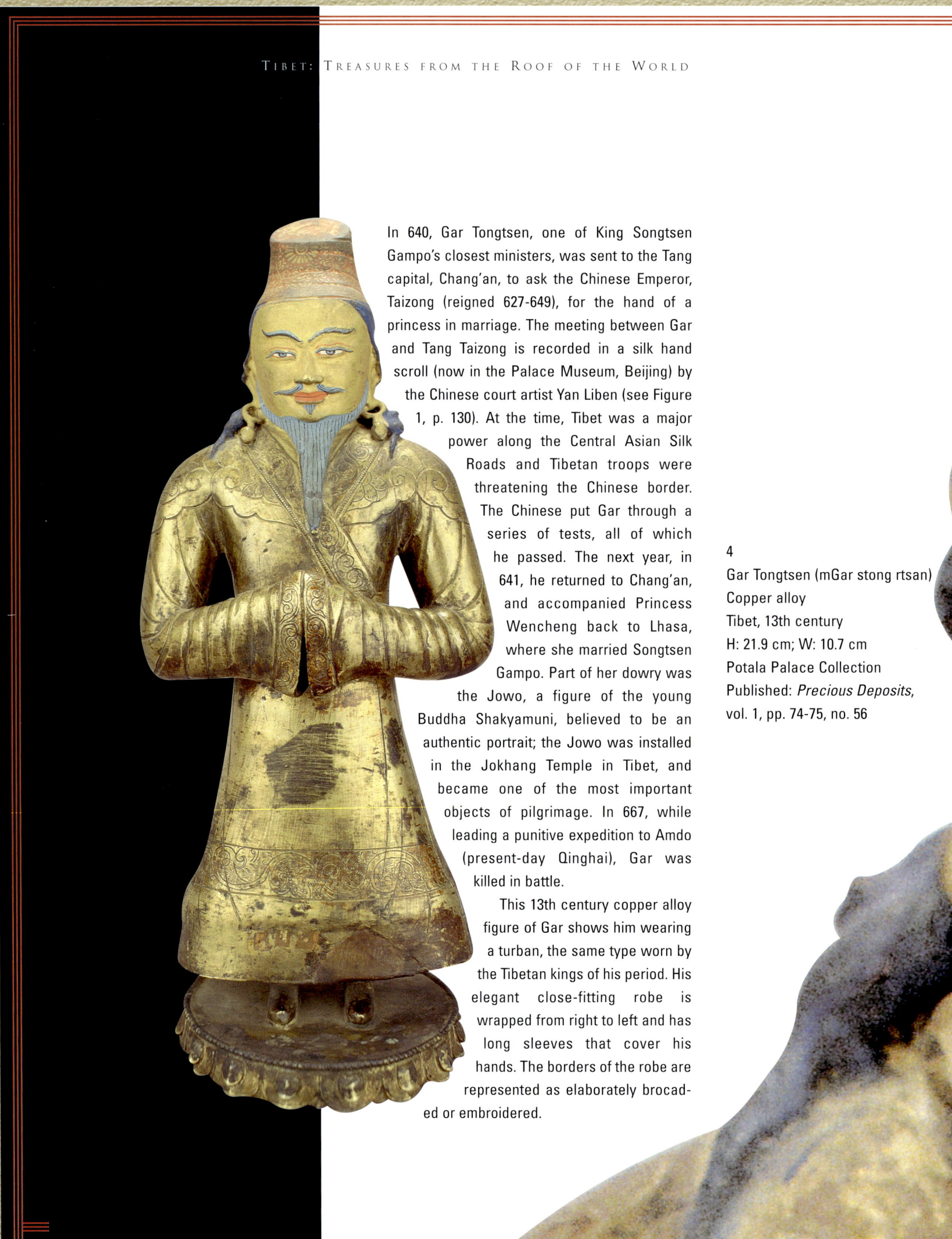

In 640, Gar Tongtsen, one of King Songtsen Gampo's closest ministers, was sent to the Tang capital, Chang'an, to ask the Chinese Emperor, Taizong (reigned 627-649), for the hand of a princess in marriage. The meeting between Gar and Tang Taizong is recorded in a silk hand scroll (now in the Palace Museum, Beijing) by the Chinese court artist Yan Liben (see Figure 1, p. 130). At the time, Tibet was a major power along the Central Asian Silk Roads and Tibetan troops were threatening the Chinese border. The Chinese put Gar through a series of tests, all of which he passed. The next year, in 641, he returned to Chang'an, and accompanied Princess Wencheng back to Lhasa, where she married Songtsen Gampo. Part of her dowry was the Jowo, a figure of the young Buddha Shakyamuni, believed to be an authentic portrait; the Jowo was installed in the Jokhang Temple in Tibet, and became one of the most important objects of pilgrimage. In 667, while leading a punitive expedition to Amdo (present-day Qinghai), Gar was killed in battle.

This 13th century copper alloy figure of Gar shows him wearing a turban, the same type worn by the Tibetan kings of his period. His elegant close-fitting robe is wrapped from right to left and has long sleeves that cover his hands. The borders of the robe are represented as elaborately brocaded or embroidered.

4

Gar Tongtsen (mGar stong rtsan)
Copper alloy
Tibet, 13th century
H: 21.9 cm; W: 10.7 cm
Potala Palace Collection
Published: *Precious Deposits*, vol. 1, pp. 74-75, no. 56

TIBET: TREASURES FROM THE ROOF OF THE WORLD

5
The Three Buddhist Kings
Thangka, colors on cotton
Tibet, 19th century
H: 90 cm; W: 144 cm
Tibet Museum, Lhasa
Published: *Treasures from Snow Mountains*,
pp. 64-66, no. 11; *Tibet Museum Catalog*, p. 78, no. 1

Tibet: Its Land and History

The Three Dharma Kings of Tibet, Songtsen Gampo, Trisong Detsen, and Ralpachen (Tritsug Detsen) appear wearing turbans, which was an early Tibetan style. Songtsen Gampo (ca. 618-650), (center), holding a lotus, is recognizable by the head of Amitabha in his headdress. He is accompanied by his two ministers. Thomi Sambhota, who devised the Tibetan alphabet based on a Sanskrit alphabet he studied in India, is seen here with a book in his hand. Minister Gar Tongtsen, shown holding a staff, accompanied Princess Wencheng from China to Tibet. To the left of this group is Trisong Detsen (ca. 740-798), who has the attributes of Manjushri, the Bodhisattva of Wisdom (sword and book). Ralpachen (reigned 814- 836), to the right, bears a *vajra* on his left shoulder and hence represents the Bodhisattva Vajrapani. Together, the three are manifestations of the Three Great Lords (*rigsum gonpo*) of Tibet: Avalokiteshvara, Manjushri, and Vajrapani, representing the compassion, wisdom, and secret power of all Buddhas.

At the very top of the thangka are (from left to right: the Fifth, Sixth, and Seventh Dalai Lamas and White Tara. On the bottom are three groups of fierce deities charged with protecting the Dharma and its followers. Under Trisong Detsen, are the Six-armed Mahakala on top, Yama and Yami (Lord of Death and his female counterpart), and Vaishravana (a God of Wealth). Below Songtsen Gampo is Palden Lhamo on her all-seeing mule. On the right are Rahu, chief of the planetary deities, and Begtse, a fierce worldly protector. There is also a wrathful deity with a trident and dish of jewels, riding a gray mare. He is the White Brahma (Lhachen Tsangpa Karpo, Sita-Brahma), a patron of the Tibetan people and trusted protector of Songtsen Gampo and the Tibetan government. Except for Rahu, these protective deities are among the Drakche Gye (Eight Ferocious Ones).

These three kings are known as the Three Dharmarajas (Kings of the Dharma) because of their extraordinary contributions to the establishment and growth of Buddhism in Tibet. Songtsen Gampo's two principal wives, a Nepalese Princess, Bhrikhuti, and a Chinese Princess Wencheng, brought Buddhist images with them as part of their trousseaux and contributed to the king's efforts to promote Buddhism. Princess Wencheng brought the Jowo (Jo Rinpoche), a figure of the Buddha Shakyamuni, the main image of the most significant temple in Tibet, the Jokhang in Lhasa. Trisong Detsen brought Padma Sambhava and Shantarakshita from India and with their help, established the first monastery, Samye. Ralpachen ("the long-haired") was a lavish patron of Buddhism; he was known for his piety because he allowed monks to sit on his outspread long hair, hence his nickname.

6
Padma Sambhava
Slate
Tibet, 17th century
H: 69 cm; W: 44 cm
Formerly in the Norbulingka
Tibet Museum, Lhasa
Published: *Well-Selected*, no. 61; *Tibet Museum Catalog*, p. 98, no. 3

The great teacher, Padma Sambhava ("Lotus Born"), a native of Uddiyana of India (present-day Swat in northern Pakistan), came to Tibet at the invitation of King Trisong Detsen (reigned 755-797) in the middle of the 8th century. At that time, Trisong Detsen and the Indian monk Shantarakshita were building Samye Monastery. They experienced great difficulty, because their work during the day was destroyed by the local demons at night. In despair, the two invited Padma Sambhava, who had a reputation for taming demons, to help them. Not only did Padma Sambhava tame the demons, he also extracted an oath from the two to protect Buddhism and persuaded them to help in the construction work.

The slate carving, formerly in the Norbulingka, shows Padma Sambhava seated in his palace in the Glorious Copper Mountain, a paradise on a rocky island surrounded by waves. He wears his distinctive headdress with upturned lappets, decorated with the sun and moon, and topped by an eagle's feather (an ancient symbol of penetrating vision).[1] His right hand grasps the *vajra*, and his left supports a skull bowl. At the crook of his left elbow rests the *khatvanga* staff, topped by a trident over three heads in various stages of decay. These heads, one freshly severed, one shrunken, and the other a skull, symbolize the conquest of desire, hate, and ignorance. The two kneeling ladies beside him are his two consorts, Mandarava, an Indian Princess, and Yeshe Tsogyal, a Tibetan Queen, both recognized as great adepts in their own right. The palace is guarded by the Guardian Kings of the Four Quarters, only three of whom are visible.

The Nyingma, oldest among the orders of Tibetan Buddhism, was based in part upon the teachings of Padma Sambhava.

---

[1] Marylin Rhie and Robert Thurman, *Wisdom and Compassion: The Sacred Art of Tibet* (New York; San Francisco: Asian Art Museum of San Francisco and Tibet House in association with Harry Abrams, 1991), p. 167.

Milarepa (1040-1123), "Cotton-Clad" Mila, was one of the most famous yogins and poets in the history of Tibet. He was the foremost disciple of Marpa the Translator (1012-1096) and many of the teachings of the Kagyu order passed through him. In his youth, Milarepa took up black magic in order to punish the enemies of his family; he killed some of them and brought hailstorms to destroy their crops. Finally, he came to his senses, and to save himself from falling into hell, he decided to practice the Dharma in order to purify himself. In the course of searching for teachers, he found Marpa, who would become his master. After assigning Milarepa to perform herculean tasks for six years, Marpa succeeded in purifying his disciple of the effects of his misdeeds and finally initiated him into Buddhist teachings.

The beloved poet-saint Milarepa is shown in the pose of royal ease (Sanskrit: *maharaja lila asana*), with one leg raised and the other bent at the knee. His left hand is lowered over his knee, while his right hand is raised to his ear, either to hear his own singing better or to listen to the words of his *dakini* teachers and consorts. The very emaciated figure is seated on the skin of an antelope, the usual symbol of someone who meditates. The skeletal condition of his body is due to the intensity of his ascetic practice, when he subsisted solely on nettle leaves, which turned his complexion green.

7
Milarepa
Copper alloy
Tibet, 16th - 17th century
H: 16.5 cm; W: 13.3 cm
Potala Palace Collection
Published: *Precious Deposits*, vol. 2, pp. 48-49, no. 26

8
Rangjung Dorje, the Third Karmapa (1284-1339)
Copper alloy
Tibet, 16th century
H: 20 cm; W: 13.5 cm
Tibet Museum, Lhasa
Published: *Tibet Museum Catalog*, p. 96, no. 2

This gilt copper alloy figure of the Third Karmapa, Rangjung Dorje, shows him seated in *vajra* position with both hands resting on his knees, middle fingers touching the ground.[1] Rangjung Dorje was one of the greatest of the seventeen Karmapas who have appeared to date. In 1301, at the age of 18, he climbed Mount Everest (Jomolungma) and entered into a solitary meditation retreat in an ice cave. Inspired by the realizations gained on this retreat, he studied extensively in the Kagyu and Nyingma schools, and unified the two systems in his new Karma Nyingtik tradition. He is renowned for prolific writings on Buddhist philosophy and practice, natural science and medicine. When the great Mongol Emperor Togh Temür died in 1332, Rangjung Dorje was asked to preside over the coronation of the new Mongol Emperor, Toghon Temür, who then became his disciple.

The Kagyu order is based on the teachings of the Indian masters Tilopa and Naropa. It was established in Tibet through the efforts of Naropa's disciple, the Tibetan translator, Marpa (1012-1096), who went to India seeking the authentic teachings of the Buddha. His follower, the "Cotton-Clad" Milarepa and Milarepa's disciple Gampopa, popularized these teachings in Tibet, and the order rapidly evolved into twelve sub-orders. One of the most influential of these is the Karma Kagyu order under the leadership of the Karmapas. The line of Karmapas began with Dusum Khyenpa (1110-1193), who established their home monastery at Tsurphu about fifty miles east of Lhasa. Dusum Khyenpa was asked by his disciples to take rebirth in Tibet and continue to guide them. He agreed, and several years after his death, a young boy (Karma Pakshi) proclaimed himself the reborn Karmapa, and answered questions only Dusum Khyenpa and his intimate disciples would know. In this way, the unique Tibetan institution of reborn Lamas (Tibetan: *tulku*) began.

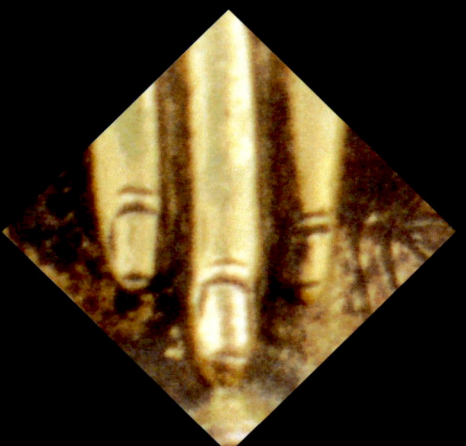

The Karmapas are distinguished in their portraits by the black hat, which was first given to the Fifth Karmapa, Dezhin Shegpa (1384-1415), by the Chinese Ming Dynasty Emperor Yongle, who reigned from 1403 to 1424. This black hat (Tibetan: *gomsha*), which has passed from Karmapa to Karmapa down to the present day, is ornamented with the sun and moon and the double *vajra,* and purportedly is made from the hair of *dakinis* (mystic female "sky walkers"). In this 16th century portrait, the Third Karmapa wears the black hat as a posthumous sign of his position.

[1] The Second Karmapa, Karma Pakshi, is also typically portrayed in this position. However, he is shown with his trademark goatee in most portraits. The Third Karmapa, Rangjung Dorje, may be portrayed in positions other than what appears here, however, this is one of his distinguishing poses. See: Khempo Sangyay Tenzin and Gomchen Oleshey, *The Nyingma Icons: A Collection of Line Drawings of 94 Deities and Divinities of Tibet* (no. 41). Published in *Kailash: A Journal of Himalayan Studies,* vol. III, no. 4 (1975): 363.

9
Portrait of Shakya Yeshe (1354-1435)
Silk embroidery
China, Ming Dynasty, Xuande reign (1426-1435)
H: 162 cm; W: 98 cm
Tibet Museum, Lhasa
Published: *Tibet Museum Catalog*, pp. 40-41, no. 3; *Wenwu* 9 (1985)

Shown here are two imperially-commissioned portraits of the prominent Lama Shakya Yeshe (1354-1435), one of the eight greatest disciples of Tsongkhapa, the founder of the Gelug order. In 1408, Emperor Yongle, of the Ming Dynasty, sent an invitation to Tsongkhapa to visit the Ming capital. Tsongkhapa refused the invitation, so in 1413, Yongle sent a second invitation. This time, Tsongkhapa delegated Shakya Yeshe, who arrived in Nanjing the next year. There, he built temples, initiated monks and, in 1415, was given the title Da Ci Fawang (Tibetan: Byams chen chos rje, "Dharma King of Great Loving Kindness"), one of several princely religious titles given by Yongle to great Tibetan Lamas. Shakya Yeshe received bountiful gifts from Emperor Yongle, including a black hat, which is clearly visible in the second of his two portraits included in this exhibition (no. 10). Shakya Yeshe, renowned for his fund-raising abilities, used the gifts he brought back from China to help found Sera Monastery in 1419.

In 1429, Shakya Yeshe returned to China, during the reign of Emperor Xuande (1426-1435), this time to the new northern capital at Beijing, where he demonstrated his abilities as a healer by curing the emperor's ills. He also toured the sacred mountain Wutaishan, Mongolia, and Amdo (present-day Qinghai province). In 1434, the emperor granted him another, even more exalted title (consisting of thirty-eight Chinese characters). The next year, in 1435, he died on his way home to Tibet.

The first of these two images (see no. 9) is embroidered silk and shows the lama as a younger man, seated in meditation on a lotus throne, with his hands in a gesture of preaching, carrying two lotuses at shoulder level, which support the bell and *vajra*. His hair is knotted into a chignon and he wears a three-leaf crown. He is surrounded by an elaborate "throne of glory," surmounted by Garuda (the mount of the Indian deity Vishnu and enemy of the *nagas*). In the upper corners of the embroidered portrait are images of White Tara and Vajradhara. The portrait was apparently remounted with embroidered silk that was once part of a Qing Dynasty imperial robe.

The second and later of these two portraits is a slit-silk tapestry, which can be dated to the Xuande period (1426-1435), on the basis of the lengthy, woven title, which appears in both Chinese and Tibetan.[1] This portrait shows Shakya Yeshe in the same posture and gesture as the previous portrait, but here, he is cloaked in a sumptuously detailed robe with dragon designs and wears the Five-Buddha black hat (three Buddhas are visible here), recorded as a gift from Emperor Yongle. He sits on a Chinese-style throne similar to those seen in Ming Dynasty imperial portraits. On a typical Ming-style red lacquer table behind him, are an incense burner in the form of an ancient bronze vessel and an incense container. The large red seal that dominates the space above Shakya Yeshe's right shoulder replicates the Chinese-language seal given to him by Emperor Xuande.

10
Thangka of Shakya Yeshe
Silk
China, Ming Dynasty, Xuande reign (1426-1435)
H: 108 cm; W: 63.5 cm
Norbulingka Palace Collection
Published: *Precious Deposits*, vol. 3, pp. 150-151, no. 55

[1] The Tibetan title, which differs very little from the Chinese, reads: "Endowed with manifold sublime activities, wise and lucid, abiding in highest reality, pure of wisdom, all-illuminating, all-pervading, protector of the nation, propagator of the teachings, totally virtuous, Dharma King of Great Loving Kindness, possessor of supreme cognition in the West, Tathagata, Great Buddha of Perfect Omniscience."

This square jade seal bears a crouching mythical beast and was made for the Yuan Dynasty *guoshi* (National Preceptor). Its inscription is written in Phagpa script. After Phagpa was named National Preceptor, these titles became more and more honorific. The title *guoshi* became *Guanding guoshi* (Empowered as National Preceptor), and was later changed to *Da Yuan guoshi* (National Preceptor of the Great Yuan).

11
Seal of the Yuan Preceptor, Supervisor of Buddhist Affairs
Jade
China, Yuan Dynasty (1260-1368)
H: 10 cm; L: 12 cm x 12 cm
Tibet Museum, Lhasa
Published: *Tibet Museum Catalog*, pp. 30-31, no. 3;
Golden Treasures, pp. 22-23

Tibet: Its Land and History

The imperial edict of Ming Dynasty Emperor Yongle reign (1403-1424), is written in ink on five-color brocade, woven with cloud motifs. The Chinese language version, written from right to left, and read from top to bottom, appears first, as was standard during the Ming and Qing Dynasties: the edict from the emperor, who rules the country by the mandate of heaven, proclaims the following…

The edict goes on to confer the post of Commander of the U Tsang region (Central Tibet) to Chokyi Kyirong (Chos kyi rong), followed by the date: the tenth day of the fifth month, the eleventh year of the reign of Emperor Yongle (equivalent to 1413). The Tibetan version is written in long-tail script (Umey, dbu med), and reads from left to right.

12
Imperial Edit
Silk
China, Ming Dynasty, Yongle reign, dated 1413
H: 32 cm; L: 330.5 cm
Tibet Museum, Lhasa
Published: *Tibet Museum Catalog*, pp. 36-37, top

13
Seal of the Fifth Dalai Lama
Sandalwood and iron
China, Qing Dynasty, 17th century
H: 8.8 cm; L: 11.2 cm; W: 11.2 cm
Tibet Museum, Lhasa
Published: *Tibet Museum Catalog*, p. 141, no. 4

Ngawang Losang Gyatso (Ngag dbang lo bzang rgya mtsho, 1617-1682), the Fifth Dalai Lama, was the greatest ruler of Tibet. With the help of the Mongol Gushri Khan, he was able to unify Tibet and was the first ruler to hold both spiritual and temporal power. He had the Potala Palace built on the Red Hill, over the ancient palaces of the Tibetan kings, and he made the Gelug order (to which he belonged), supreme over other religious orders.

In 1647, the Great Fifth Dalai Lama was invited to China by the Manchu Emperor Shunzhi (reigned 1644-1661) of the new Qing Dynasty. He arrived in the first month of 1653, and the emperor showered him with a thousand gifts, among them this seal, inscribed in three languages (Chinese, Manchu, and Tibetan). The seal bears the title (in Chinese): Seal of the Dalai Lama, Buddha of Great Compassion in the West, leader of the Buddhist faith beneath the sky, holder of the *vajra* (Vajradhara) (*Xitian dashan zizai fo suo ling tianxia shijiao putong wazhila dala dalai lama zhi yin*).

The seal, which is carved of sandalwood and reinforced with iron, appears to have been heavily used.

14
Edict of the Qing Emperor Daoguang (reigned 1821-1850)
Addressed to the Seventh Panchen Lama
Gold album, dated to the 18th year of Daoguang (1838)
China
L: 23.2 cm; W: 9.9 cm
Tibet Museum, Lhasa
Tibet Museum Catalog, p. 34, no. 1

In 1838 this golden album was sent to the Seventh Panchen Lama, Tenpai Nyima (1781-1852), by the Qing Dynasty Emperor Daoguang. The inscription, engraved into joined gold plates, is written in the four official languages of the Qing empire —Manchu, Chinese, Tibetan, and Mongolian. In sum, the edict states that the ancestral lands, the farms, and the people of Tashilhunpo Monastery would be forever and irrevocably under the jurisdiction of the Panchen Lamas.

The Seventh Panchen Lama was born in 1782 in a noble family in southern Tibet. In 1784 he was enthroned as the seventh incarnation in the Panchen Lama lineage and the Eighth Dalai Lama, Jampel Gyatso (1758-1804), became his teacher. After the Eighth Dalai Lama died, the Seventh Panchen Lama oversaw the discovery of the Ninth, Tenth, and Eleventh Dalai Lamas.

TIBET: ITS RELIGION AND RITUAL
ROBERT W. CLARK

The sacred objects in this collection have religious and ritual significance rooted in the ancient tradition that derives from the teachings of Buddha Shakyamuni (6th century BCE, see no. 53). The Buddha taught that living beings wander from lifetime to lifetime, taking rebirth according to their thoughts and deeds (*karma*). This process of "beginningless" and "endless" rebirth is called *samsara*. Birth within *samsara* is fraught with misery. Birth, sickness, old age, and death entail misery. Not getting what you want, and getting what you don't want, are both miserable and unavoidable. Every type of rebirth, whether human, animal, divine or infernal, has its own particular range of miseries. Every experience of every living being is either miserable by nature, or leads to misery. Happiness in *samsara* is always transitory; even the greatest pleasures and most enviable situations are fleeting, always ending in loss and downfall.

This rather sour assessment of life is the point of departure of all the Buddha's teachings. Buddhism, therefore, does not appeal to those convinced that true and lasting happiness will be found in worldly life, that there is a god or messiah who will provide salvation or that death will put an end to all of one's problems. Buddhism is most compelling to those who fear not the finality of death, but its vacuity; who fear the existential misery of living forever in a universe that has no meaning; or who fear to be reborn again and again, endlessly and helplessly in frail bodies always subject to heat, cold, hunger and every type of pain. The Buddha addresses these fears by showing the causes of all miseries and the way they can be eliminated. The state in which they are fully eliminated is called *nirvana*. This is the subject of much of Buddhist literature and art (For example, see no. 88, where this great "game of birth and death" is presented in graphic form, together with the steps whereby *Nirvana* is attained).

The ultimate state of *nirvana,* called *Buddhahood,* encompasses the welfare of both oneself and others. One's own welfare is attained by the wisdom that cuts off the causes of one's bondage to the *samsara*. The welfare of others is accomplished by the compassion that rejects the solitary peace of a limited *nirvana* in order to work continuously to free all beings from the miseries of *samsara.*

Two things are required to attain the blissful state of *nirvana*: the elimination of defilement and the increase of good qualities. Defilements result from activities motivated by ignorant states of mind (*klesha*) such as greed, anger, delusion, pride and envy. Good qualities arise from merit and wisdom. Merit is produced by generosity, morality, patience, virtuous effort and mental concentration. The greatest merit arises when these are practiced with the motivation of the *Bodhisattva*. This motivation, called *bodhicitta,* recognizes each and every being as one's own kind mother in some past lifetime. It seeks the highest welfare and happiness for each of them and, therefore, pursues the state of perfect enlightenment (*Buddhahood*) in order to accomplish that goal of universal enlightenment. Wisdom arises from the persistent and thorough analysis of phenomena. The Buddha taught that this analysis leads to the realization that nothing whatsoever exists inherently. All things arise only in dependence upon causes and conditions, and are therefore empty of any true existence (although they have an ephemeral, relative existence). The full realization of this principle of *dependent arising* eliminates the basis of all greed, hatred, ignorance and other sources of defilement. This is taught extensively by the Buddha in the *Prajnaparamita Sutras* (see no. 38).

Each of the objects displayed in this collection can be understood as an instrument intended to accomplish the goal of Buddhist meditation, ritual and philosophy, which is to eliminate defilement and to increase merit and wisdom. Some, such as images of Buddhas and Bodhisattvas, do this by inspiring faith and serving as objects of worship. Others, such as sacred vases (see nos. 43 & 44) and hand-held instruments (see nos. 19, 20 & 26) are used in rituals as auxiliaries to meditation.

Many of these objects are the finest examples of their type. Made for Dalai Lamas, many were gifts from kings and emperors. In the hands of an enlightened being, such as the present Dalai Lama, they are objects of mystical power that dispel the darkness of ignorance and bestow the blessings of countless Buddhas. For those of lesser attainment, these types of sacred objects are used to develop good qualities and eliminate defilements. Take, for example, the prayer wheel (see no. 24). It is filled with a scroll upon which is written invocations of the Bodhisattva Avalokiteshvara (see no. 74). These invocations are in the form of that Bodhisattva's mantra, "Om Mani Padme Hum (seen in the large blue Sanskrit syllables in no. 75)." In the hands of a person whose mind is filled with compassion for all beings, it is believed that each spin of a mantra in the wheel invokes an emanation of Avalokiteshvara. One prayer

wheel could easily have up to one hundred thousand mantras written on the scroll. A person might spin the wheel thousands of times in one meditative session. In this manner, hundreds of millions of Avalokiteshvara emanations are sent forth to encompass the welfare of others. The meaning of the mantra is not found in its translation. Tibetans use the original Sanskrit mantras rather than translating them into Tibetan. A mantra is a set of sacred syllables that connect a person with a Buddha or Bodhisattva. Each Buddha and Bodhisattva has at least one unique mantra.

A Buddha begins as an ordinary person. At some point, this ordinary person develops a sense of compassion for other beings that can no longer tolerate seeing their endless suffering in the rounds of birth and death. When that person is so moved by compassion that the wish to free all beings from misery becomes the motive for every thought, word and deed, at all times, even in dreams, that person is said to have entered onto the path to Buddhahood and to have become a Bodhisattva. Being a Bodhisattva entails an unshakeable resolve to free all beings from *samsara,* and is informed by the understanding that one cannot free anyone from *samsara* so long as one remains trapped by oneself. Therefore, a Bodhisattva seeks the powerful and transcendent state of Buddhahood as a means for helping others, and as the prerequisite for freeing others from all misery. In a process that usually continues over the course of many lifetimes, the Bodhisattva builds up great stores of merit and wisdom through diligence in generosity, patience, ethics, meditative concentration and analytical wisdom. At some point, all good qualities are attained, and all defilements exhausted. In this manner, a Bodhisattva attains Buddhahood through abandoning all selfish goals and defiled actions, and striving in the highest way for the benefit of all.

There are a great number of Buddhas, Bodhisattvas, and deities, both peaceful and wrathful in the vast Buddhist pantheon, only a few of whom are seen in this collection. Each of them represents an individual who pursued the path to enlightenment, and having attained it in a limited or complete manner, continues to exhibit many of the personal qualities and characteristics that made them unique. Although all Buddhas have realized the limitless wisdom of enlightenment, they retain individual qualities that make them more or less accessible to any given individual. Some people, upon seeing an image of Buddha Shakyamuni, are moved to faith. Others have greater affinity with a Tara, Vajrapani or Avalokiteshvara.

Avalokiteshvara is known as Bodhisattva. However, like the other great Bodhisattvas such as Manjushri (see no. 72), Maitreya (see no. 70), and Tara (see no. 81), this does not necessarily indicate a lesser status than a Buddha. These are called tenth stage Bodhisattvas, meaning that the path to Buddhahood has been completed, but the appearance of a Bodhisattva is retained. By attaining Buddhahood, this world of illusion, the *samsara,* is completely transcended. The ordinary flesh and blood body is left behind, and the limitless, formless Dharma body (*Dharmakaya*) is attained. However, this Dharma body can be perceived only by another Buddha. Ordinary beings, those who really need the help of a Buddha, cannot perceive it. Therefore, a Buddha manifests or emanates form bodies (*Rupakaya*) to interact with others in accordance with that compassionate resolve (*bodhicitta*) that led to Buddhahood.

Buddhas are associated with certain Bodhisattvas who are considered their emanations, or often simply their disciples. Buddha Amitabha, for example, is associated with the Bodhisattvas Avalokiteshvara and Tara (see no. 76 where Buddha Amitabha is seen as the uppermost of the eleven heads of Avalokiteshvara. In no. 81 Amitabha (in the Amitayus form) is seen right above Tara's head). However, only another Bodhisattva who has attained at least the first of the ten Bodhisattva stages (*bhumi*) can perceive one of these great Bodhisattvas. Ordinary beings lack the merit and the purity of perception to perceive these transcendent beings. Therefore, the great Bodhisattvas themselves manifest forms in the ordinary world to guide ordinary beings. Examples of this are the Dalai Lamas, who are associated with Avalokiteshvara as his emanations or special emissaries. A Buddha may directly emanate a human form. Examples of this are the Panchen Lamas and the first of the Tibetan *Dharmarajas,* King Songtsen Gampo (618-650). Images of Songtsen Gampo (see nos. 2 & 3) show Buddha Amitabha in his crown.

Buddhas manifest not only in the form of Bodhisattvas and great human masters like the Dalai Lamas, but in ordinary objects. Material objects, for example, may be understood as manifestations of the Buddhas. The Buddha taught that when the delusions of ignorance that cloud the minds of ordinary beings are fully lifted, the "ordinary world" is experienced as the blissful state of *nirvana*. All problems and miseries arise from the fundamental ignorance that misperceives reality. All Buddhist practices, such as meditation, ritual, and sacred art, are intended to help eliminate ignorance; to decode reality. In sacred art, this process of decoding reality depends on understanding the Buddhist symbolic system of the five Buddhas (*pañcabuddha / sangs rgyas lnga*) whereby every color, element, symbol, and direction has a profound meaning.

Name	Consort	Color	Element	Symbol	Direction	Klesha	Wisdom
Vairochana	Akashadhatis	white	space	Wheel	Center	delusion	ultimate
Akshobhya	Lochana	blue	water	Vajra	East	anger	mirror-like
Ratnasambhava	Mamaki	yellow	earth	Jewel	South	pride	equanimity
Amitabha	Pandaravasini	red	fire	Lotus	West	greed	discrimination
Amoghasiddhi	Samaya Tara	green	air	Sword	North	envy	accomplishment

These five Buddhas, with their associated features, represent the five approaches to the decoding of reality. That decoding is necessary for the attainment of the state of enlightenment that transcends the *samsara* and encompasses the welfare of beings. Together they form the indivisible whole of the Buddhist path. They are organized visually in the form of a *mandala*. There are many forms of *mandalas* (see no. 17) this is a mandala intended for offering rituals). Stupas are a type of three-dimensional *mandala*. The crystal stupa (see no. 16), is a model of the famous Bodhnath stupa in the Kathmandu Valley. The Mahabodhi stupa (see nos. 56, 57 & 58), like the Bodhnath stupa, is a *mandala* of the five Buddhas that include a pantheon of deities and iconographic map of the cosmos and the path to enlightenment.

A *mandala* has quadrilateral symmetry. When presented in color, the eastern quadrant is blue, the south yellow, the west red and the north green. The center is typically white, though in some mandalas, the center may be blue and the east white. Each of these five sections is associated with one of five Buddhas who function as archetypes in the symbolic system of Buddhist *tantra*. Like all Buddhas, they have personal histories of their lifetimes of practice as Bodhisattvas before becoming Buddhas. However, they are best known in Buddhist lore as archetypes of one aspect of Buddhahood. As such, each is associated not only with a direction and a color, but with a dynamic process of purification and transformation. Amitabha, for example, purifies the negative qualities of greed and worldly desire, allowing the innate wisdom of perfect discrimination to arise. Vairochana Buddha (see no. 59) eliminates the most fundamental defilement, ignorance, so that the innate wisdom of ultimate reality may arise. Each of the five Buddhas has a consort. She embodies his particular wisdom, and he embodies the compassionate methods that transform the negative quality (*klesha*) into that wisdom.

Each of the five Buddhas has a special realm, called a *pure land* that is his own mandala. From his abode in the center of the mandala, he emanates forms to aid living beings in attaining liberation from *samsara*. In his *pure land*, each Buddha is surrounded by his Bodhisattvas who assist and join him in his work of salvation. Avalokiteshvara, for example, is included in the *pure land* mandala of Amitabha. All Buddhas, Bodhisattvas, protective deities and *yidams* (Supreme Being) are included in one or another of these five Buddha families. The *yidam* Vajrabhairava (see no. 61) is included in the family of the Buddha of the East, Akshobhya. Although each Buddha, Bodhisattva, protective deity and *yidam* has a primary identification with one of the five Buddhas, they all must fully integrate all five. This is because all five wisdoms must be fully present before one can attain enlightenment. This is shown in the crowns of all Buddhas, Bodhisattvas, protective deities and *yidams*. Each has a crown with five jewels, or five skulls for more wrathful deities. These represent the five Buddhas, and often the images of the five Buddhas or their symbols will be seen in the crown. This is the case with the five Buddha crown worn (see no. 34) by *tantric* practitioners in the course of rituals and, with the sacred crown (see no. 51) worn by *tantric* masters (*vajracarya*). This integration of all five Buddhas is seen explicitly in the iconography of the *yidams*. For example, Guhyasamaja (see no. 62) wears the five Buddha crown and holds the five attributes (symbols) of the five Buddhas in his hands. A wrathful deity such as Mahakala (see no. 77) is often shown wearing the crown with five skulls.

The wrathful deities in the Buddhist pantheon may be fierce protectors, such as Achala (see no. 85) and the Mahakalas (see nos. 86 & 87), or ferocious yidams such as Vajrabhairava (see no. 61). They wear crowns of skulls, robes of flayed skin and garlands of severed heads. They are associated with much of the frightful imagery of *Tantric* Buddhism such as ritual daggers (see nos. 21, 22 & 23), human skulls (see no. 48), and dancing skeletons. How, one might ask, does this represent a religious system conceived in loving kindness and compassion consummated in universal salvation?

Questions about wrathful gods, frightful imagery and the use of human bones in ritual objects can be sensitive for both religious and social reasons. The sacred art of Tibet is part of a living sacred tradition. Taken out of its religious and social context (a Buddhist shrine or meditation hall), this art can raise questions in the minds of viewers. Many of these wrathful elements would never be on public display in Tibet. They would be viewed only by those in a religious community, who had developed the requisite levels of compassion for all beings, and realization of the emptiness of all worldly forms, and then been given the requisite rituals of empowerment and transmission.

To put these types of objects on public display, even in a Buddhist country like Tibet, risks some misunderstanding. Images of beings who appear demon-like, and who possess fearsome attributes, could lead the uninitiated to question the commitment of Buddhism to its fundamental ethics of compassion and avoidance of harm to living beings. While it is not possible in a brief format such as this to elucidate the full range of meaning of these things, it may be possible to clear away some obvious misconceptions.

Why human bones? During ancient times in India and Tibet, cemeteries were desolate places set apart from villages where corpses were placed above ground rather than buried. Buddhist yogins would commonly take up residence in the cemeteries. There they could best learn the great lesson of the transitory nature of the physical body and of all compounded things. The wearing of bone ornaments and the use of skull cups and other implements of human bone is characteristic of these yogins. The skull and other human bones are a potent symbol of the impermanence of life and the need to exert oneself on the spiritual path undistracted by concern for the fleeting things of this world. They also possess a great deal of psychological and spiritual power (*mana*) that can be employed to advantage in ritual and meditation. For these reasons, they are used as ritual implements in the *Tantric* Buddhism of India and Tibet.

Why wrathful gods? Who are the victims whose heads, skins and intestines adorn these fearsome forms? Initiates are led to understand the profound layers of symbolism and allegory bound up in each of these complex images. The "victims" of these gods, such as the skulls or heads strung around their necks, the flayed human skins worn as clothing or used as saddle cloth, or the figure writhing under the feet of a ferocious divinity, must be understood in the context of their symbolism. Each of them represents some aspect of inner delusion to be confronted in meditation and eliminated, cut off, and severed by practicing strict morality, generating great compassion, and realizing highest wisdom. To assume that these "victims" are worldly enemies of Buddhism misses the point entirely.

Buddhism is based on the ethic that understands each and every living being to desire happiness and comfort, and to eschew suffering and misery in all its forms. However, because of ignorance and delusion, beings pursue these goals in unskillful ways. Not understanding the subtleties of cause and effect (*karma*), their pursuit of happiness often establishes the causes of misery. For the Buddhist, every being is equally deserving of that happiness and freedom from sorrow. The Bodhisattvas' path is to take upon oneself, personally, the burden of bringing about happiness for all. However, ignorant persons cannot be easily led on a path that demands abstaining from all harm to others and limiting one's own desires. Under the spells of greed, anger, delusion, pride and envy, beings are difficult to tame. The wrathful deities, with their fearful attributes, embody powerful *tantric* techniques to awaken beings from the slumber of ignorance. They are Bodhisattvas and Buddhas, and as such, have the unshakable resolve to do whatever is necessary to lead each individual being to salvation. They are free of any trace of harmful act or intent, but rather embody the most dynamic forces of compassion and wisdom.

The potent symbolism of the fearsome imagery of Tantric Buddhism, therefore, requires viewers to make a special effort to avoid harmful assumptions and misconceptions and, instead, establish one's view of these things in a basic understanding of Buddhism and an appreciation of the rich and dynamic sacred tradition that provides many potent symbols to aid in inner transformation.

Some of these symbols are seen in the images and objects in this collection. There are different levels of significance to each object. In brief, they have outer, inner and secret meanings. An outer meaning of a painted or bronze image could be the depiction of a historical figure (For example, see no. 7, an image of Milarepa (1040-1123)). The inner meaning is found in the faith inspired by viewing the image, in the instruction conveyed by his posture, gestures and attributes, as well as in the reflection on his life story and teachings. The secret levels of meaning are associated with the ways in which an image or object actually embodies the body, speech or mind of an enlightened being. Ritual and religious uses of these objects depend upon all three levels of meaning to bring about the reduction of defilement and the increase of merit and wisdom. This is shown in a famous Tibetan account that illustrates the dynamic power of objects of faith.

Some years ago, there was an elderly woman who lived near a small village in Tibet. Her son was a merchant who traveled between Tibet and India. She was a devout Buddhist, who spent hours every day in front of her little altar in prayer and meditation. She never had an opportunity to travel to the holy land of India to worship the Buddha in the places of pilgrimage. Earlier, domestic duties demanded her presence. Now, old age prevented her travel. She therefore decided to ask her son to bring a sacred object back from the Buddha's homeland.

"When you go to India, please bring me a relic of the Lord Buddha for my altar." He agreed, and set out on the long journey. In India he passed the great sites of the Buddha's birth, enlightenment, teaching, and passing away (*parinirvana*). However, he was caught up in buying and selling and completely forgot his mother's request. When he returned home, she was very disappointed. The next year, he again promised to bring her a sacred relic. This time the demands of commerce totally occupied his mind, and again he forgot his sacred commission. The mother's disappointment was even greater.

As he prepared for the next journey, she said, "I am a most unfortunate woman, dogged by old age and cursed by fate (*karma*) never to see even a trace of the Lord Buddha. What is the use of prolonging such a senseless life?" She then took him over to a nearby precipice. "You see that abyss? If you return this time with no sacred object, you will witness your mother casting herself to her death."

Sobered by her words, the son resolved this time to bring back a true relic of the Exalted One. His trip to India was long and difficult. Robbers haunted the roads, and the high mountain passes were plagued by bad weather. In India, he had to struggle just to break even on his trades. He returned to Tibet completely wrapped up in thoughts of business. It was only as he approached the little village of his home that he recalled the threat spoken by his mother. Clearly, he could not return empty handed. In near panic, he cast about to find something to give his mother. He had nothing. Suddenly he stumbled on the dried carcass of a dog by the side of the road. An inspiration struck him. With his knife he prized out one shiny molar from the canine skull. Cleaning it off, he wrapped it in a piece of fine Varanasi silk and placed it in a carved sandalwood box.

The old woman was delighted with the "relic of Buddha" presented by her son with great ceremony. She placed it in the center of her altar and, with a mind overflowing with joyful faith and devotion she began a serious regimen of worshipping the "sacred object." Prostrating to it a hundred times every morning, she offered it butter lamps, sparkling vessels of pure mountain water, rare fruits and fine incenses. She meditated on it as if it was the Buddha himself. Gradually the tooth began to glow with a mystical light. The veils of ignorance and delusion that had obscured her vision since beginningless time gradually melted away. Soon she joined the ranks of the enlightened ones, abandoning the toils of *samsara* and going forth to accomplish the welfare and happiness of all.

Outwardly, the sacred object was just a dog's tooth. It had an inner meaning for the elderly woman because she believed it to be the tooth of the Buddha. It therefore served as a focus and inspiration for her faith. Its secret meaning is its *tantric* significance. In *tantric* texts, the Buddha teaches that the world, *just as it is*, is a pure land of enlightenment. Every sound is the sacred word of the Buddha. Every living being is a sublime deity. The refusal or inability to see this is the fundamental defilement and the source of all misery and *samsaric* bondage. *Tantric* practice, therefore, cultivates the ability to perceive all things as transcendental. To perceive them as such requires increased merit and wisdom.

The sacred objects in the collection each function on these three levels. Outwardly, they each have a provenance, a history, and a physical composition. The inner meaning is found in their symbolism and ritual use. Their secret meaning is the manner in which they actually are the body, speech, mind or attributes of enlightened beings. By honoring them with faith and using them with skill, defilement is reduced and merit and wisdom accumulated. The inner meaning indicates how each object should be used. The secret meaning makes that use efficacious.

The beauty and profound significance of this collection of the Dalai Lamas' sacred, religious and ritual items is one of Tibet's great gifts to the world. Within it are some of the finest representations of the material and spiritual treasures of the ancient heritage of Buddha Shakyamuni. Much has been lost in the recent upheavals of history. May Tibet, and the sublime culture it has preserved for so long, not be lost to the world.

Sarvamangalam!

(May all living beings be happy!)

15
Kadampa *Stupa*
Copper alloy
Tibet, 14th century
H: 31.4 cm; D (base): 12 cm
Potala Palace Collection
Published: *Precious Deposits*,
vol. 3, pp. 78-79, no. 40

A *stupa* (Tibetan: *chorten*; reliquary/cenotaph) is the fundamental Buddhist monument and symbol of the faith. In India, the original *stupas* were burial mounds containing sacred relics. In Tibet, the *stupa* represents the mind of the Buddha, and is one of the three required objects on a Buddhist altar (the others are an image of the Buddha, representing his body, and a sacred text, representing his speech). There are many sizes and styles of *stupas* in India and throughout the Buddhist world. A *stupa* may be understood as a monument to the state of perfect enlightenment and represents the fully enlightened mind of a Buddha. As a historical monument, it commemorates the final attainment (*parinirvana*) of a Buddha.

This is a type of *stupa* introduced to Tibet from India with the second transmission of Buddhism in the 10th and 11th century. It is associated with the school of the eminent Indian Buddhist savant Atisha Dipamkara Shrijnana (982-1054). Atisha's disciple Drom Tonba ('Brom ston pa, 1008-1064) established the reformist Kadampa tradition, which is known for its Indian Buddhist pedigree and for the simplicity and purity of its ethics, meditations, and monastic discipline.

The bell-shaped dome of the *stupa*, called *garbha* (womb) or *anda* (egg) contains Mount Meru, the cosmic mountain at the center of the universe. It rests on a lotus pedestal and is surmounted by a high abode (*harmika*), sometimes called "the penthouse of the gods" (*devakotuva*) that represents the Trayastrimsha heaven of Indra, King of the Gods. The *stupa*'s upper portion (*yashti* or cosmic-tree) consists of thirteen parasols, symbolizing progressive stages (*bhumi*) leading to enlightenment. The axis-tree supports a parasol (*chattra*) symbolizing the Buddha's supreme status. Upon this sits a lotus bud, which in turn, supports a crescent moon (symbolizing universal compassion) and a sun (perfect wisdom). The finial is in the form of the three flaming jewels of enlightenment (*Dharmakaya*, *Sambhogakaya*, and *Nirmanakaya*) that arise out of the union of compassion and wisdom.

16
Crystal *Stupa*
Crystal, gilt copper, and turquoise
Nepal, 18th century
H: 33.5 cm; W: 14 cm
Tibet Museum, Lhasa
Published: *Treasures from Snow Mountains*, p. 128, no. 48; *Tibet Museum Catalog*, pp. 96-97, no. 4

The Buddha Shakyamuni taught that living beings in this world often require objects to support their faith and spiritual practices. These include physical, verbal, and mental support objects. It is through these support objects that the Buddha bestows his blessings and powers.

Tradition holds that the blessings and benefits that result from establishing a *stupa*—a mental support object—are immense. For example, when a *stupa* is established in a particular town, every living being in that locality, by merely seeing it, will be completely freed from the defilements of the five poisonous mental afflictions. In addition, they will be freed from the miseries of the lower rebirths (in the hells, or as animals or ghosts), and will gain the seed of the state of Buddhahood, which will then ripen through the cultivation of the path to enlightenment.

The presence of a *stupa* in an area is said to attract all that is virtuous and auspicious, and to bring peace, happiness and prosperity to that land. It protects from all that is fearful or ruinous, such as disasters of earth, water, fire, and wind, and the harm caused by weapons, poisons, pollutants, disease, animals, organisms, corrupt governments, and so forth. Regarding the benefits of the *stupa*, the Buddha said:

"It is possible to calculate the benefits of making offerings to all of the Buddhas and Bodhisattvas. However, the benefits that arise from establishing one of these mental support objects are beyond all calculation."

The Buddha also said:

"By offering merely one flower, or some pure water to a *stupa,* you will gain great benefits. In this very life, you will accumulate a vast store of merit and wisdom and will eliminate all defilements. In the next life, you will take rebirth in a Buddha's Pure Land."

This crystal *stupa* is a model of the Bodhnath *stupa* in the Kathmandu Valley of Nepal. The bell-shaped crystal body of the *stupa* rests on a series of bases, the lower one, a recessed square and the upper, lotus-shaped. A ring of *vajras* separates the two. Above the crystal dome is the square abode (Sanskrit: *harmika*), adorned in the Nepalese style with the eyes of the primordial Buddha looking out. There are thirteen parasols above the *harmika*, topped by the sun and moon, and beautifully inlaid with turquoise and other precious stones.

17
Coral Mandala Offering Set
Coral and gilt silver
Tibet, 18th century
H: 21.5 cm; D: 16.5 cm
Tibet Museum, Lhasa
Published: *Treasures from Snow Mountains*, p. 148, no. 66; *Tibet Museum Catalog*, pp. 112-113, no. 2

Mandala offering sets are usually made of metal, but the layers of this unique example are made of precious red coral beads sewn together. The mandala has a partial gilt silver repoussé base, ornamented with the seven symbolic attributes of a virtuous Buddhist emperor, interspersed with lotuses. The four layers above are strung with red coral beads highlighted with pearls. On the top is a partial gilt silver Dharma wheel on a lotus base. The center of the wheel is inlaid with turquoise.

During religious ceremonies, the mandala offering set is constructed in a symbolic offering of an idealized universe with thirty-seven separate features. These include such things as the sun and moon, and the seven symbolic attributes of a virtuous Buddhist monarch (Sanskrit: *sapta rajayaratna*; Tibetan: *rgyal srid sna bdun*)—the precious wheel, priceless jewel, cherished queen, eminent householder, glorious elephant, invaluable horse, and the illustrious military chief. The names of these thirty-seven features are recited as each of them is added to the mandala using rice and/or precious stones, bits of gold, silver, coral, and so forth. The base is held in the left hand, and the largest ring is placed on top and filled with grains or other substances. This is repeated with the middle ring and then with the small ring. Finally, the top ornament is placed at the summit of the now conical construction. It is then offered to the objects of worship, typically the assembly of enlightened beings including the Buddhas, Bodhisattvas, Supreme Beings (*yidam*), protector deities, and the lineage of Lamas from the historical Buddha (Shakyamuni), down to one's own Lama. This offering ritual is repeated as many times as possible. One hundred and eleven thousand such offerings (or abridged versions of this offering), are part of the standard "preliminary practices" Buddhists often complete before engaging in actual Tantric meditations.

18
The Precious Wheel (Tibetan: *korlo rinpoche*;
Sanskrit: *cakraratna*)
Gilt silver with precious stones
Tibet, 19th century
H: 47.5 cm; W: 22.5 cm
Tibet Museum, Lhasa
Published: *Treasures from Snow Mountains*, p. 152, no. 70;
Tibet Museum Catalog, p 182, no. 2

Buddhists use many different types of symbolic wheels in ritual settings, each one distinguished by the number of spokes: eight, twelve, sixteen, thirty-two, and one thousand. This partial gilt silver example is a one thousand spoke wheel that symbolizes the Thousand Buddhas of the present "fortunate eon" (*kalpa bhadra*). It is one of the seven symbolic attributes (Sanskrit: *sapta rajayaratna;* Tibetan: *rgyal srid sna bdun*) of a universal emperor (see no. 17). The wheel in the shape of a sun-disc plays on the analogy between the sun, whose light and warmth pervade the entire world; the universal emperor, whose power pervades the entire world; and the Buddha, whose blessings pervade the entire world. It is surrounded by a flame-shaped aureole, and its central disc is divided into thirteen concentric rings, with a turquoise stone set in the center. The aureole is filled with flowers and leafy scrolls and the flowers are ornamented with turquoise and other semi-precious stones.

Tibet: Its Religion and Ritual

TIBET: TREASURES FROM THE ROOF OF THE WORLD

19
Bell and *Vajra*
Gilt copper
China, Ming Dynasty, Xuande reign (1426-1435)
Bell: H: 20 cm; D: 10 cm
Vajra: H: 14 cm; D: 4 cm
Potala Palace Collection
Published: *Treasures from Snow Mountains*, p. 129, no. 49

The *vajra* (Tibetan: *dorje*) and bell (Sanskrit: *ghanta*; Tibetan: *drilbu*) are the most common ritual implements in Tantric Buddhism. The *ghanta* bell is held in the left hand and a matched *vajra* in the right. In Tantric practice, the *ghanta* bell embodies the feminine principle of the perfect wisdom that transcends the illusions of the world. The *vajra* embodies the masculine principle of universal compassion and the skillful means to free beings from misery and its causes.

The nine-pronged gilt *vajra* has eight curved prongs and one central prong on each end that spring from *makara* heads (mythical, crocodile-like creatures). The bell's handle consists of half of a *vajra*; the head of Prajnaparamita, the female deity of supreme knowledge; and a vase of ambrosia. Emperor Yongle, the third emperor of the Ming Dynasty (reigned 1403-1424), began the practice of casting bells and *vajras* of this type as gifts for the high Lamas of Tibet. This bell and *vajra* set were commissioned by Emperor Xuande (reigned 1426-1435) the fifth in the Ming dynastic line, who continued Emperor Yongle's policy of gift exchange with Tibet.

The jade bell and five-pronged *vajra* were made at the 18th century Manchu, Qing Dynasty court, probably as a gift to the Eighth Dalai Lama. Mimicking different media metal objects reproduced in jade; jade objects reproduced in ceramic; and so on, was a specialty of court workshops during Emperor Qianlong's reign (1736-1795). Emperor Qianlong was an enthusiastic devotee of Tibetan Buddhism, and maintained an active relationship of tribute and gift-giving throughout his long reign, that was explicitly modeled on the system created in the early Ming Dynasty. This jade set may well have been designed to replicate a similar bronze set of Emperor Yongle, which the Eighth Dalai Lama gave to Emperor Qianlong.

20
Bell and *Vajra*
Jade
China, Qing Dynasty, Qianlong reign (1736-1795)
Bell: H: 16 cm; D: 9 cm
Vajra: H: 10 cm
Potala Palace Collection
Published: *Treasures from Snow Mountains*, p. 131, no. 51

A *purba* is a ritual dagger, an important ritual object believed to have been introduced in the 8th century by Padma Sambhava (see no. 6). The purba has a triple-edged blade used to dispatch the three great enemies. Ordinary enemies may be converted to friends by such means as generosity, kindness, and compassion. However, unseen enemies, such as the three great enemies (one's own greed, hatred, and ignorance) cannot be controlled by external means. The *purba* uses the special methods of Tantric practice to focus the power of a wrathful god, such as Hayagriva or Mahakala, on the unseen enemy within. Many different *purbas* may be deployed in the practice of mandalas (diagrammatic images of the sacred world, which also represent the palace of the deity, and the mind and body of the Buddhist practitioner), when they are used to stabilize the mandala's main points and overcome obstacles to the approach to enlightenment.

The handle of the 12th-13th century brass *purba* (see no. 21) depicts Vajrakila holding a curved knife and skull cup. His torso is adorned with snake ornaments. The bottom portion of the triangular blade has *makara* heads on each side, between which are three flayed animal skins. The *purba* is inserted into a base in the form of the demon of ignorance, whose entrails—symbolizing hatred, greed, envy, and so on—can be seen spilling out of his body. The entire assemblage sits on a triangular base in the form of flames, which bears a lotus pedestal. This *purba* was formerly kept at the Norbulingka, the Summer Palace of the Dalai Lamas.

The pair of gilt bronze *purbas* from the Potala Palace (see no. 22) has handles with the visage of a fierce, Mahakala type deity. In these later, 17th - 20th century *purbas*, the blade has entwined serpents between the three blades and only one *makara*.

The set of 21 painted wooden *purbas* from the Potala Palace consists of one main *purba* with the head of the main deity, and a retinue of smaller *purbas* with the heads of real and mythical animals (bear, dog, deer, horse, goat, tiger, *makara*, and others). Each *purba* in the retinue represents an auxiliary to the main *purba*, which has the image of a ferocious Mahakala-type deity. Each of the *purbas* allows the Buddhist practitioner to invoke the power of that divinity, and focus it on the corresponding part of the mandala to control a specific type of obstacle to good fortune, longevity, spiritual development, and enlightenment.

21
Purba (Ritual Dagger)
Brass
Tibet, 12th - 13th century
H: 24 cm; W: 10 cm
Tibet Museum, Lhasa
Published: *Well Selected,* p. 154, no. 129; *Treasures from Snow Mountains*, p. 123, no. 44; *Tibet Museum Catalog*, p. 180, no.3

22
Pair of *Purbas*
Gilt bronze
Tibet, 18th century
H: 62 cm; L: 11.3 cm
Potala Palace Collection
Published: *Gems of the Potala*, p. 242

23
5 *Purbas* from a set of 21
Painted Wood
Tibet, 18th - 19th century
H: 30-20 cm; L: 6-3.5 cm
Potala Palace Collection
Published: *Treasures from Snow Mountains*, pp. 124-125, no. 45

The prayer wheel is a device that provides an efficient way of focusing prayers. A coil of mantras (mystic, mind-protecting spells associated with an enlightened deity), often tens of thousands, printed from woodblocks on long scrolls, are rolled up and placed within the cylinder. The meditator spins the wheel, using the weight on the end of the chain to accelerate and sustain the spinning. Like other Buddhist ritual devices, the prayer wheel is a support (Tibetan: *rten*) for meditation. With each revolution of the wheel, the meditator visualizes the mantras going forth to benefit others. Each of the hundreds of thousands of mantras becomes the deity of that mantra and goes forth to encompass the welfare and happiness for limitless living beings. The most common mantra in Tibetan prayer wheels is the six-syllable mantra of the Bodhisattva Avalokiteshvara: "Om Mani Padme Hum."

Prayer wheels come in all sizes, some hand-held, others designed for table-top or other stationary use. The hand-held prayer wheel (no. 25), which is exquisitely crafted of silver with partial gilding, belonged to a Dalai Lama or a person of high rank. Due to years of handling, the ivory handle has developed a warm patina. The body of the wheel is inscribed with the six-syllable mantra (Om Mani Padme Hum) and *hrih*, the seed-syllable of Avalokiteshvara. The tabletop prayer wheel (see no. 24) is especially sumptuous. It consists of a chased silver cylinder with a spindle emerging from the top, which is turned to set the wheel in motion.

24
Table Prayer Wheel
Silver
Tibet, 19th century
H: 19 cm; D: 12.5 cm
Potala Palace Collection
Published: *Treasures from Snow Mountains*, p. 140, no. 59

25
Prayer Wheel
Gilt Silver
Tibet, 19th century
L: 36 cm; D: 9 cm
Norbulingka Collection
Published: *Treasures from Snow Mountains*, p. 139, no. 58; *Tibet Museum Catalog*, p. 211, no. 4

A *damaru* is a small hand-held drum used in ritual and meditation practices. It is held in the right hand, and the wrist is rotated back and forth so that the strikers rapidly beat the two drum skins. At the same time, the ritual bell (*ghanta*) is often rung by the left hand. The most typical use of these is as a musical offering to whichever deities are being addressed in the ritual.

This *damaru* of jade nephrite is crafted in the shape of two crania, designed to resemble an actual skull drum. The drum skin is dyed turquoise and painted with designs in gold and other colors. The two strikers are crocheted red silk and the top of the multipart tassel is embroidered with auspicious symbols and ends in five separate silk
tassels in red, yellow, blue, white, and green. The jade body of the drum and the intricate weaving of the tassel attachments strongly suggest that this drum was a gift to the Dalai Lama from Emperor Qianlong (reigned 1736-1795).

26
Hand Drum (*Damaru*)
Nephrite, hide, gold, semi-precious stones, and silk
China, Qing Dynasty, Qianlong reign (1736-1795)
H: 6.5 cm; D: 11 cm
Potala Palace Collection
Published: *Treasures from Snow Mountains*, p. 132, no. 52

Conch shells have been in ritual use in Tibet at least since the introduction of Buddhism. The white conch is one of the "Eight Auspicious Symbols" of Buddhism. A conch was presented by Indra to Shakyamuni Buddha after his Enlightenment in request for his teaching. The conch therefore symbolizes the proclamation of the Dharma (the Buddha's teaching). When Buddhist disciples request a formal teaching of the Dharma, they offer a conch to the teacher. Its loud, deep sound is used to summon monks to an assembly. Unlike most seashells, this rare type of conch coils to the right.

One of a pair of right-turning conches, once preserved in the Norbulingka, this conch and its mate have an interesting history. The eight trigrams in high relief decorate the wings of the trumpets among auspicious clouds. The mouthpiece of this trumpet reads: *Jiaqing longyin*, or "the dragon sings in celebration," while the other reads: *faxiang huxiao*, "the tiger roars auspiciously." It is unusual, that this pair of Tibetan ritual trumpets bears typical Chinese Daoist decoration, and that the inscriptions are associated with the tiger and dragon, the *yin* and *yang* guardians of ancient China. What is most interesting, is that while one trumpet bears a Chinese inscription on the back stating that it was respectfully made by Zhongyi Sanran (a Daoist name) on the twenty-fifth day of the first month of the year *gengchen*, the thirteenth year of the reign of Emperor Chongzhen (equivalent to 1640), the other has a Tibetan inscription stating that the pair were an offering from Geleg Rabtan, son of the King of Batang. Batang, ethnically Tibetan, is now part of China's Sichuan province. The fact that Geleg Rabtan signed his Daoist name and used Daoist motifs on Buddhist sacred trumpets suggests he was influenced by both Buddhism and Daoism.

27
Ritual Conch Trumpet (one of a pair)
Conch shell and gilt silver
China, Ming Dynasty, Chongzhen reign,
dated 1640
L: 35 cm; W: 21 cm
Tibet Museum, Lhasa
Published: *Well-Selected*, p. 120, no. 90;
Treasures from Snow Mountains, p. 138, no. 57; *Tibet Museum Catalog*, p. 106, no. 2

This rare right-turning conch has been carved with the Seven Buddhas of the Past, with a eulogy by the Qing Dynasty Emperor Qianlong (reigned 1736-1795), which is also recorded in his collected works:

> Conch of the endless sea,
> Sublime instrument of Indra's heaven,
> Used to sound the chant,
> Words of truth, words of power,
> Shakyamuni plucks a flower,
> Kasyapa plays the music,
> To the ten directions throughout the three times,
> Different sounds, one meaning,
> Put the mind to rest, display its brightness,
> Practice the vast Mahayana and take profound refuge in the Buddha's excellence.

The imperial eulogy demonstrates that this conch was a gift to the Dalai Lama from Emperor Qianlong.

28
Ritual Conch Trumpet
Conch
Tibet (1736-1795)
H: 10.5 cm; L: 18.5 cm
Potala Palace Collection
Published: *Treasures from Snow Mountains*, pp. 136-137, no. 56

29
Pair of Conch Trumpets
Conch, gilt silver, turquoise
Tibet, 18th century
H(1): 23.5 cm; L (1): 48 cm; W(1) 13 cm
H(2): 25.5 cm; L (2): 43.5 cm; W(2) 13 cm
Potala Palace Collection
Published: *The Potala Catalog*, pp. 180-181

Conch shells have been in ritual use in Tibet at least since the introduction of Buddhism. These types of shells are well known in India where various religions use conch shells for ritual. The value of this type of shell is that it turns to the right, unlike nearly all other sea shells, which coil to the left.

The conch is one of the Eight Auspicious Symbols of Buddhism. A white conch shell was presented by the King of Gods, Lord Indra, to Shakyamuni Buddha afterr the Enlightenment at Bodh Gaya. The right coiling white conch symbolizing the proclamation fo the Dharma Indra presented it to the Buddha as he requested that Buddha proclaim the Dharma in this world system. To this day, an honored Buddhist teacher may be offered such a conch shell by his disciples when they request a formal teaching of the Dharma.

This pair of conches has typical Tibetan decoration on the silver flanges. The mouthpiece improves the conch's acoustic qulities, and the silver flange is designed to make the appearance more impressive.

Tibetan oboes (*gyaling*) come in pairs. This outstanding pair from the Potala Palace is adorned with precious and semi-precious jewels. A *gyaling* is fingered like a wooden flute or a recorder and has a split reed that fits at the very top. There are no reeds present here, perhaps because the reed is fragile and was often changed during heavy use. The *gyaling* is played only in pairs. *Gyaling* means "royal oboe" and it is played to indicate that something very grand is taking place or someone very important is arriving. When a king or a great Lama is entering an assembly, a pair of *gyalings* will sound. There is always a lead player (first *gyaling*) and an accompanying player (second *gyaling*). The second *gyaling* must watch the fingers of the first *gyaling* and play exactly what he plays. The fraction of a second delay makes for a rich echoing sound.

30
Gyaling Horns
Gold on silver, wood, turquoise and jewels
Tibet, early 20th century
H: 59 cm; D: 15 cm
Potala Palace Collection
Published: *Precious Deposits*, vol. 5, pp. 226-227, no. 138

TIBET: ITS RELIGION AND RITUAL

31
Long Horn (one only)
Silver
Tibet, 17th - 20th century
H: 160.5 cm; W: 23.7 cm
Potala Palace Collection
Published: *Precious Deposits*, vol. 4, p. 146, no. 61

This horn is from a matched set of Tibetan long horns (*gdung chen*). They are played for ceremonial occasions at Tibetan monasteries, typically accompanied by large bronze cymbals and bass drums. They are over two hundred and eighty centimeters long when extended. The sound of the long horn recalls the voice of the legendary six-tusked white elephant associated with the coming of a Buddha into the world. The two horns are played at slightly different pitches, emulating the sound of the bull elephant calling to his mate, whose answering voice is a little higher. In the esoteric science of Tantra, the long horns emulate the sounds of the internal winds entering the mystic channels.

The long horn is set on this stand when played in a temple. When played in a procession, an acolyte carries the large end of the horn with a rope handle. Figures of the Lords of the Cemetery adorn the stand, indicating that the sound of the sacred long horn is heard both in this world and the next, and serves as a guide for spirits of the dead on their journey between those worlds.

32
Long Horn Stand
Gilt Copper
Tibet, 17th - 20th century
H: 101 cm; L: 79.2 cm
Potala Palace Collection
Published: *Precious Deposits*, vol. 4, pp. 146-149, no. 62

This pair of silver ritual trumpets is modeled after human thighbones. The body of the horn is wound with silver thread, and the mouthpiece issues out from the jaws of a *makara* (mythical crocodilian creatures). Used in Buddhist ceremonies, such as musical offerings to deities, they are typically accompanied by other instruments of the sacred orchestra such as long horns, *ghanta* bells, *damaru* hand drums, *gyaling* horns, long horns, bass drums, bass cymbals, and regular cymbals. Trumpets made of human thighbones are used to summon all types of living beings—including every manner of ghost and goblin—to the great feast of the *Chod* ritual.

33
Pair of Thighbone-Shaped Trumpets
Gilt silver and jewels
Tibet, 19th century
L: 48 cm; D (mouth): 6.2 cm
Tibet Museum, Lhasa
Published: *Treasures from Snow Mountains*, p. 142, no. 61;
Tibet Museum Catalog, pp. 210-211, no. 2

This crown is worn during certain Tantric empowerments and rituals. The five segments represent the Five Buddhas. Each section, bordered by two strands of seed pearls, has an elaborate gold pedestal supporting the turquoise symbol of one of the Five Buddhas, surrounded by a jeweled halo. From left to right they are: the jewels of Ratnasambhava (south); the eight-spoke wheel of Vairochana (center); the *vajra* of Akshobya (east); the lotus of Amitabha (west); and the sword of Amoghasiddhi (north). During initiations, each Buddha is asked to give his particular empowerment to the initiate, and then to take his seat in the crown on the initiate's head.

When this crown was in the Norbulingka, it was accompanied by a black ritual yogin wig. The wig is made of wool fashioned to resemble hair. Half of the hair falls down the shoulders and the remainder is gathered in three topknots, one above the other, adorned with strings of pearls and a jeweled finial.

34
Five Buddha Crown
Cloth, gold, pearls, turquoise
Tibet, early 20th century
H: 21 cm; L: 57 cm
Tibet Museum, Lhasa
Published: *Well-Selected*, p. 118, nos. 87-1, 2; *Treasures from Snow Mountains*, p. 135, no. 55, *Tibet Museum Catalog*, p. 212, no. 1

93

35
Amulet Box (*Gau*)
Gold, silver, pearls and turquoise
Tibet, 17th - 18th century
H: 21 cm; L: 16 cm; Thickness: 9 cm
Tibet Museum, Lhasa
Published: *Well-Selected*, p. 118, no. 88; *Treasures from Snow Mountains*, p. 147, no. 65; *Tibet Museum Catalog*, p. 182, no. 1

A *gau* is an amulet box with a removable back into which a sacred image is placed, along with such things as mantras, relics, and sacred medicines. A cord is attached to the brackets on the sides, so it may be worn around the neck as a portable altar, for blessings and protection and to maintain spiritual connections with deities and Lamas. When not worn on the body, it is placed on an altar at home.

This shrine shaped *gau* came from the Norbulingka and contains a gilded image of the Buddha Amitayus. The gold work on the front cover of the *gau* is especially fine. It shows the Buddha Shakyamuni on top, and Palden Lhamo on the bottom, with eight dancing goddesses between them. The inner section of openwork design, outlined with small pearls, depicts Garuda on top, two dragons on the sides, two lions on the lower corners, and two deer kneeling in front of a Dharma wheel, the symbol of the Buddha's teaching.

36
Amulet Box (*Gau*)
Gilt Silver
Tibet, 19th century
H: 26 cm; W: 10.5 cm; L: 22 cm
Potala Palace Collection
Published: *Treasures from Snow Mountains*, p. 146, no. 64

This exquisitely modeled silver and partial gilt *gau* frames a bas-relief of an architectural shrine that is surmounted by a *serto*, the emblem of transcendence often found on the roof of a Buddhist shrine. This roof has two *makaras*. On the two sides of the ogival opening (where a small image of a deity could be displayed), are two flanking dragons that climb pillars. Six offering vases stand at the bottom of the opening. Beneath, two silver lions support the shrine model. Framing the entire shrine is a field of foliage and flowers worked in silver with the Eight Auspicious Symbols picked out in gilt. The offerings to the five senses (mirror for sight, fruit for taste, yoghurt for smell, musical instrument for sound, and a piece of silk for touch) are arrayed below the shrine model. The outer border consists of leafy scrollwork.

    This larger type of *gau* is intended specifically for a man; there are two lugs on either side designed to accommodate a strap that hangs across the chest. When its owner was at home, the *gau* would have been placed on a domestic altar. The back is detachable to allow objects to be placed inside. This *gau*'s contents are missing, but it would have contained an image of a Buddha and any of various sacred objects, such as barley grains given by a Lama, mantras, relics, woodblock-printed protective charms, and sacred medicines.

In ancient India, Buddhist sutras were written on palm leaves, the traditional material used before the introduction of paper. The pages of this manuscript are finely painted with Buddhas and their disciples. The text is written in a form of East Indian script from Bihar known as Lantsa in Tibet, and thus the manuscript is likely to have come from the Pala region of east India. Characteristic of these palm leaf manuscripts (*pothi*) is that two holes have been drilled for the string that is used to bind the pages together. The wooden covers protecting the sutra are a later addition from Tibet. They are carved with images of two mythical birds (*hamsa*) and scrolling foliage.

The *Ashtasahasrika Prajnaparamita Sutra* (Perfection of Wisdom in Eight Thousand Quatrains) is the most popular of the many long versions of the *Prajnaparamita Sutra*. It avoids the extensive repetitions of the longer versions, while providing detailed explanation missing from shorter versions, to facilitate understanding of this most profound aspect of Buddhist philosophy.

37
Ashtasahasrika Prajnaparamita Sutra
Palm leaves and gilt wood
India, Pala period, 11th - 12th century
L: 56.3 cm; W: 6.5 cm
Tibet Museum, Lhasa
Published: *Well Selected*, p. 46, no. 18; *Treasures from Snow Mountains*, pp. 114-115, no. 40

This sacred text was produced for the Third Dalai Lama, Sonam Gyatso (1543-1588), whose gilded and bejeweled portrait illumines the left side of the page. It was one of the most precious possessions of the Dalai Lamas down to the present Dalai Lama, His Holiness Tenzin Gyatso. Sonam Gyatso was the first to be called "Dalai Lama." His name "Gyatso" is translated in English as "Ocean" and in Mongolian as "Dalai." His disciple, the Mongol leader Altan Khan, therefore referred to him as the "Dalai Lama." The name is given posthumously to his two previous births.

The golden letters on this page are Tibetan; however, they spell out the Sanskrit title of this book: *Aryasuvikrantavikramipariprccha Prajnaparamitanirdesasutra*. This means, "The *Prajnaparamita* sutra on the questions of Suvikrantavikramin." Suvikrantavikramin was a distinguished disciple of Buddha Shakyamuni. This text records his questions about *Prajnaparamita,* and the Buddha's response. In general, the *Prajnaparamita* sutras present the Buddha's teaching on the essential nature of reality and how it may be realized. Until it is fully realized, one is caught up in the illusions of the conventional world (*samsara*) and is subject to every type of misery from lifetime to lifetime. There are many different *Prajnaparamita* sutras, varying in length and detail more than in their essential message. This particular *Prajnaparamita* sutra stands out among the many versions as the most advanced. In its seven chapters, the most profound points of Buddhist philosophy are analyzed in great detail, giving logical arguments and lucid descriptions and inspiring analogies.

On the right side of the page is the four-armed Goddess Prajnaparamita. She holds a *vajra* in her right hand, and a *Prajnaparamita* text in her left. The *vajra* is the embodiment of the enlightened mind and the symbol of the method of realizing it. The text contains the practical instructions on how enlightenment is realized. *Prajnaparamita's* remaining two hands are in the gesture of elucidating the profound truth of enlightenment. This goddess is the deity of the *Prajnaparamita* sutras. She is known as the *Yum* (mother) of all Buddhas. The text itself is called "The Mother" because all Buddhas are "born" from the study and practice of the *Prajnaparamita.*

38
Prajnaparamita Sutra
Gold and colors on paper
Tibet, 18th century
L: 80 cm; W: 32 cm
Potala Palace Collection

Tibet: Treasures from the Roof of the World

TIBET: ITS RELIGION AND RITUAL

The sutra is bound by two pieces of wood, and then coated with red cinnabar lacquer, which is incised and filled with gold in the Chinese *qiangjin* ("engraved gold") method.

The edges of the pages forming the text block are painted on each of the long sides with eight dancing figures—the eight offering deities. The title of the section of the work is written on one of the short sides of the text block in Tibetan and Chinese. The inside text is written in Tibetan, but it is also transcribed (not translated) line by line in Chinese characters. This suggests that this volume was prepared at the Chinese Ming Dynasty court and was designed to provide non-readers of Tibetan with an approximate pronunciation of the Tibetan phrases. The main title in Tibetan says simply that the text is a collection of preliminary practices. They are the rituals of Amitayus, the Buddha of Limitless Life, whose crowned images, one seated and one standing appears on either side of the title. The rituals are Tantric empowerments and practices aimed at clearing away obstacles to long life.

39
Ritual Text on the Buddha Amitayus
Gilt and lacquered ivory covers with paper pages
China, Ming Dynasty, 15th century
H: 14cm; L: 30.5 cm; W: 11.5 cm
Tibet Museum, Lhasa
Published: *Golden Treasures*, p. 229

103

TIBET: TREASURES FROM THE ROOF OF THE WORLD

Butter lamps are used for ritual offerings. Donating a butter lamp to a monastery and lighting a butter lamp are means of increasing one's merit. Shaped like a chalice, the butter lamp has a flaring mouth, a narrow waist, and a bottom formed by lotus petals. This finely made example is adorned with turquoise.

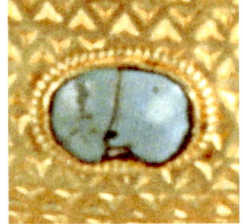

There are two popular styles of butter lamps: Kalsang (named after Kalsang Gyatso, the Seventh Dalai Lama) and Tupten (named for Tupten Gyatso, the Thirteenth Dalai Lama). This Tupten-style butter lamp, according to the inscription on the base, was made as an offering to the Fourteenth Dalai Lama.

A wick is formed from unprocessed cotton and a straw. The cotton is wrapped around the straw, and the straw set in the small hole in the middle of the basin of the lamp. The wick is placed so its top is slightly above the rim of the lamp. The lamp is then filled with clarified butter from the milk of a *dri* (female yak), and placed on an altar as an offering to the Buddha, Dharma, and Sangha.

40
Butter Lamp
Gold and turquoise
Tibet, early 20th century
H: 33 cm; D (mouth): 30 cm; D (foot): 25 cm
Potala Palace Collection
Published: *Treasures from Snow Mountains*, p. 150, no. 68

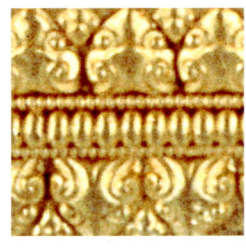

Tibet: Its Religion and Ritual

41
"Monk's Hat" Pitcher
Cloisonné enamels and
partial gilt on copper
China, Ming Dynasty
(1368-1644)
H: 22.5 cm; D(mouth): 12 cm;
D(ring foot): 8 cm
Norbulingka Collection
Published: *Treasures from Snow Mountains*, p.179, no. 90; *Tibet Museum Catalog*, pp. 200-201, no. 3

In China and the West, this type of vessel, based on Tibetan metal and wooden prototypes, is called "monk's hat" pitchers, perhaps because the shape of the spout and collar resemble hats worn by certain monks in China. This form of pitcher was particularly popular from the middle of the 15th century onward. In Tibet, they are made in a variety of sizes and are used for such things as regular water offerings and for dispensing tea at monastic assemblies.

The underglaze cobalt blue porcelain pitcher (no. 42) came originally from Norbulingka. Its collar and spout are decorated with a floral scroll, the neck has the Eight Buddhist Symbols, and the shoulders of the body have lappets in the shape of *ruyi* (wish-granting fungi), and there is an auspicious prayer-poem in Tibetan that runs around the middle, which reads:

> May you be blessed with good fortune in the morning,
>
> May you be blessed with good fortune at night,
>
> May you be blessed with good fortune at noon,
>
> May your days and nights always be blessed with good fortune,
>
> May you ever be blessed with the good fortune of the Three Jewels!

This prayer-poem, which stresses blessings in this life, must have caught the fancy of both the Ming and Qing Dynasty emperors, who had it woven into presentation scarves, embroidered onto thangkas, and inscribed on porcelain.

Although the pitcher has lost its lid and the thumb guard that originally stood upright at the top of its handle, the signs of imperial manufacture are still clear: the base is inscribed in Chinese with the six-character mark of Ming Dynasty Emperor Xuande, who reigned between 1426 and 1435. He continued to foster close tribute relations with Tibet throughout his reign.

In China, the manufacture of cloisonné enameled metalwork began in the Ming Dynasty with Emperor Jingtai (reigned 1450-1456). This remarkable cloisonné example (no. 41), complete with its lid, is similar in its decoration of stylized lotuses to contemporaneous porcelains. The lotuses take the form of medallions set against a field of floral scrolls. The lotus petals on the shoulder, recall the pedestal bases on Buddhist figural bronzes of Ming Dynasty Emperor Yongle (reigned 1403-1424). These two pitchers were imperial gifts from China. The cloisonné example has a red lacquered wooden box decorated with floral motifs in gold.

42
"Monk's Hat" Pitcher
Porcelain with under glaze cobalt blue decoration
China, Ming Dynasty, Xuande reign (1426-1435)
H: 22.4 cm; D (mouth): 13.5 cm; D (base): 8.9 cm
Norbulingka Collection
Published: *Well Selected*, p. 139, no. 112; *Treasures from Snow Mountains*, p. 178, no. 89; *Tibet Museum Catalog*, pp. 46-47, no. 4

TIBET: TREASURES FROM THE ROOF OF THE WORLD

43
Serkyem Ewer with interlocking peonies
Porcelain decorated with red underglaze copper
China, Ming Dynasty, Hongwu reign (1368-1398)
H: 37 cm; D (mouth): 7cm; D (ring foot): 11 cm
Norbulingka Collection
Published: *Treasures from Snow Mountains*, p. 175, no. 86; *Tibet Museum Catalog*, p. 190-191, no. 4

This porcelain Serkyem ewer (no. 43) mimics the shape of a metal vessel (no. 44) and even includes such details as the strut that joins the long, curved spout to the neck, and the loop on top of the handle for a metal chain to attach it to the lid. The decoration is typical of imperial wares of the early Ming Dynasty, especially those made during Emperor Hongwu's reign (1368-1398). The standing banana leaves around the neck, the lotus-shaped gadroons around the base, the peony scrolls circling the body, and the lotus lid with lotus-bud knob, can be found on many of the surviving vessels of this period. The dull grayish-red color produced by the reduction firing of underglaze copper is also typical of the period. This firing process requires that the kiln master reduce the amount of oxygen flowing into his kiln just as the temperature hits a precise mark. This process was often less than completely successful and underglaze red wares quickly yielded to the more reliable use of underglaze cobalt blue. This ewer is one of very few surviving examples of the technique and undoubtedly represents a gift of great rarity sent to a high Lama from the Ming court.

The tall, narrow-necked Serkyem (no. 44) ewer swells to a large belly and is supported on a lotus base. The handle is in the form of a dragon and the spout curves elegantly upward from the gaping mouth of a crocodilian *makara*. The body is decorated with the eight Buddhist symbols, which are combined into one single, interlocked design.

Ewers in this form are used in the Serkyem ritual, which is designed to propitiate wrathful protective deities. This nightly ritual is specifically directed at the wrathful protector of a monastery or individual. In the outer sense, the protector guards the monastery building or the home, but, in the inner sense, he protects the mind and practice of the monks or lay practitioner from defilements, deluded thoughts and untoward dreams. The ewer holds a strong black tea that is intended to keep the protector deity wide-awake during a night of vigilant guard duty.

TIBET: ITS RELIGION AND RITUAL

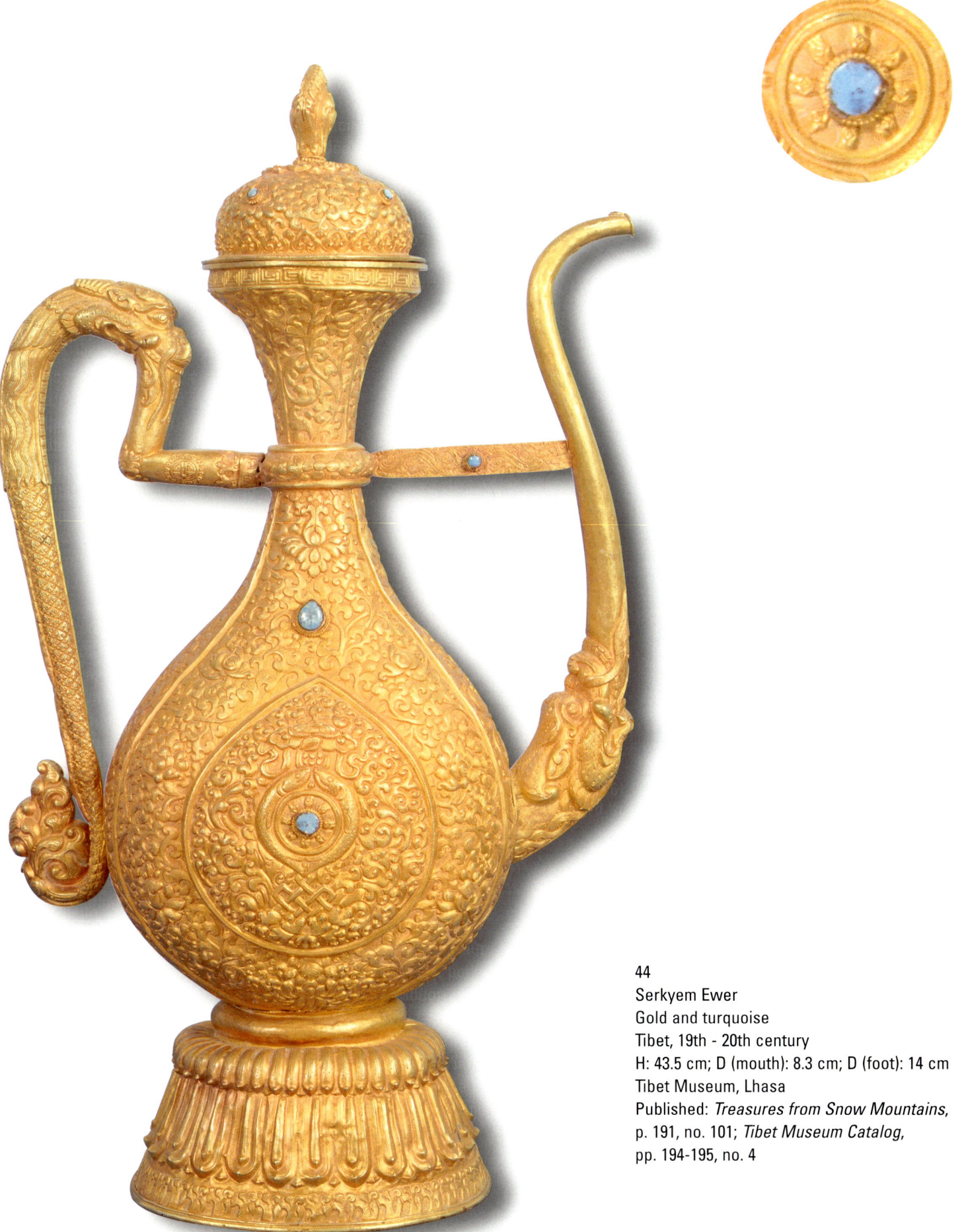

44
Serkyem Ewer
Gold and turquoise
Tibet, 19th - 20th century
H: 43.5 cm; D (mouth): 8.3 cm; D (foot): 14 cm
Tibet Museum, Lhasa
Published: *Treasures from Snow Mountains*,
p. 191, no. 101; *Tibet Museum Catalog*,
pp. 194-195, no. 4

TIBET: TREASURES FROM THE ROOF OF THE WORLD

110

45
Sacred Vessel (*kundika*)
Gold, turquoise, and coral
Tibet, 19th century
H: 21 cm; W: 10.5 cm; D (ring foot): 7 cm
Tibet Museum, Lhasa
Published: *Treasures from Snow Mountains*, p. 159, no. 75;
Tibet Museum Catalog, p. 192, no. 3

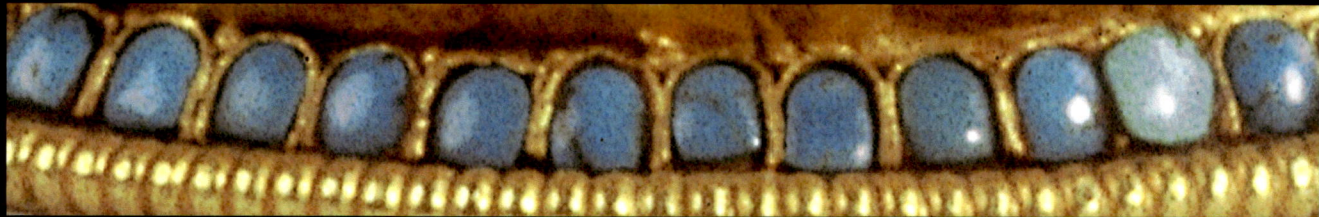

This type of elegant vessel, originating in India, is called a *kundika* (Tibetan: *ril ba spyi blug*). What seems to be the spout actually serves as the handle and is also the opening where the vessel is filled. The narrow vertical spout rises from a lotus-shaped base and is capped with a coral top. The vessel is elegantly decorated with turquoise inlays.

This type of vessel is an attribute of Maitreya, the future Buddha. From it he bestows the nectar of immortality and enlightenment. This sacred vessel is used to conclude monastic ceremonies and daily to conclude the noon meal, which is the last of the day. Before going forth into the world, the monk cleanses himself of all selfish and worldly motivations. As an outward sign, he receives the sacred nectar from this vessel. Only after taking a drink from this vessel is a monk or Lama free to get up and leave the sacred precincts.

The vessel spout, lid, body and base are all in the form of a lotus, the symbol of purity. The "nectar" is dispensed through the top of the spout and, as the monk drinks from the vessel, he is symbolically purified of worldly defilements (*klesha*) such as ignorance, anger, greed, pride, and jealousy.

46
Empowerment Ritual Vessel (Tibetan: *bumpa*)
Gold, turquoise and coral
Tibet, 19th century
H: 22.5 cm; D (mouth): 9 cm; D (base): 9.5 cm
Tibet Museum, Lhasa
Published: *Treasures from Snow Mountains*, p. 158, no. 74; *Tibet Museum Catalog*, p. 192, no. 2

This bulbous vessel with a flat top has a spout that rises out of the mouth of a gaping *makara*. The lid is decorated in relief with the Eight Auspicious Symbols, alternating with turquoise ornaments. This type of vessel, as here, is often fitted with a textile covering. Originally, the vessel contained a cone-shaped wand, topped by peacock feathers and used for sprinkling sacred nectar on images, offerings and initiates. The officiating Lama or his assistant also uses the vessel to dispense sacred nectar into his disciples' cupped hands. The nectar is composed of saffron-infused water mixed with the twenty-five vase ingredients (see nos. 49 & 50). The underside of the flat top is gripped by the fingers and nectar is poured from the spout. Disciples take a sip of the nectar of empowerment to transform them internally and put the rest on their head to receive external blessings.

47
Ritual Water Pot
Gilt Silver
Tibet, 18th - 19th century
H: 10 cm; W: 17 cm; D (bottom): 19 cm
Tibet Museum, Lhasa
Published: *Treasures from Snow Mountains*, p. 199, no. 109;
Tibet Museum Catalog, p. 206, no. 3

The flat top of this ritual pot is removed and inverted to serve as a dish for balls of *tsampa* (roasted barley flour). The *tsampa* is moistened with consecrated water to provide ritual offerings of purified food. These are provided for the recently deceased, who may return to their former homes in search of a meal before proceeding on to their next rebirth. They are also used to feed hungry ghosts (*preta*) who are unable to obtain food or drink unless it has been consecrated for their use.

The handle is placed on the side of the pot rather than opposite the spout. In rituals for feeding hungry ghosts and individuals who have died within the last forty-nine days, the Lama or lay practitioner inserts his or her finger into the loop handle, leaving the other fingers free to swing the *tingsha* cymbals used to summon spirits to the consecrated meal.

This ritual bowl made from a human skull is used in Tantric rituals as the attribute of certain deities. The skull is lined and edged in gold and has the sun and moon, a conch shell, and the six-syllable mantra, "Om Mani Padme Hum," carved in low relief on its outer surface. The Tibetan inscription on the label of the storage container records that the cup was made from the cranium of Tenpei Wangchuk (also known as Kedrup Chenpo), a great scholar and adept, and that it was offered to the Dalai Lama by Chungtsang Tulku of Drakyab Monastery in Chamdo in Eastern Tibet.

The triangular base supporting the skull cup is in the shape of a fire mandala (the sphere of the fire element), upon which sits a tripod formed of three freshly severed human heads. Skull cups are used for inner offerings (not for the outer offerings of flowers, incense, and so forth). These inner offerings are symbolic of the five aspects of the physical body and the five aspects of the mind. In ritual, these substances are symbolized by other materials, such as precious herbs and rare essences of flowers, combined with alcohol, tea, and other liquids. The skull cup, functions as the crucible for transformation of the elements of the ordinary body and mind into the body and mind of the enlightened being. In ritual, the *vajra* on the gold crown-shaped lid, which symbolizes enlightened body, speech, and mind, enter into the mixture of the five meats and five nectars and effect the transformation.

48
Kapala (Skullcup)
Tibet, 19th century
H: 25.5; W: 18.5 cm; L: 19 cm
Tibet Museum, Lhasa
Published: *Well-Selected*, p. 115, no. 82;
Treasures from Snow Mountains, p. 153, no. 71;
Tibet Museum Catalog, p. 100-101

49
Vase of Longevity
Gold, turquoise, and precious gems
Tibet, 19th century
H: 29 cm; W: 14 cm; Base: 8.8 cm
Tibet Museum, Lhasa
Published: *Well Selected,* p. 119, no. 89; *Treasures from Snow Mountains*, pp. 154-155, no. 72; *Tibet Museum Catalog*, p. 192, no. 1

Originally from the Dalai Lama's Summer Palace (Norbulingka), the jewel-encrusted gold longevity vase (no. 49) is composed of three separate sections: a vase, a base, and a top ornament of five ribbons symbolizing the Five Buddhas. The leaf-shaped central "ribbon" crowning the vase bears an image of Tsongkhapa (1357-1419), the founder of the Gelug order, on one side, and of Amitayus, the Buddha of Limitless Life, on the other.

The coral longevity vase (no. 50) is even more elaborately decorated. The vase and its support are carved from red coral, and the five ribbons are gold set with turquoise, pearls, and other precious stones. The gold openwork of the larger central ribbon forms the Eight Buddhist Symbols. The ribbon is topped with an amber sun disc, and a jade crescent moon, and the ribbon encloses a lapis-filled field upon which floats a red coral figure of Amitayus, who is seated on a white jade base.

The vase of longevity is filled with the nectar of immortality and held by the Buddha Amitayus. In Tantric ritual, the longevity vase is filled with purified water dyed with saffron, which is mixed with twenty-five "vase ingredients" (Tibetan: *bumdze, bum rdzas*). The twenty-five ingredients—five sets of five (five *vajras*—enlightened body, speech, mind, activities, and qualities)—are combined in pill form. The first set of five (enlightened body) are the five medicinal substances; the second five (enlightened speech) are the five fragrant substances; the third five (enlightened mind) are the five essences; the fourth five (enlightened activities) are the five grains; and the fifth five (enlightened qualities) are the five precious substances. The officiating Lama, who becomes mystically identified with Amitayus in the course of the ritual, then touches the vase to the heads of his disciples to dispense Amitayus' powers of limitless life, which remove obstacles to longevity and spiritual maturity.

50
Coral Longevity Vase
Coral inlaid with gold and gems
Tibet 19th century
H: 25 cm; W: 17 cm
Tibet Museum, Lhasa
Published: *Tibet Museum Catalog*, pp. 106-107, no. 5

This crown, made by Nepalese Newari craftsmen, is a sumptuous display of inlaid jewels and openwork medallions set against a gilt copper repoussé base. Gilded figures of Buddhas are surrounded by elaborately filigreed and bejeweled haloes, inlaid with pearls, lapis lazuli, turquoise, rubies, and emeralds. This type of crown is still worn by Nepalese *vajracaryas* (lay Buddhist masters of the *vajra*), when they perform important rituals that involve realizing themselves as Buddhas. The goal of these rituals is to empower all living beings with the blessings of enlightenment. Other similar crowns are found in the Art Institute of Chicago, the Los Angeles County Museum of Art, the Virginia Museum of Fine Art, and the Musée Guimet, Paris. The Guimet crown is dated by inscription equivalent to 1145 and its similarity to the present crown suggests it must have been made at about the same time.

The Five Buddhas (Vairochana, Akshobhya, Ratnasambhava, Amitabha, and Amoghasiddhi) are arrayed around the crown. All five are represented in their divine form (Sanskrit: *Sambhogakaya*). The Buddha directly above the wearer's forehead is Vairochana and above him is Akshobhya. Akshobhya is the lineage lord of the *Vajra* Family of Buddhas and the teacher of most of the Tantric rituals. He therefore has a central place on the crown.

51
Sacred Crown
Gilt copper with inlays of turquoise, rock crystals, rubies, and pearls.
Nepal, 11th - 12th century
Overall H: 33 cm; W: 21.5 cm
Potala Palace Collection
Published: *Precious Deposits,* vol. 1, pp. 126-127, no. 79; See also Pratapaditya Pal, *Nepal, Where the Gods Are Young* (New York: The Asia Society, 1975), pl. 51; Ian Alsop, "Repoussé in Nepal," *Orientations* (July 1986): 14-27, fig. 6

52
Dance Costume
Silk, bone
Tibet, 19th century
Hat: H: 29 cm; D: 13 cm
Costume: H: 148 cm; L: 100 cm
Potala Palace Collection

The elaborate apron and crown (Tibetan: *rugyen, rus pa'i rgyen*), the dominant features of this dance costume, are made of human bones. Its design is modeled on the bone ornaments of the *dakini*, female deities of Enlightenment, who give special teachings to adepts. Wearing these garments during the *cham* dance, Lamas transform themselves into deities.

The dancer wears a wig consisting of three piled up topknots with strands of hair hanging over the shoulders. The crown covering the wig has five skulls that represent the transformation of the Five Poisons into the Five Wisdoms. The long, full sleeves of the robe are made of strips of sumptuous brocaded silk, and the silk apron that covers the body of the robe bears a large appliquéd image of the fierce deity Mahakala, with his three eyes and fangs. The apron has a border of skulls alternating with *vajras,* and ends in a rainbow-colored fringe. Over the silk apron, the dancer also wears a second, bone apron, made of carved bone ornaments in various shapes strung with bone beads. The bone terminates with small bells.

SACRED ARTS OF TIBET

T E R E S E   T S E   B A R T H O L O M E W

In Tibet, religion is a way of life. Tibetan Buddhism permeates every aspect of Tibetan culture, especially its art. The sacred sculptures and paintings of this exhibition function as a support for the Buddhist faith, for they inspire Tibetans to acquire the ideal qualities represented in these images.

Paintings
In Tibet, paintings take many forms. They can be painted directly on the walls of monasteries, similar to the frescoes of Europe, or they can also be painted on large pieces of prepared cloths, and then adhered to the walls. The paintings shown in this exhibition are called thangkas, literally "something that is rolled up." They are painted on cotton and framed in brocade. They can be rolled up when they are not in use, and transported with ease. A thangka, used as an aid to meditation, can be woven, embroidered, or appliquéd. Paintings can range from miniature images that can be inserted into an amulet box, to gigantic ones that require hundreds of people to carry them and are shown once a year during religious festivals. Some paintings are the size of playing cards; they come in sets and are known as *tsakali*, used by teachers when they instruct their students during initiations.

Thangkas were mainly painted by itinerant artists who traveled all over Tibet, working for monasteries as well as for private patrons. Monks, such as some of the Karmapas, were also talented painters. The Tenth Karmapa Choying Dorje (1604 –1674) was a famous artist and there are several extant paintings attributed to him.[1] In general, thangka artists do not sign their work. For the artist, painting a sacred image is an act of merit and the person who commissions it also accrues merit.

Thangkas are commissioned for many reasons: for use in religious practice, for long life, as a thanksgiving for having recovered from illness, or for the accumulation of merit. The person who commissions the thangka supplies the material. The quality of the pigments, the amount of gold used for embellishment, the richness of the brocade utilized for mounting the painting, all depend on the wealth of the person commissioning the thangka.

The process of painting a thangka can be summarized as follows:

1. Thin hide glue (yak skin glue) is applied to the unbleached cotton, cut to the required size, the edges sewn with thin strips of bamboo, and then laced firmly to a wooden frame. The glue waterproofs the cotton, so that it will not absorb the colors.
2. Sizing of chalk and glue is applied to both the front and back. When dried, it is polished with a smooth stone on a hard level surface, until the grain of the cloth is hardly visible.
3. The images to be painted are drawn with charcoal. The lines are then gone over with a fine brush dipped in black or red ink. The proportions of the images are set down in sacred texts and have to be followed precisely. In the background, however, the artists can give free rein to their creativity (Figures 1 and 2).

Opposite Page:
Figure 1
Thangka Painter, 1937
Photo: Theos Bernard
The Theos Bernard Collection,
Gift of the Eleanor Murray Estate.
Phoebe A. Hearst Museum of Anthropology,
University of California Berkeley,
(XXVIII-19).

Figure 2
Tibet, 1937
Photo: Theos Bernard
The Theos Bernard Collection,
Gift of the Eleanor Murray Estate.
Phoebe A. Hearst Museum of Anthropology,
University of California Berkeley,
(LVIII-33).

4. Tibetan artists make their own brushes from yak and goat hair. Some use sable brushes imported from China.[2] Colors are made from minerals and plants, and mixed with yak skin glue. Light background colors are applied first, such as the sky. The central image follows: the lotus throne first, then the clothes, and finally the body of the deity. The final touches consist of detailing in gold, and polishing the gold lines with a piece of agate. The eyes are the last things to be painted.

5. The finished thangka is sewn into a mounting of Chinese brocade and a thin gauze curtain is sewn on top. To display the thangka, the curtain is rolled up and tucked into a string across the top, with the middle part arranged nicely in a loop. Two long ribbons draping from the top are for securing the thangka in a windy area, otherwise, they hang down as decorations. On the back of consecrated thangkas the words "Om," "Ah," and "Hum," are written over the body, speech, and mind centers of the main image and sometimes on the subsidiary images. In some cases, there are prayers written on the back as well, and handprints of the monk doing the consecration.

Included in this exhibition are thangkas that are embroidered, woven, and appliquéd. They, like the painted thangkas, have to follow precisely the proportions of the images set down in the sacred texts. The embroidered thangka of Cittavishramana Avalokiteshvara (see no. 73) is simple and stately, while that of the Sarvavid Vairochana (see no. 60) is sumptuous in its ornamentation. The names and genders of the creators of these two fine works are unknown. In China embroidery is usually done by women, but in the Himalayas, men too do this type of fine work. Tibetan embroidery often included small pieces of pearls, turquoise, and coral. The 7th century Trandruk Monastery, the principal shrine of the Yarlung Valley in Tibet, possesses a thangka sewn entirely of pearls, depicting Princess Wencheng (one of the two wives of King Songtsen Gampo) as the incarnation of White Tara. *Kesi* "slit silk" tapestry, such as the portrait of Shakya Yeshe (see no. 10) and the Chakrasamvara (see no. 65) are Chinese in origin, and are masterpieces made by the imperial workshops of the Ming Dynasty. Pieces in such pristine condition no longer exist in China but, because of Tibet's dry climate, these remarkable thangkas have been preserved.

Figure 3
Unrolling the giant thangka during the Yoghurt Festival
Photo: Terese Tse Bartholomew.

Appliqué thangkas, such as the White Tara in this exhibition (see no. 81) are made entirely of brocaded silk and satin. In a painted thangka, the brushwork outlining each element is of utmost importance. For an appliqué thangka, this outlining is done with the 'horse thread,' horsehair wrapped with silken thread used for edging the individual pieces of brocade. Appliqué is the preferred method of making a gigantic thangka, such as the two *kyigus* covering a space of about 75 feet x 40 feet, displayed on the lower faces of the Potala Palace on the thirtieth day of the second month. Drepung Monastery near Lhasa shows its large thangka during the Yoghurt Festival in summer, when it is draped over the hillside (Figure 3). These are just two examples of the many giant thangkas used in the great monasteries of Tibet. Tashilhunpo Monastery, seat of the Panchen Lama, has its own high wall for displaying gigantic thangkas (Figure 4).

Gyeten Namgyal (1912-), a tailor who worked for the Thirteenth Dalai Lama and who became Namsa Chenmo (Great Master of Clothes), and ran the workshop catering to the Dalai Lama's needs under the Fourteenth Dalai Lama, discussed in his memoir how such gigantic appliqué thangkas were made.[3] He was in charge of the two thangkas created shortly after the Fourteenth Dalai Lama was enthroned. It took sixty tailors eight months to complete the job. Gyeten Namgyal also supervised the making of appliqué thangkas for Norbulingka. The most difficult one requested by the Fourteenth Dalai Lama was a complex Kalachakra thangka (for a similiar deity see nos. 66, 67 & 68). Eight tailors worked on it for one year! However, not all appliqué thangkas were made by male tailors. The mother of Qing Dynasty Emperor Qianlong (reigned 1736-1795), a devout Buddhist, made an appliqué thangka of the Green Tara, now on display in the Yonghegong in Beijing.

Figure 4
Gigantic appliqué Thangka at Tashilhunpo Monastery, 1937
Photo: Theos Bernard
The Theos Bernard Collection, Gift of the Eleanor Murray Estate.
Phoebe A. Hearst Museum of Anthropology, University of California Berkeley,
(XXIX-27).

In smaller thangkas, like the White Tara, the brocade pieces were sometimes pasted instead of stitched. The process of making an appliqué thangka is usually more difficult than painting. As a result, the iconography in appliqué thangkas is generally less complicated. There are peaceful and wrathful gods in the thangka of the White Tara (see Figure 5). White Tara (4), as the main deity of this thangka, sits in the center, and is larger in size than the accompanying gods and goddesses. In thangkas, the central deity or figure can also sit off to one side, like King Songtsen Gampo (see no. 3). Size determines the major deity. As a peaceful deity, White Tara sits in meditation and her hair is blue in color, as opposed to the wrathful White Achala (7) with orange- color hair, brandishing a sword below. White Tara and the peaceful gods above (1-3) all have lotus-shaped eyes. White Tara's outer (see no. 5) halo is bordered with a rainbow and flowers. Achala and the wrathful yellow god of wealth below have bulging eyes and flaming haloes for burning off ignorance.

The peaceful gods at the top of the thangka are, from left to right: the goddess Ushnishavijaya (1), the Buddha of Boundless Life, Amitayus (2), and the supreme deity Sitasamvara (3). White Tara and the three peaceful gods above sit on white moon disks (represented by white brocade with gold designs), while the two wrathful gods below sit on red sun disks (represented by red brocade with gold designs). In front of White Tara is the peaceful offering of the five senses (6): a mirror for sight, cymbals for hearing, fruit for taste, a conch with yoghurt for smell, and a piece of silk for touch. The proper offerings to a wrathful deity is a large skull containing the wrathful offering of the five senses, with tongue, ears, eye balls, nose, and heart.

The presence of the three gods of longevity, Amitayus, White Tara, and Ushnishavijaya, together with the Yellow god of wealth, suggests that this thangka was commissioned for the purpose of obtaining wealth and longevity.

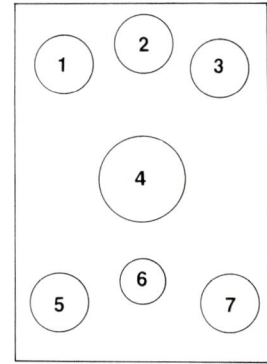

Figure 5
Line drawing of White Tara appliqué thangka illustration.
Illustration: Terese Tse Bartholomew.

Sculptures
Tibetan sculptures, like the images in thangkas, have to follow the proportions stipulated in the sacred texts. Clay and metal are the most commonly seen sculptural materials in Tibet; rarer materials such as wood, ivory, horn, turquoise and coral are also used. The Newars of Kathmandu Valley in Nepal were, and still are, the best craftsmen of the Himalayas; they are famous for lost-wax casting and repoussé work, and their use of semi-precious stones and skill at mercury gilding are beyond compare. The Newars were often itinerant craftsmen who traveled from place to place, working wherever there was a need for sculptures, such as when a monastery was under construction and needed images for its altars. During the 13th

century, Anige (1243 - 1306), a famous artist-prince from Nepal, decorated the Sakya Monastery and, later on, he and his students were invited to Dadu (near present-day Beijing) to work for the Mongol Kublai Khan, who founded the Chinese Yuan Dynasty. (See Patricia Berger, "Diplomatic Gifts.") Some of the Newars who worked in Tibet settled down and married Tibetans and their descendants continued their craft. In Lhasa, the Dalai Lamas, at least the Thirteenth, had craftsmen in his direct employ.

The standing Buddha (see no. 53) is a fine piece of Newari lost-wax casting. The model for the piece was an Indian sculpture of the Gupta period (4th - 6th century). Gupta sculptors of India had successfully perfected the image of the Buddha and their model was closely followed by the Newars of Nepal. The proportions, the hair and ears, the stance of the body, the thin garment revealing the body below, all followed Gupta prototypes.

The Newars were, and still are, masters of repoussé — the method of forming an image by hammering a thin sheet of copper. The piece of copper is embedded in a bed of pitch, a mixture of wax, resin, and brick powder. Using a small hammer and a large assortment of chisels and punches, the metal is worked from the back and then from the front.[4] The end result is further embellished with turquoise, coral, and other gems, and then fire gilded. The Newars are known for their finishing work with gold. The gold is first dissolved in mercury, finely ground into a paste, and then brushed onto the sculpture, which has been thoroughly cleaned beforehand. During the heating process, the sculpture is turned constantly so that it is evenly heated and the surface is brushed with a metal brush. The heat evaporates the mercury, leaving the gold behind, and the gold surface is given a final polish. The sacred crown (see no. 51) is a superb example of the Newars' work. The small images of the Buddhas and other decorations on the crown are finely made using the repoussé technique. The image of Vairochana is especially impressive, with its halo of seed pearls, radiating lotus petals of lapis lazuli, and outer border of flowers in green and red stones. He is borne on the back of Garuda, who has ruby eyes and a lapis lazuli beak and bites two snakes inlaid with seed pearls. The fine repoussé work, the careful shaping of the stones, the skillful setting, and fine mercury gilding, resulted in a masterpiece of Newari metalwork.

The Newars guarded their secret of mercury gilding through the centuries. Heinrich Harrer, in *Seven Years in Tibet*, mentioned how jealously the Nepalese gold and silversmiths of Lhasa guarded their secret. During their stay in Lhasa, Heinrich Harrer and Peter Aufschnaiter were invited to regild some images in a temple. Luckily they were able to find a recipe for preparing gold paint from gold dust in one of the books from the nobleman Tsarong Sharpe's library. Various chemicals were ordered from India for this project.[5]

Some of the large statues of Tibet are several stories high and repoussé, which is relatively lightweight, and is the method generally employed for creating these giant images. The statue of Maitreya, the Buddha of the Future, at Tashilhunpo Monastery is a good example. This statue, twenty-seven meters high, is the tallest Maitreya image in Tibet. It was commissioned by the Ninth Panchen Lama (reigned 1892-1937) in 1914 and took four years to complete. The gilt metal statue is made in sections that are riveted together and it is supported inside by a tall juniper tree trunk (Figure 6).

Tibetan dress their images in rich brocades, ornament them with jewelry, and paint their faces with cold gold and colors, even in cases when the images are already mercury gilded (For example, see no. 84, Goddess Vajravarahi). Cold gold, as opposed to mercury gilding (also known as fire gilding), is a paint composed of fine gold dust mixed with yak skin glue. Once painted, the face of the deity has a matte appearance. The lips, eyes, and eye brows are also painted in color. The eyes are outlined in red, giving them a realistic appearance. The hair of peaceful deities is painted blue, and that of wrathful deities painted orange (see no. 86).

One of the duties of newly appointed ministers, according to Heinrich Harrer, was to present a gold butter lamp, as well as silk costumes to the deities in the Jokhang, the cathedral of Lhasa.[6] Many of these costumes were made of the finest Chinese silk brocades. Sumptuous jewelry also ornaments the important sculptures of Tibet, such as Jo Rinpoche, the statue of the young Buddha Shakyamuni in the Jokhang, and the sandalwood statue of Avalokiteshvara, Lord of Mercy, in the Potala.[7]

One of the most intricate sculptures in this exhibition is a Vajrabhairava Mandala (see no. 61). It was housed originally in the Potala and has more recently been on view at the Tibet Museum. When closed, this magnificent piece resembles a lotus bud emerging from a bell-shaped base, supported by curling leafy tendrils, with the sun and moon symbols resting on the topmost leaves. When the elaborate top is removed, the eight petals open up, revealing the buffalo-headed Vajrabhairava, with his nine heads, sixteen legs, and thirty-four arms standing in the center of a cosmic diagram. While the form of this sculpture originated during the Pala Dynasty (8th - 12th century) of eastern India, it was actually manufactured in the imperial workshops of Ming Dynasty China. The piece was commissioned by Emperor Yongle (reigned 1403-1424), as a present for a high monk of Tibet. The workmanship of the piece is superb and every inch of it is of the highest craftsmanship. The shape is basically Indian, the iconography Tibetan, and the square faces of the images and their jewelry are typical of the hybrid works of the Ming Yongle period. The style of the workmanship, however, is Nepalese, as is the fire gilding. Anige came to China during the reign of Kublai Khan and he trained a generation of Chinese students. During the reign of Emperor Yongle, it is possible that there were Nepalese craftsmen in the Ming imperial workshop or it may be that this piece was made by the second or third generation of Anige's Chinese students. The complex nature of this object thus generates speculation on the identity of its creators and highlights the diverse cultural sources that come together in the artful objects used in the practice of Buddhism in Tibet.

Figure 6
Sculpture of Maitreya the
Buddha of the Future,
Tashilhunpo Monastery.
Photo: gettyimages.com/creative

DIPLOMATIC GIFTS

Patricia Berger

"The king…did not give for the sake of wealth, he did not give for the sake of a gift given in return, he did not give for the sake of diplomacy, he did not give for the sake of outward appearance, he did not give for the sake of happiness, he did not give for the sake of power, he did not give for the sake of fame, he did not give for the sake of obtaining a daughter, but it was for the sake of omniscient knowledge." Nagashena, *Milindapanho* (Milinda' Questions, 1st century C.E., translated by I.B. Horner)

On December 11, 640, the Tibetan minister Gar Tongtsen arrived at the Tang capital, Chang'an, with gifts of five thousand ounces of gold and "precious baubles," to request the hand of a Chinese princess in marriage for Tibet's King Songtsen Gampo.[1] This was not the first Tibetan mission to Chang'an, nor was a princess all that the king sought. He also had a long wish list that included requests that the Tang emperor send Chinese scribes to Lhasa and that members of the Tibetan royal family be admitted to the state university, an ambitious plan designed to

Figure 1
Yan Liben (ca. 600-674), *Tang Emperor Taizong Greeting the Tibetan Ambassador* (Chinese: *Bunian tu*: The Imperial Hand Carriage), hand scroll, ink and colors on silk (Palace Museum, Beijing).

make the Tibetan nobility fluent in Chinese culture, language, and learning. Gar's embassy is vividly pictured in a painting done at the time, a piece of inspired reporting by the Tang court official and painter Yan Liben (Figure 1). The painting represents the moment when the slightly-built Gar, hands folded in an elaborately brocaded robe and visibly ill-at-ease, first appears flanked by two hefty Tang officials before the huge figure of Tang Emperor Taizong (reigned 627-649), who sits on a platform carried by a bevy of slender beauties. The discrepancy in scale may represent wishful thinking on the part of the Chinese court; Tibet was then and would remain for centuries a formidable military force in Asia and more than just a thorn in China's side. Perhaps for this reason, Gar's request met with imperial approval—Taizong named him "Great Protecting General of the Right—and in March, 641, he was allowed to accompany the Princess Wencheng back to Lhasa, where she wed the Tibetan king.

Princess Wencheng was a devout Buddhist, as was Songtsen Gampo's Nepalese wife, Bhrikhuti, and tradition holds that the two ladies soon consorted to convert the king to Buddhism. They succeeded admirably: Songtsen Gampo soon became one of the most avid royal patrons Buddhism has ever had, eventually building one hundred and eight monasteries (a sacred number) throughout Tibet. Among the objects in Wencheng's rich dowry was the ultimate gift: a golden image of the Buddha Shakyamuni, which was ensconced in the Jokhang in Lhasa. Known as the Jowo (or Jo Rinpoche), this figure is still the ultimate object of devout pilgrimage in Tibet. Said to be an authentic portrait of the Buddha, the Jowo has been shrouded in rich brocades and jewels and his face has been refreshed multiple times with new layers of gold, which have completely transformed its original, presumably Chinese, style (see Terese Tse Bartholomew, "Life in Lhasa, the Holy City," Figure 1, the Potala Palace).

Though the Jowo has come to be seen as the most meaningful gift to pass from China to Tibet, a sacred object beyond art historical evaluation, this single statue did not completely satisfy the desire of Tibet's kings for Chinese things. During the reign of Tang Gaozong (649-683), another embassy returned to Chang'an to request that the court send technicians to teach Tibetans the secrets of silk production, papermaking, and wine brewing. In reply, Gaozong, who actively supported Buddhist causes, granted Songtsen Gampo the title "Baowang" ("Precious King," also at the time a well-known epithet for the Buddha of the Western Paradise, Amitabha).[2] Even later, more requests were sent (and met) for princesses. With all the movement between Lhasa, Chang'an, and other Asian capitals, a new pattern emerged in Asian diplomacy, where Buddhism and Buddhist objects had a significant role to play.

Buddhist Gift-Giving
In Buddhist practice, gift giving (Sanskrit: *dana*) is a central, spiritual virtue that recognizes not only the wishes or needs of the recipient, but also the value of the giver's proper spirit of generosity. The Buddha Shakyamuni's attainment of enlightenment was built upon a myriad of lifetimes, spent giving of himself, and even offering his own flesh to help other beings. Immediately after his enlightenment, the Buddha was showered with gifts as the heavens rained down offerings in the form of fragrant flowers, sweet dew, and other auspicious signs. The Buddha—whose enlightened, benign presence in the world was itself a gift beyond measure—went on to build his entire monastic establishment on the concept of the gift. Wealthy laymen, who did not have the inclination to become monks, could still accrue karmic merit by funding monasteries. Even impoverished devotees could give in small but valuable ways, by sharing a bowlful of food with an itinerant monk or by offering their services to a monastic community. Gifts were meant to be presented with an open heart and no expectation of return. But, in fact, laymen understood that the work of monks—their meditations, scholarship, and devotional practices— created reservoirs of spiritual merit, as well as worldly benefits, for the entire community. Their work was worth supporting through material gifts of food, clothing, architecture, and works of art, often with the donor's name prominently inscribed.

Early Buddhist Patronage in Tibetan-Chinese Border Regions
The relationship between Tibet and China was crafted in the border regions. Some of the earliest evidence anywhere of elite Tibetan patronage of Buddhism survives in the area around the Chinese cave-temple site, Dunhuang, located in modern Gansu province, in the northwest corridor leading from China into the Central Asia. Dunhuang, a multiethnic way station on the Silk Road, came under Tibetan control between 781 and 847. The Tibetan period at Dunhuang followed years of constant warfare along the border that peaked with the Tibetans' capture of the Tang capital Chang'an in 763 and their enthronement of a Chinese emperor of their choosing. Dunhuang had been the site of temple building, painting, and sculpture from the late 4th century on, but, during the Tibetan period, Tibetan donors first made an appearance in cave murals there, wearing their distinctive robes and turban-like hats (For similarly dressed figures, see nos. 2, 3, 4 & 5).[3] By the end of the Tang Dynasty, esoteric, Tibetan-style Buddhist images—even mandalas—could be seen side-by-side with more typically Chinese Buddhist paintings and sculptures. The art of Dunhuang began to display a new hybrid character, a mixture of Tibetan and Chinese styles and subjects that represented the shifting needs of Dunhuang's ethnically diverse donors.

In 1038, the area around Dunhuang came under the control of the Tangut people (Tibetan: Minyag). The Tanguts spoke a Tibetan dialect, but they invented a graphic script that resembled Chinese; they were fluent in Chinese, and they established a Chinese-style imperial government with the Chinese-style dynastic name Xixia (Western Xia). They were remarkably innovative in their creative borrowing of Chinese models. However, many of the structures that governed Buddhist relations between Tibet and China in the succeeding imperial dynasties—the Yuan, Ming, and Qing—were based on Xixia—that is, non-Chinese—precedents. The Xixia emperors were avid Buddhists, supporting Buddhist masters from surrounding states in an ongoing series of projects to translate sacred texts into their own language. At the cave-site of Yulin, not far from Dunhuang, Tangut Buddhists established a series of cave-temples that provide a clear visual record of the nature of Xixia imperial patronage in the 12th century. In one of the cave murals at Yulin, the Xixia emperor appears twice, once in the sacred enclosure of the mandala of the deity Ushnishavijaya, where he acts as an attendant to the goddess at the center, and presents himself as an initiate into her Tantra.

Mandalas such as the one at Yulin, focusing on deities unknown in the pantheon of Tang Dynasty Tantric Buddhism, reflect the renewed importance of Tibet as an innovative center of Tantric studies in the 11th and 12th centuries. The Tibetan Kagyu order, in particular, played an important role in promoting Tantric Buddhism in Xixia. In the late 12th century, the last years of the dynasty, the Xixia emperors welcomed Lamas of the Tibetan Kagyu order. Visual evidence for this close relationship comes from a silk tapestry portrait of the founder of the Tsalpa suborder of the Kagyu, Gungphang Lama Shang (1123-1194), a product of Xixia workshops made as a gift to a Tibetan monastery (Figure 2). This portrait is very similar in technique to an image of Achala (see no. 85), also probably a gift from Xixia to Tibet. Another influential Kagyu Lama, Xinbizhihai, was memorialized at Yulin. He was one of several National Preceptors (*guoshi*)—National Buddhist Masters—appointed by the Xixia emperors. This office was already in place in this border region before 1038 and, following Xixia precedent, the Yuan and Qing emperors subsequently established Preceptors for their own dynasties.[4]

Figure 2
Portrait of Gungphang Lama Shang, silk tapestry (*kesi*). After *Xizang tangka* (Tibetan Thangkas), pl. 62.

Though Xixia was obliterated during Chinggis (Genghis) Khan's last campaign in 1227 (Chinggis actually died in Xixia territory the same year), the state Buddhist institutions its emperors built were powerful models for the Mongols' Chinese-based Yuan Dynasty, which was established by Chinggis' grandson, Kublai Khan, in 1260.

The Mongols and the Art of Diplomacy
The Vajrayana (*Vajra* Vehicle) or Tantric Buddhism practiced in Tibet accepts the idea that enlightenment can, and, indeed, will occur in this material world. Far from asserting that the world we experience everyday is not real, Tantric Buddhism acknowledges the material world of the senses, while understanding that the enlightened mind perceives a more profound reality. This paradox of the Double Truth—the simultaneous existence of this everyday world and another, deeper appreciation of its true nature that only the enlightened mind can comprehend—has had significant impact on Asian statecraft. More than one Asian ruler, including the Xixia, Mongol, Ming, and Qing emperors, wanted to be recognized as an enlightened Universal Wheel-Turning King (Sanskrit: *cakravartin*), whose reign would usher in the next Buddhist era. For many of these rulers, Vajrayana Buddhism, with its promises of enlightenment and, perhaps even more importantly, of supreme transformative power, continued to be a major tool in state-building.

The particular efficiency of Tantric practice in producing results in this lifetime was what convinced Kublai Khan (1215-1294) to undertake initiations into the Tantras. Instrumental in his conversion was his forward-looking wife, Chabi, and Phagpa Lama (1235-1280), a master of the Tibetan Sakya order. Phagpa, together with his uncle Sakya Pandita (1182-1251) and brother, Chana Dorje, were been "guests" (meaning "hostages") of Kublai Khan's brother, Möngke Khan, whose court was in former Xixia territory. In 1260, at Chabi's suggestion, Phagpa initiated Kublai Khan into the Hevajra Tantra. In return, Kublai gave Phagpa the title of National Preceptor, following Xixia precedent, as well as the honorific title Da Bao Fawang (Great Precious Dharma King), which would be revived in the Ming Dynasty. The two sat on seats of equal height, as "sun and moon," symbolizing their separate but equal authority, the Khan's over secular matters and his guru's over religion. So began their *choyon* (*mchod yon*) relationship of Lama and patron, which was given material authority in the seal that Kublai presented to his guru (see no. 11, the Jade National Preceptor's Seal), which is written in the "square" Phagpa script Phagpa himself developed) when he made him administrator of Tibet. The relationship was secured when Kublai Khan offered Phagpa the gift of an unusual right-turning conch shell, which was said to have been passed down from the Buddha Shakyamuni himself. This exact gift of a conch would be repeated over and over again during the Manchu Qing Dynasty (1644-1912) (see nos. 27, 28 & 29).

The Mongol capital, which Kublai Khan established at Dadu (modern Beijing), and the summer court at Shangdu (known in the West as Xanadu), were both sites of extensive Tibetan style construction projects. In response to a clearly felt absence of artistic talent trained in the intricacies of Tibetan Buddhist iconography, Phagpa Lama invited the young Nepalese artistic prodigy Anige (1243-1306) and a troop of artisans to Dadu. Anige eventually came to head up Kublai Khan's department of artistic works and was even accorded a Chinese wife and full Confucian honors upon his death. During his long career, Anige designed architectural projects in Beijing, including the still-extant, though much restored, White Stupa (Baita), at the Miaoying Temple, one of the earliest reinforced masonry structures in Asia. He and his able staff painted numerous temple frescoes and produced large numbers of sculptures; some using specifically Tibetan materials, and Anige was even entrusted with designing posthumous tapestry portraits of Kublai and Chabi, which were meant to be used in regular sacrificial rituals after their deaths. He also served as director of the southern ceramic kilns at Jingdezhen, for which he provided designs for blue-and-white porcelains destined to be "bestowal gifts" given by the Yuan imperial government to their relatives and allies in the Near East.

Anige may also have been the genius behind the creation of a golden image of the Supreme Being (*yidam*), Mahakala, in his role as Gurgyi Gompo (Lord of the Tent—the Mongolian and Tibetan words for "tent," *gur* and *ger*, are very similar). The 12th -13th century bronze Mahakala included in this exhibition (see no. 86) must be very much like this golden image.[5] Fabricating this golden Mahakala was Phagpa's idea; it was designed as a war standard for Kublai Khan to use in his campaign against Chinese resistance in the south.[6] Mahakala was Kublai Khan's own *yidam* (tutelary deity) and the Lord of the Tent, in particular, was especially beloved by Phagpa's Sakya order. This golden image was destined for a long career among the Mongols and their successors. Sometime after the fall of the Mongol Yuan Dynasty in 1368, the Mahakala-image made its way into former Tangut territory, whence it was brought to Inner Mongolia in the early 17th century, just as Mongolian hopes for a new empire were rising again. In 1636, this charismatic Mahakala came into the hands of the Manchus, who were also intent on the same goal. The Manchus established the image in a mandala-shaped temple-complex in the center of their capital at Mukden (modern Shenyang, Liaoning province) and, when they completed the conquest of China, they brought the Mahakala to their new northern Chinese capital at Beijing. There it rested at the Pudu (Universal Passage) Temple, just east of the Forbidden City, until the Boxer Rebellion in 1900, when it was apparently looted. Its present location is unknown.

Kublai Khan's death in 1294 brought to the throne a series of emperors who all maintained the Lama-patron relationship established by their dynastic founder. Advised by Tibetan and Mongolian Lamas, the later Mongol rulers were also just as eager to be seen as great Buddhist donors. In 1345, the last Yuan Emperor Toghon Temür (reigned 1333-1367) commissioned the building of a massive stupa-gate, the Guojieta (Stupa that Straddles the Road), near the Great Wall at Juyong Pass, just north of the capital at Dadu (Figure 3). All that remains of this construction is the arched gateway; the stupa, if ever completed, has long since disappeared. The gate is elaborately decorated with relief sculpture on the entrance archway, which bears a *garuda*-bird with wings outstretched, gnashing its beak on a struggling snake, and, on the inside walls of the vaulted passage, the Guardians of the Four Quarters and mandalas of the Five Buddhas. There is also a lengthy inscription in six languages (Lantsa/Sanskrit, Tibetan, Phagpa/Mongolian, Chinese, Tangut/Xixia, and Uighur). Only the Mongolian version identifies Kublai Khan as an emanation of Manjushri, the Bodhisattva of Wisdom. This assertion was made in the face of the rapid disintegration of the Mongols' Chinese-based empire in the south, a last-ditch effort to claim something akin to the divine right to rule China, based on the belief long held in China that Manjushri dwelled at Wutaishan (the Five-Terrace Mountains), in what is now Shanxi province. This posthumous claim had tremendous appeal in later centuries for the emperors of the early Ming and Qing Dynasties, who would also adopt Manjushri's mantle of transcendent wisdom.

Figure 3
The Juyong Gate,
north of Beijing.
Photo: Patricia Berger

The Early Ming Emperors and Tibet
The founder of the Ming Dynasty, Zhu Yuanzhang (Hongwu, 1368-1399), had been a Buddhist monk before his political ascendancy. It was his fourth son, the usurper Zhu Di, known as Emperor Yongle ("Eternal Happiness") (reigned 1403-1424), and who redeveloped close ties between the Chinese empire and Tibet. Yongle's desire to do so may have arisen because of his early life spent in the region around modern Beijing, where he was established as the Prince of Yan in 1370. The young prince built lasting ties with the Mongolian aristocracy, many of whom were practicing Buddhists with close relations in Tibet. Yongle's reign was internationalist in character—he sent expeditions into Central Asia and launched exploratory seafaring missions, headed by the eunuch Zhang He, which traveled in massive fleets as far as the east coast of Africa.[7]

Yongle's Confucian courtiers strongly disapproved of his interest in Tibetan Lamas. Despite their objections, he clearly saw the advantages of using Tibetan Buddhism to create support for his usurpation of the throne (which resulted in the presumed death of his predecessor and nephew, Jianwen). In 1407, the emperor invited the Fifth Karmapa of the Kagyu Black Hat order, Dezhin Shegpa (Helima, 1384-1415), to Nanjing to preside over a great plenary mass designed to conclude the funeral rituals for his father, Hongwu, and his mother.[8] This mass, conducted at Nanjing's Linggu Monastery, produced a series of miraculous displays in the sky that suggested to onlookers that the imperial couple were emanations of the Bodhisattvas Manjushri and Tara. They attributed these events directly to the Karmapa's charismatic power and Yongle had the events recorded in a long, inscribed hand scroll, which was sent to the Karmapa's monastery at Tsurphu (see, e.g., Figure 4). During his stay in Nanjing, the Fifth Karmapa was also given the title Da Bao Fawang (Great Precious Dharma King). He went on to repeat the funerary mass at Wutaishan, where similar miracles were observed.

The early Ming emperors had some of their favorite Lamas immortalized in portraits, two of which are included in this exhibition. In 1408 and 1415, Yongle sent invitations to visit his southern capital at Nanjing to the great Lama Tsongkhapa, founder of the Gelug order. All of his overtures were declined, but Tsongkhapa's disciple; Shakya Yeshe, did visit the Ming court at Nanjing in 1415, where he was granted a black hat and the title Da Ci Fawang (Dharma King of Great Loving Kindness).[9] This exalted status is recorded in the Yongle-period embroidered portrait of Shakya Yeshe. Returning to Tibet in 1416, Shakya Yeshe (see no. 9) used grants given by Yongle to build Sera Monastery. He continued this mutually beneficial relationship, journeying to China again during the reign of Emperor Xuande (1426-1435), this time to the new northern capital at Beijing. In 1434, Xuande, grateful for Shakya Yeshe's medical advice, granted him an even more exalted title consisting of thirty-eight Chinese characters. The event is memorialized in a woven portrait, in which the Lama wears the black hat Yongle gave him two decades earlier (see no. 10). The portrait is also impressed with a seal that records Shakya Yeshe's new title.

Figure 4
The Fifth Karmapa's Visit to Nanjing, hand scroll, ink and colors on paper, detail, section 1. After *Precious Deposits*, volume 3, no. 48, p. 94.

Ming Dynasty Emperor Yongle's reign, in particular, is known for the brilliant gifts the emperor commissioned for his favorite Lamas. Aside from textile images, the gilt bronze sculptures produced at the Yongle court, inscribed with the special mark used only for religious gifts ("Donated"—rather than simply "Made"—during the reign of Yongle of the Great Ming"), are noted for their graceful naturalism and exquisite detail. Two sculptures in this exhibition, the Manjushri Namasamgiti (see no. 72) and the three-dimensional Vajrabhairava Mandala (see no. 61) bear the Yongle reign mark and represent the extraordinary vividness of the new, hybrid Tibeto-Chinese style that was designed by Chinese, Nepalese, and Tibetan artists specifically to serve the ritual functions of Tibetan Buddhism. Both sculptures represent forms of Manjushri, who, as Yongle worked so hard to demonstrate, was embodied in the Ming founder, Hongwu. No doubt Yongle dearly hoped he also would be recognized as an emanation of the same Bodhisattva (and, indeed, he was by Mongolian Buddhists, even in the early 20th century).

Among the other spectacular gifts the early Ming emperors sent to Tibet were underglaze copper red and cobalt blue porcelains, sophisticated, white-bodied, translucent ceramics the secret of which was closely guarded by Chinese potters. This new ceramic style first became popular during the Yuan Dynasty, when immense amounts of blue-and-white porcelain were created for domestic use and for export throughout the Mongol empire. Many new shapes were introduced into the Chinese ceramic artist's repertory in the 14th and 15th centuries specifically to serve the ritual needs of Tibetan Buddhism. Among these were various water vessels, including the Serkyem ewer, a type that can be traced to Central and Western Asian metalwork, but was reproduced in the early Ming Dynasty, in the difficult and rare underglaze copper red technique (see no. 43). Another type of water vessel, the monk's-hat pitcher, has a flanged rim that resembles the brim of monastic headgear. This shape was particularly popular in the 15th century (for example, see no. 42, the blue and white porcelain pitcher) and was produced in more than one medium, including colorful cloisonné enameled metal (see no. 41).

By the Xuande reign, the relationship between the Ming emperors and Tibetan Lamas, expressed in the glorious titles granted by the emperors and given material form in the exchange of luxurious and practical gifts, was a well-established mechanism for ensuring some degree of Ming control of Tibetan politics (see no. 12, Yongle's beautifully decorated and phrased but ultimately business-like edit of 1413), as well as access to Tibetan markets and Tibetan herds. This exchange all but ended with the death of Emperor Chenghua (reigned 1465-1487) and was not reinstated until the Ming Dynasty fell to the Manchus in 1644.

Gifts of the Qing Emperors

The Manchu imperial Aisin Gioro clan established formal relations with Tibetan and Mongolian Buddhist monks of the Sakya order in the 1630s, years before they completed the conquest of China and founded the Qing Dynasty (1644-1912). Qing court records are filled with information regarding gifts to Tibetan Lamas and grants to Tibetan monasteries. The Qing emperors' generosity to Tibet can be explained in several ways. The system of gift-exchange enabled a modicum of remote control over this inaccessible Himalayan realm, but it also permitted the Qing emperors to sustain the notion that they were the fulfillment of a prophecy first stated by the Third Dalai Lama, Sonam Gyatso (1543-1588): that a great ruler, an emanation of Manjushri, would unite China, Mongolia, and Tibet into a vast empire, brought together under the aegis of the Gelug order. This brilliant, historically resonant idea was further amplified when the Great Fifth Dalai Lama, Ngawang Losang Gyatso (1617-1682), joined the Fourth Panchen Lama (1570-1662) in 1640 in a letter addressed to Abahai, the soon-to-be Qing dynastic founder, which began with the salutation: "Manjushri Great Emperor."[10]

In 1652, the Fifth Dalai Lama visited Abahai, now reigning as Emperor Shunzhi (1644-1661), at his new capital, Beijing. The visit was preceded by years of negotiation, beginning in 1648, when the Manchus sent letters of invitation to the Dalai and Panchen Lamas. The envoy, it is said, brought presents representing the emperor's sincere intention, including belts of gold set with jade and ceramic vessels modeled on Tibetan wooden tea urns. (see no. 115)[11] The Panchen Lama declined to travel, citing his advanced age (he was nearly 80 at the time) but, in 1652, the Dalai Lama and his entourage began the long trek. The first audience between the Qing conqueror and the great Dalai Lama took place in the Forbidden City in the first month of 1653, with Shunzhi granting the Dalai Lama a seat and accepting his gift of horses and various other objects. The event is recalled in a mural now in the main audience chamber of the Potala Palace, where the two rulers are shown seated in the center of a bird's-eye view of the Forbidden City, arranged to resemble a mandala (Figure 5). When the Dalai Lama departed Beijing in early 1653, Shunzhi gave him saddles, horses, gold, silver, pearls, jade, and satins, as well as the highly honorific title "Buddha of Great Compassion in the West, leader of the Buddhist faith beneath the sky, holder of the *vajra* (Vajradhara)," recorded in Tibetan, Manchu, and Chinese on a wood and iron seal that was also presented by Shunzhi (see no. 13).

Although it is impossible to plumb the depths of the Manchu Qing emperors' hearts and discern whether their interest in Tibetan Buddhism was sincere or merely expedient (or perhaps both), the outpouring of gifts to Tibetan and Mongolian Lamas and the degree of attention the Manchus paid to Tibetan monastic establishments in China, Mongolia, and Tibet was unprecedented. At no time was this more apparent than during the long reign of the fourth Qing Emperor, who reigned as Qianlong (1736-1795). Qianlong's interest in Buddhism of all

Figure 5
Emperor Shunzhi of the Qing Dynasty and the Fifth Dalai Lama in the Forbidden City, Beijing, mural, Great Western Audience Chamber, Potala Palace. After *Precious Deposits*, vol. 4, no. 2, p. 11.

types is well-documented. He built numerous temples within and beyond the confines of the Forbidden City, some for his own use, some for his devout mother, but all of them designed to serve the specific ritual requirements of Tibetan Buddhism. At the Manchus' summer retreat, Chengde (Rehol), located in the mountains northeast of Beijing, he erected replicas of Tibet's greatest monastic institutions—including the Dalai Lama's Potala, the Panchen Lama's Tashilhunpo, and Tibet's first monastery, Samye.[12] His capital housed as many as several hundred incarnate Lamas at a time. Many of them lived at the Yonghegong, the princely palace where Qianlong had been born and which he converted into a monastery for Mongolian monks in 1744; others stayed at the Huangsi (Yellow Temple), which was renovated to prepare for the visit in 1780 of the Sixth Panchen Lama (who unfortunately died there of smallpox the same year). Still other Lamas occupied the dozens of monasteries that were built all over Beijing and in the surrounding hills.

Following precedents set by Kublai Khan, Ming Emperor Yongle, and his own grandfather, Kangxi (reigned 1662-1722), and acting on the recommendation of his own Tibeto-Mongolian guru, Rolpay Dorje, his National Preceptor and childhood friend, Qianlong made pilgrimages to Wutaishan (where, it is said, he had visions of Manjushri) and supported vast translation projects that resulted in the publication in Manchu of the Tibetan Buddhist scriptural and commentarial canon. He also established a method to control the source of Tibetan Buddhist political power: the system of finding and installing reincarnations of powerful Lamas. In 1757, Qianlong deputized his guru Rolpay Dorje to Tibet to oversee the selection of the Eighth Dalai Lama (Jampel Gyatso, 1758-1804). It is likely that the brilliant thangka of Avalokiteshvara of the Six Syllables (see no. 75), was woven for this event and carried to Lhasa as part of the emperor's many gifts to the new incarnation. Embroidered copies of the same image were distributed among other great Tibetan monasteries, while another copy was kept in the imperial collection in Beijing as a record of the original gift (it is now in the National Palace Museum, Taiwan).

However devout or cynical the Qing emperors might have been in their relations with Tibet, many of the objects in this exhibition suggest that they continued to give gifts and titles even well into the 19th century, for reasons of diplomacy, outward appearance, power, and fame, and perhaps for omniscient knowledge, as well.

This may be the oldest object in the exhibition. It replicates the characteristics of 6th century Indian Gupta images of the Buddha, such as the transparent robe, the lack of an *urna* (the mark on the forehead), the striations and flaring of the robe, the rounded modeling of the figure, and the graceful standing posture. The Buddha's right hand is in the open-palmed gesture of bestowing the blessings of the teaching. His left holds a corner of the robe indicating that he is conferring the precepts of monastic discipline. His standing posture indicates that he is going forth into the world for the sake of living beings. Images of the Buddha in Tibet are characteristically seated in the cross-legged meditation posture. This type of standing image was highly honored because it was associated with the Buddha coming to Tibet from India, as did the many great Buddhist teachers who crossed the Himalaya from the 6th - 12th century.

A similar figure is S131 in the collection of the Los Angeles County Museum of Art. See: Pratapaditya Pal, *Indian Sculpture* (Los Angeles: Los Angeles County Museum of Art, 1986), vol. 1, pp. 61, 254. See also: Los Angeles County Museum of Art 1975, pp. 21, 147; Pal 1975a, p. 51; Pal 1978b, p. 110; von Schroeder 1981, pp. 216-17; Pal 1984, p. 201.

53
The Buddha Shakyamuni
Gilt copper
Nepal, 7th - 9th century
H: 28.5 cm; L (base): 5.8 cm
Tibet Museum, Lhasa
Published: *Tibet Museum Catalog*, p. 174, no. 1

54
The Buddha Shakyamuni
Gilt copper alloy
Tibet, 14th - 15th century
H: 59 cm; W: 41 cm; L: 32 cm
Tibet Museum, Lhasa

The Buddha Shakyamuni is the historical figure who lived in India in the 6th and 7th centuries BCE. Two of the main characteristics that identify this image as the Buddha Shakyamuni include the crown protrusion on his head (Sanskrit: *ushnisha*) characteristic of all Buddhas, and the *urna*, a round twist of hair between his eyebrows. His left hand is in the gesture of meditation (Sanskrit: *dhyana mudra*) and, in some similar examples, supports an alms bowl, which, together with the robe falling from one shoulder, marks him as a monk. The Buddha Shakyamuni's right hand is in the gesture of contacting the earth (Sanskrit: *bhumisparsha mudra*), he made at the moment he manifested enlightenment under the Bodhi tree. His left hand in the gesture of meditation indicates he remains ever in a state of perfect meditative stabilization. This shows that a Buddha is able to function in the world and teach living beings the path to enlightenment without ever stirring from his state of perfect awareness. The right hand touching the earth indicates that a Buddha calls the earth and all beings in the world, to witness his enlightenment. This means that, after striving on the spiritual path for three countless eons, he has overcome all faults and perfected all virtues. Not even the greatest of the worldly gods and demons (represented by Mara) can dispute the authenticity of his attainment.

Arranged like a tree with a leaf-shaped halo, this altar piece depicts the Buddha Shakyamuni in the center, flanked by his two great disciples, and surrounded by the sixteen *arhats*, their two helpers, and the four guardian kings.

    The Buddha Shakyamuni is identified by his hand gestures: left hand palm up in meditation, and the right lowered in the earth-touching gesture, calling the Earth as a witness at the moment of his victory over Mara. As a peaceful deity, the hair of the Buddha is painted blue. His two disciples, named Shariputra and Maudgalyayana, carry alms bowls and staffs.

    The sixteen *arhats* were the disciples of the Buddha who served as patriarchs of the Buddhist Church when the Buddha left his earthly abode. They are enlightened beings entrusted with the duty of propagating and protecting Buddhist faith. Wearing the robes of monks, they are depicted on lotus pedestals. In the Tibetan tradition, the sixteen *arhats* are later accompanied by two other figures, their supporters, for a total of eighteen: Dharmatala carries a load of books on his back, while the rotund Hvashang is surrounded by young boys. Their images appear above those of the four guardian kings, who sit in a row beneath the Buddha. These kings protect the four directions and are shown as warriors, befitting their protective roles.

    Although Buddha Shakyamuni and the *arhats* are favorite subjects for paintings, they are seldom seen together in a tree-shaped sculpture as they are in this unique example. Images sitting on tree branches do occur in Buddhist art. In the 7th century, the Seven Buddhas of the Past were already sitting in tree branches in Chinese bronze images. In this exhibition, the large metal mandala of Vajrabhairava holds a number of Buddhist images aloft among its leafy branches.

55
The Buddha Shakyamuni, His Two Chief Disciples, and Sixteen
Arhats
Copper alloy with cold gold
Tibet, ca. 13th century
H: 32 cm; W: 20 cm
Tibet Museum, Lhasa
Published: *Tibet Museum Catalog*, pp. 94-95, no. 5

These two models replicate the Mahabodhi Temple, the site where the Buddha Shakyamuni attained enlightenment. This temple, is located in Bodh Gaya, in the state of Bihar, east India. The site of Bodh Gaya was, and still is, the foremost pilgrimage site of the Buddhist world. It was there that the Buddha Shakyamuni sat under a *bodhi* tree (*ficus religiosa*) and attained enlightenment. It soon became a pilgrimage site and a temple was built near the tree. The date when the temple was first constructed is subject to debate, but, judging from the first of these models, it was built in a north Indian style, with a tower on each of the four corners, and a fifth high tower built over the main sanctuary. When Muslims conquered Bihar in the late 12th and early 13th centuries, many Buddhist monuments were destroyed, but there is evidence that some rebuilding of the temple was undertaken at the behest of the King of Burma in the last years of the 11th century.[2] At this point, the shape of the main doorway of the temple was altered to accommodate three Burmese-style ogival arches. A major restoration of the Mahabodhi Temple took place in 1881, when an Englishman, Sir Edwin Arnold, spearheaded a movement to restore the site to its original form.[1] A model of the original temple found near the site was actually used as a blueprint to rebuild the temple.[3]

It was believed that small models of the Mahabodhi Temple, such as the stone example, seen here (see no. 56), were made for the pilgrims who came to worship at this major site, and who brought them back to their homes as mementos or even as ritual images. The stone model, with its small images highlighted in gold, was no doubt brought back to Tibet by a Tibetan who had visited the Mahabodhi Temple. Given the ogival arches at the doorway of the iron example (see no. 57), it must have been based on a model made after the late 11th century Burmese restoration. It may well be only one component from a larger model of the entire temple complex. In Tibet, there are many examples of these miniature Mahabodhi Temples, including a wooden one in the Potala. A wooden set showing the entire temple complex, a gift from Ming Dynasty Emperor Yongle of China (reigned 1403-1424), was once kept at Narthang Monastery in eastern Tibet.[4] When the Indian Rahula Sankrityayana stayed at Narthang in 1936-1937, he saw two sets, Emperor Yongle's gift and a stone model with Tibetan inscriptions.[5]

Today the Mahabodhi temple is once again the foremost pilgrimage site in the Buddhist world, with temples of various Buddhist countries built all around it. Tibetans in exile have made this an important place for their worship and ceremonies are performed there regularly.

[1] Susan L. Huntington and John C. Huntington, *Leaves from the Bodhi Tree: The Art of Pala India (8th - 12th centuries) and Its International Legacy* (Dayton: The Dayton Art Institute in Association with the University of Washington Press, Seattle and London, 1990), p. 529.

[2] John Guy, "The Mahabodhi Temple: Pilgrim Souvenirs of Buddhist India," *The Burlington Magazine*, v. 133 (June 1991): 356-367.

[3] Geri H. Malandra, "The Mahabodhi Temple," in Janice Leoshko, ed., *Bodhgaya, The Site of Enlightenment*, (Bombay: Marg Publications, 1988, p.10.

[4] Heather Karmay, *Early Sino-Tibetan Art* (Warminster, England: Aris and Phillips Ltd., 1975), p.92.

[5] Jane Casey Singer, "Bodhgaya and Tibet," in Janice Leoshko, ed., *Bodhgaya*, p. 148.

57
Model of the Mahabodhi Temple
Iron and gold
Tibet, ca. 11th century
H: 39.5 cm; D (base each side): 13.5 cm
Tibet Museum, Lhasa
Published: *Precious Deposits*, vol. 4, pp. 160-161, no. 67

56
Model of the Mahabodhi Temple
Stone
Tibet, 11th century
H: 13 cm; L: 7.5 cm
Potala Palace Collection

The Buddha Shakyamuni, wearing an elaborate crown, is seated on his *vajra* seat under the towers of the Mahabodhi Temple at Bodh Gaya, where he manifested enlightenment. This posture of the Buddha seated in meditation, with his left hand on his lap and his right hand pointing at the earth (earth-touching gesture, *bhumisparsha mudra*), indicates the moment of his enlightenment and his victory over Mara. Two Bodhisattvas attend him. At the top of his elaborate throne is the bird Garuda, who is shown swallowing snakes. There are *hamsa* (mythical birds of India) on the crossbar and a lion throne below. The hoards of Mara come to attack Buddha from the left, balanced by the nine Hindu planetary deities on the right.

Surrounding the central square are white stupas (see nos. 15 & 16) adorned with scenes from Shakyamuni's life and deities of various forms. A four-armed form of the guardian Mahakala, painted blue, appears in the shrine below. Two monks, accompanied by ritual objects, are portrayed sitting in the lower left hand corner; they may have commissioned the painting.

The Mahabodhi Temple, unlike the two stone and iron examples (see nos. 56 & 57), is elaborately depicted with hundreds of enshrined Buddhas on the exterior walls and towers of the temples. The real temple at one time had over a thousand such images in niches. Tibetans believed that the Mahabodhi Temple was built about one hundred years after the Buddha passed into nirvana. Inside the temple was a chapel enshrined with a life-size image of Buddha Shakyamuni (Tibetan: *jowo jangchu chenpo*, Sanskrit: Mahabodhi—Lord of Great Enlightenment). To see this image was said to bring great bliss.

58
The Mahabodhi Temple at Bodh Gaya
Thangka, colors on cotton, brocade mounting
Tibet, 18th century
L: 83 cm; W: 105.5 cm
Formerly in the Potala Palace
Tibet Museum, Lhasa
Published: *Xizang tangka* pl.106;
Tibet Museum Catalog, pp. 58-59, no. 2;
Golden Treasures, p. 64

59
The Buddha Vairochana
Copper alloy
Tibet, 14th - 15th century
H: 27 cm; L: 24 cm; W: 11 cm
Tibet Museum, Lhasa
Published: *Tibet Museum Catalog*,
p. 177

Vairochana is one of the Five Buddhas (Pancha Jina: Ratnasambhava, Amitabha, Amoghasiddhi, Vairochana, and Akshobhya). The Five Buddhas embody the five essential aspects of the Enlightened Ones (Buddhas), and are the organizing principle of the symbolic system of esoteric Buddhist texts (Sanskrit: *Tantra*) and rituals. All Tantric deities belong to the "family" of one or another of these Five Buddhas.

Vairochana's name means "giver of illumination." He is the Buddha of the Wheel of Dharma *(Dharmachakra)*. The wheel symbolizes the Buddha's central function of teaching the Dharma in order to free beings from their ignorance and thereby free them from the toils of *samsara*, the world of illusion. Vairochana holds his hands in the gesture of teaching the Dharma *(Dharmachakra mudra)*. The principle function of images like this is as an aid to meditation. Looking at the expression of Vairochana's face and the disposition of his body, the meditator realizes the Buddha as the supreme teacher, the perfect union of limitless love and compassion with ultimate, all-knowing wisdom.

150

60
Sarvavid Vairochana Mandala
Thangka, embroidered silk with gold couching, pearls, coral, and turquoise
China, Qing Dynasty, 18th century
H: 193 cm; L: 89 cm
Tibet Museum, Lhasa
Published: *Precious Deposits*, vol. 4, pp. 99-101, no. 39

The four-headed, white-bodied Sarvavid Vairochana (the *yidam* or Supreme Being form of Vairochana, and a main deity in the Drikung Kagyu order) is seated in the center of the mandala-palace, surrounded by rings of other Buddhas. The mandala palace has four entrances and outer courts that contain victory banners, canopies, and flags. The meditator approaches the inner group around Sarvavid Vairochana from the outside in: passing through a ring of flames and a ring of *vajras* symbolizing adamantine will. Instead of the eight cemeteries usually seen around the outer perimeter of mandalas, there is a ring of four guardians, *mahasiddhas* ("great adepts"), Ganesha (the elephant-headed god), and so on. In the next layer, multicolored lotus petals open outward; then banners unfurl; then the terraces of the palace, strung with garlands of actual seed pearls, are arrayed with four entrances, each watched by guardians; then rings of monks and nude dancing figures stand, all leading to the center courtyard where Sarvavid Vairochana and rings of Buddhas sit with their hands in an array of different symbolic gestures.

In the sky above is Shakyamuni in the earth-touching gesture (*bhumisparsha mudra*), accompanied by the future Buddha Maitreya (with his Dharma wheel and sacred vessel) on the left, and Manjushri (with sword and book) on the right. In the mountainous landscape below, from left to right are the guardian Vaishravana (with a flag and a mongoose spitting out pearls), the guardian Vajrapani (making a threatening gesture while holding his namesake *vajra*), and the luck-bringing goddess Tseringma, riding on a white horse and holding a divination arrow and a golden vase. In the outer ring are the flames that burn away obstructions to enlightenment.

61
Vajrabhairava Mandala
Gilt copper
China, Ming Dynasty, Yongle reign (1403-1424)
H: 82 cm
Potala Palace Collection
Published: *Well*-Selected, no. 44; *Treasures from Snow Mountains*, pp. 84-89, no. 22; *Tibet Museum Catalog*, pp. 110-111; *Precious Deposits*, vol. 3, pp. 262-266, no. 99; Ulrich von Schroeder, *Buddhist Sculptures in Tibet*, vol. 2, pp. 1264-1265, no.350

The buffalo-headed Vajrabhairava, who stands at the center of this mandala, is a fierce form of Manjushri, the Bodhisattva of Wisdom. He has nine heads, sixteen legs, and thirty-four arms, each one displaying a different attribute. All of these attributes can be deployed in his function as a universal savior or Supreme Being (Tibetan: *yidam*), who delivers all beings from the rounds of birth and death (Sanskrit: *samsara*) and establishes them in the state of highest enlightenment. The uppermost of his nine heads is that of Manjushri. Various Buddhist traditions teach that he is an emanation or manifestation of Manjushri, and that he honors his Guru by carrying him on top of his head.

The many heads indicate that Vajrabhairava can see all points of view and understand all aspects of reality. The two horns show mastery over the Two Truths (conventional and ultimate). The thirty-four arms, each wielding a different attribute, demonstrate Vajrabhairava's abilities to help each living being according to his or her individual needs. The sixteen legs indicate his standing in the realization of the sixteen types of Emptiness (Sanskrit: *shunyata*). He stands on top of all the worldly gods and powers (symbolized by the animal figures) who embody worldly ways and who perpetuate *samsara*. Vajrabhairava stands upon a solar cushion representing his illumination of the world and his ability to banish the darkness of ignorance. He is on a lotus throne symbolizing his transcendence of all the defilements of the world.

This three-dimensional, gilt copper alloy mandala is based on a lotus-shaped prototype from the Pala kingdom of Eastern India (8th - 11th century). The buffalo-headed Vajrabhairava Ekavira ("Solitary Hero," meaning he appears without his consort), rests within a closed lotus bud that rises above a filigreed tree whose branches bear images of the offering goddesses, accompanied by serpent deities below. Each petal of the lotus is decorated on the exterior with one of the Eight Cemeteries and their inner surfaces serve as flame-shaped haloes for multiple, nearly identical, two-armed Vajrabhairava figures (four of the petals have a single figure and four have two, for a total of twelve). The central deity, the surrounding twelve, two-armed Vajrabhairava, and the small, energetic figures, the main deity tramples beneath each of his sixteen feet are revealed when the hinged parasol at the top of the mandala is released and the petals of the flower open.

This elaborate gilt artifact was a gift from Ming Dynasty Emperor Yongle (reigned 1403-1424), who cultivated the relationship of the Chinese imperial court with Tibet's great Lamas, by means of a carefully orchestrated program of invitations to the Ming capitals at Nanjing and Beijing (not all of them accepted) and repeated gift-giving. On the interior of the lotus, right in front of the image of Vajrabhairava, is the mark of Yongle's reign, written in Chinese: *Da Ming Yongle nian shi* ("Donated during the reign of Yongle of the Great Ming"). A second, identical inscription appears between the two registers of the base. This three-dimensional mandala was once kept on the third floor in the northern section of the Red Palace, Lhasa.

62
Guhyasamaja
Thangka, colors on cotton
Tibet, 18th century
H: 162.5 cm; L: 97.6 cm
Norbulingka Collection
Published: *Golden Treasures*, pp. 82-83; *Tibet Museum Catalog*, p. 152, no. 1

The blue-bodied Guhyasamaja (Tibetan: Gsang ba 'dus pa) holds his green-bodied consort Sparshavajra and sits upon a sun disc on a lotus pedestal. The attributes he and his consort hold in their three pairs of hands are the same. Their main hands, of which only his are visible, hold the *vajra* and bell, and the other hands hold a flaming sword, lotus, wish-granting gems, and the Dharma wheel. Guhyasamaja and his consort sit in the middle of a mandala, surrounded by thirty-three images of various deities, surmounted by the triad of Tsongkhapa, the founder of the Gelug order, and his two disciples, indicating that this is a painting done for the Gelug order.

Tradition holds that Guhyasamaja's tantra is the oldest Buddhist tantra, taught by the Buddha Shakyamuni on the morning after his enlightenment. The name "Guhyasamaja" means "Secret Assembly," which indicates that all the enlightened ones are embodied in him. This is indicated in his iconography by the attributes in his six hands and the identical ones held by his consort. These are the attributes of the Five Buddhas, plus the bell. Because Guhyasamaja is part of the *vajra* family of the Buddha Akshobhya, he holds the male *vajra*, Akshobhya's main attribute, in one of his main hands and the female bell of wisdom in the other. Unlike Guhyasamaja himself, who has a very peaceful countenance, his consort Sparshavajra has an energetic ferocity and intensity. Their union represents the coming together of wisdom, the female attribute, and compassion, the male—the perfect union of wisdom and compassion that characterizes the enlightened state. The *Guhyasamaja Tantra* is the "king of Tantras," the highest, most esoteric, and most complex of all Buddhist teachings. Because tradition holds that it was the first Tantra, it is also believed to be the prototype for all other Tantras.

Chakrasamvara (Tibetan: 'Khor lo sdom pa) is most often called Demchok. He is blue in color, and embraces his red-bodied consort, Vajravarahi (see no. 84). He has four heads and twelve arms, while Vajravarahi has a single head and two arms. Chakrasamvara's two main hands, which embrace his consort, cross in front of his chest holding the *vajra* and bell in the gesture of uniting wisdom and compassion. He stands on a red sun disc on a multi-colored lotus with his left leg bent and right leg extended. Among his many attributes, a few stand out: the severed four-faced head of Brahma, and the elephant skin, representing his slaying of the demon of ignorance. Chakrasamvara treads on Kalaratri, goddess of the night, who represents nirvana, and Bhairava, who symbolizes *samsara*. The pair embodies the Buddha's rejection of the limited, selfish state of attaining nirvana just for oneself, as well as the endless cycle of samsaric rebirth. The goal is the attainment of Buddhahood, in which one avoids nirvana out of compassion for all beings and avoids *samsara* through the realization of its pernicious nature. In the Gelug system, Chakrasamvara counts as one of the three main *yidam* (Supreme Beings), along with Vajrabhairava and Guhyasamaja. Vajrabhairava is generally practiced first, because he is considered to be most effective in eliminating obstacles on the path. Chakrasamvara is practiced second, because of his effectiveness in building up the good qualities needed for enlightenment. Guhyasamaja is practiced last in order to integrate fully all the elements and aspects of the path to attain highest enlightenment.

The *kesi* (slit silk) thangka (no. 65) is a masterpiece of late 14th - early 15th century Chinese weaving, superbly representing the complexity of Chakrasamvara's iconography. The dry climate of Tibet has served to preserve the thangka in all of its original brilliance. This woven version explodes with vivid detail: a brightly feathered *garuda* biting two snakes surmounts the flaming halo surrounding the pair of deities and *makaras* with lotus blossoms emerging from their gaping mouths sit on columns to the sides of the throne, while heavenly deities borne by rainbow clouds throw down flower garlands from above. Such attention to imaginative realization is characteristic of the courtly textiles of the Chinese Ming Dynasty during the late 14th and early 15th centuries, when contact between the imperial court and the great Lamas of Tibet was particularly close.

The bodies of the Tibetan 18th century copper image of Chakrasamvara and his consort have (no. 64) not been gilded and thus they form a striking contrast with the turquoise and gold jewelry worn by Vajravarahi and with the flaming halo that surrounds them both. The flaming halo serves as a protective barrier against obstructions, distractions, obstacles, and other demons, while attracting all the blessings and powers of the Buddhas in all directions. The more recent example, which can be dated to the late 19th or early 20th century, demonstrates the continuation of an extraordinary metalworking tradition in Tibet even in modern times. The spectacular crown and earrings of both deities, all inlaid with precious gems, are modeled in a style popular in the first part of the 20th century.

63
Chakrasamvara
Gilt copper, with turquoise and precious stones
Tibet, late 19th - early 20th century
H: 94.5 cm
Norbulingka Collection
Published: *Treasures from Snow Mountains*,
pp. 102-103, no. 33

64
Chakrasamvara
Gilt copper and turquoise
Tibet, ca. 18th century
H: 28 cm; L: 15.8 cm
Norbulingka Collection
Published: *Precious Deposits*, vol. 4,
pp. 124-125, no. 51

65
Opposite Page
Chakrasamvara
Thangka, *Kesi* "slit silk" tapestry
China, Ming Dynasty (1368-1644)
H: 143.2 cm; L: 93 cm
Potala Palace Collection
Published: *Treasures from Snow Mountains*,
pp. 60-62, no. 9

66
Namchu Wangden (*rNam bcu dbang ldan*):
The Kalachakra Symbol
Thangka, embroidered silk
China, Ming Dynasty, 16th - 17th century
H: 69 cm; L: 46.5 cm
Tibet Museum, Lhasa
Published: *Xizang tangka*, no. 83;
Treasures from Snow Mountains, p. 70, no. 13;
Tibet Museum Catalog, p. 60, no. 3

67
Kalachakra Mandala
Thangka, colors on cotton
Tibet, 18th century
H: 103 cm; L: 78 cm
Tibet Museum, Lhasa
Published: *Treasures from Snow Mountains*, pp. 67-69, no. 12; *Tibet Museum Catalog*, pp. 68-69, no. 5

68
Kalachakra
Thangka, embroidered silk
China, Ming Dynasty, 14th - 15th century
H: 162.5 cm; L: 97.6 cm
Potala Palace Collection

Sacred Arts of Tibet

These three images (see nos. 66, 67 & 68) represent three very different ways of depicting one of the most important *yidam* (Supreme Beings who act as personal deities) in Tibetan Buddhism—Kalachakra, the Wheel of Time. It is said that the Buddha Shakyamuni himself preached the Kalachakra Tantra, which was taken to Shambhala, a remote, ice-bound kingdom located somewhere in the far north. This scripture (and the ritual practice that reverences and embodies it), teaches that Shambhala will have thirty-two kings, the last of whom, Rudrachakrin, will face an apocalyptic conflict that will ultimately usher in the next *kalpa*, a new age over which a new Buddha will preside. Aside from its profound spiritual meaning, the Kalachakra Tantra has worldly significance as well, in that is prophesizes the coming of a golden age of peace, prosperity, and enlightenment. Today, the Fourteenth Dalai Lama continues to offer teachings on the Kalachakra Tantra at Bodh Gaya, the Indian city where the historical Buddha Shakyamuni attained enlightenment, and other sites.

The earliest of the three Kalachakra images included in this exhibition \(see no. 68) is an embroidered silk thangka that focuses on Kalachakra himself. He is shown *yab yum* (father-mother) with his consort, Vishvamata. There is a small image of the blue-bodied Gurgyi Gompo (Mahakala, Lord of the Tent (see no. 87)) in the bottom register, fourth from the right, and the Lamas shown seated in the upper registers are members of the Sakya order. These figures indicate that this thangka was made for the Sakya order. This exquisitely embroidered image was probably produced in the late 14th or early 15th century at the command of the Chinese Ming Dynasty court as a luxurious gift to one of the great Lamas of the Sakya order.

The second thangka (see no. 67) is a complete Kalachakra mandala, a Tibetan product of the 18th century. Here, the tiny joined figures of Kalachakra and Vishvamata, surrounded by a ring of flames, occupy the center of an elaborate mandala palace, where the twelve kings of Shambhala and fourteen high Lamas, including the Dalai and Panchen Lamas of the Gelug order and other figures in their lineages, each identified by inscription, occupy the register above the palace. In the lower register, on the left, is a fierce, twenty-four armed figure with four-heads, a heavy, blue body, and central hands with bell and *vajra* in the gesture of uniting wisdom and compassion. Another pair of his hands holds a sword and shield. On the right in the same register is an armored, wealth-bringing god with a red face, who holds a spear and a mongoose and rides on a blue mule.

The third Kalachakra image (see no. 66) is far more abstract, in that it gathers together the subject matter of the Kalachakra in seven letters and three other forms, together known as the Powerful Ten—Namchu Wangden (*vNam bcu dbang ldan*). One form is stacked upon another in this symbolic representation; each of the seven letters, written in Sanskrit Lantsa script, along with the three additional forms, is presented in a different color. This embodiment of the Kalachakra is often seen as a decorative element in Tibet, where it is placed over doorways or found at the beginning of books.

The "Powerful Ten" is the symbol of Buddhist Tantra in general and of Kalachakra ("Wheel of Time") in particular. This construction is also the "seed syllable" of Kalachakra, meaning that its form embodies the essence of this Supreme Being (*yidam*). The power of its ten components lies in their combination and integration of all the elements of Buddhist cosmology, practice, and philosophy. This cosmology is the "outer" meaning of the Powerful Ten—the practice constitutes the "inner" meaning, and the philosophy the "other" meaning.

The Kalachakra (1) symbol can be charted as follows:
The two extra symbols are the syllable (**2**) "E" pronounced like the "ay" in May; and the syllable "Vam (**3**)." The "E" stands for the male god Kalachakra and represents universal compassion. "Vam" stands for Kalachakra's consort, the goddess Vishvamata, and represents perfect wisdom. They accompany the Kalachakra symbol to demonstrate that the state of Enlightenment combines the compassion that keeps an enlightened person (a Buddha) active in the world with the wisdom that prevents one from becoming attached to the world.

The ring of fire (**4**) is the fire of wisdom that protects one who has attained the enlightened state from inner and outer obstacles. Once one has defeated the inner obstacles of the kleshas (greed, anger, ignorance, pride, envy, etc.) no outer obstacles will arise. The threefold significance of each of the ten elements from top to bottom can be charted as follows:

 1   2   3  4

Figure	Name	Color	Outer	Inner	Other
	Nada	dark blue	space	central channel	mind mandala
	full moon	White	consciousness	left channel	body mandala
	crescent	Red	outer body/sun	right channel	speech mandala
	HAM	Blue	formless realm of gods	crown chakra	mirror-like wisdom
	KSHA	Green	form realm of gods	secret (genital) & emptiness	wisdom of bliss
	MA	Red with four direction colors	Mt. Meru & the four worlds of the desire realm	spine, bone joints	the garland of light & the five walls & five elements
	LA	Yellow	earth mandala	navel chakra hips	wisdom of reality
	VA	White	water mandala	heart chakra knees	wisdom of discrimination
	RA	Red	fire mandala	throat chakra lower legs	wisdom of equanimity
	YA	Black	wind mandala	forehead chakra soles of feet	all accomplishing wisdom

69
Buddhist Shrine with Three Images
Gilt copper
China, Qing Dynasty (1644-1911)
H: 82 cm; L: 91 cm; W: 44 cm
Norbulingka Collection
Published: *Precious Deposits*, vol. 5, pp. 112-113, no. 54

During the Qing Dynasty, it was the custom for the emperors, who were followers of Tibetan Buddhism, to have elaborate shrines built for their statues, especially when they were gifts from the Dalai or Panchen Lamas.[1] These shrines were usually constructed in three styles: in imitation of Chinese architecture, in the shape of a stupa, or crafted in auspicious shapes such as peaches and double gourds. Made of precious material, these shrines could contain from one to nine images.

The golden pavilion enshrining three images imitates Chinese architecture, but also shows Tibetan influence. While the roof emulates the typical Chinese tile work and ridge pole with ornaments, the central ornament chained to two half eagles-half men or *garudas* (Tibetan: *khyung*) are typically Tibetan. The *makaras* (mythical crocodile-like animal associated with water and fertility) strung with bells at the ends of the eaves are also Tibetan; they protect the building from the elements. Below, four dragon pillars support rolled up curtains over the three shrine doors, which are elaborately worked with the eight auspicious motifs and jewels. The three images, from left to right, are: a Ming Dynasty Yongle period (1403-1424) Manjushri, the Bodhisattva of Wisdom; a crowned Buddha Shakyamuni in earth-touching gesture from western Tibet, which may date to the 11th - 13th century; and a seated Maitreya, the future Buddha, probably central Tibetan and dating to the 15th - 16th century.

Such a shrine could well have been a gift from the emperor of China (possibly Manchu Qing Dynasty Emperor Qianlong (reigned 1736-1795) to a Dalai Lama.

[1] Wang Jiapeng, "Buddhist Shrines," in Hung Shih Chang and Jessica P. P. Hsu, eds., *Buddhist Art from Rehol, Tibetan Buddhist Images and Ritual Objects from the Qing Dynasty Summer Palace at Chengde* (Taipei: Jeff Hsu's Oriental Art, 1999), pp. 258-259.

TIBET! TREASURES FROM THE ROOF OF THE WORLD

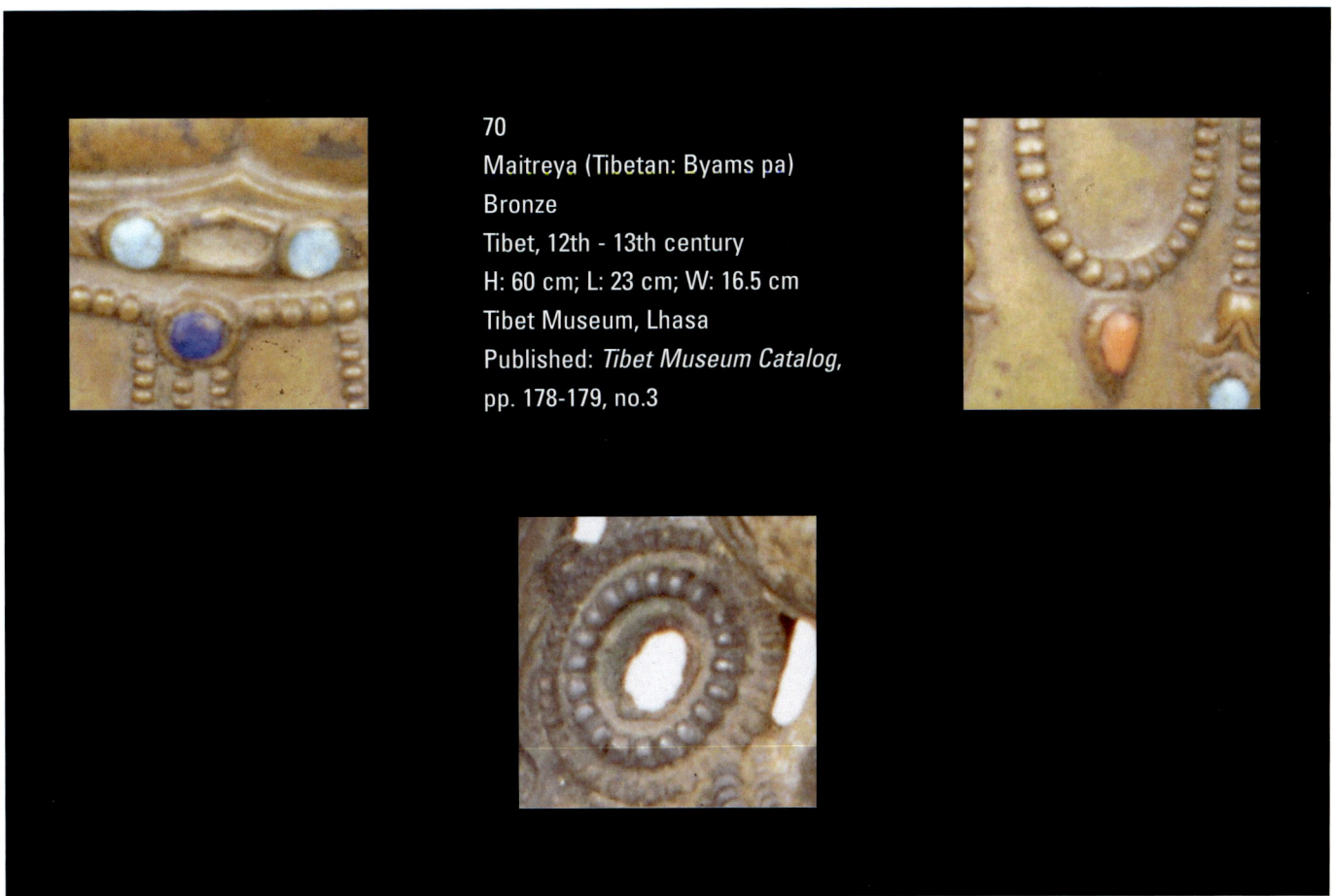

70
Maitreya (Tibetan: Byams pa)
Bronze
Tibet, 12th - 13th century
H: 60 cm; L: 23 cm; W: 16.5 cm
Tibet Museum, Lhasa
Published: *Tibet Museum Catalog*, pp. 178-179, no.3

Maitreya (Tibetan: Byams pa), the next Buddha to appear in the world, stands upright on a lotus pedestal in the "thrice bent" pose: his legs are straight, but his torso tilts to the left and his head inclines to the right. In his lowered right and raised left hands are lotus blossoms, the left one supports a sacred vessel whose waters wash away defilement and bestow immortality. This indicates Maitreya's power to remove the defilements of birth and death and overcome all misery (For example of this type of vase, see no. 11). Maitreya wears a tight-fitting garment. His hair, dressed in a high chignon, is crowned by a three-leaf crown. He wears large earrings, necklaces, and armlets that are reminiscent of Buddhist statues of the Pala period (8th - 11th century) in eastern India. Two lotus stems, rising from the pedestal, form a sinuous halo around him.

Maitreya's face is painted with cold gold, a process where gold dust is mixed with glue. Cold gold has a matte surface, unlike the shiny surface of mercury gilding. In Tibet, it was common practice to give the images under worship a new face when the old one showed wear and tear.

Buddhists believe that at present the Dharma of Buddha Shakyamuni is still active in the world. However, when the world falls far deeper into darkness and strife, the Dharma will no longer be available. Maitreya, whose name means "loving kindness," will then descend into the world from his celestial abode, Tushita, and bestow the Dharma for the salvation of all beings.

The *dharani* (sacred spells) of Maitreya are found in the Action *Tantras* (Sanskrit: *Kriya Tantra*; Tibetan: *bya rgyud*). The color of his body, the attributes of his head and arms, and so on, are specified in the *Net of Illusion Tantra (sgyu 'phrul dra ba)*. As a member of the Buddha's circle of the Eight Great Bodhisattvas, Maitreya is found throughout the *Tantras*, both early and late.

71
Bodhisattva
Gilt copper
Tibet, 13th - 14th century
H: 59 cm; L: 14 cm; W: 16.5 cm
Tibet Museum, Lhasa
Published: *Tibet Museum Catalog*, pp. 174-175, no. 4

Shown here is one of the Eight Great Bodhisattvas, the "Eight Great Spiritual Sons Next to Buddha" (*nye ba'i sras chen brgyad*). The Eight Great Bodhisattvas are enlightened beings, who appear in the world in order to save sentient beings. This Bodhisattva stands upright on his lotus pedestal, with his right hand raised in the gesture of reassurance (Sanskrit: *abhaya mudra*), and his left lowered in the gesture of gift-giving (*varadha mudra*). His hair dressed in a high knot, the scarves flying behind his ears, and his jewelry is reminiscent of the 8th - 11th century Pala style of eastern India. In the absence of any attributes in his hands, it is not possible to identify him more precisely.

In Tibetan temples where the main image is the Buddha Shakyamuni, the Eight Great Bodhisattvas are shown standing, four on each side of the Buddha. They are: Manjushri (Bodhisattva of Wisdom), Vajrapani (Bodhisattva of Sacred Power), Avalokiteshvara (Bodhisattva of Compassion), Kshitigarbha (Earth Treasure), Sarvanivarana Vishkambhin (Destroyer of All Sins), Akashagarbha (Sky Treasure), Maitreya (Bodhisattva of Loving Kindness), and Samantabhadra (All-Benevolent).

Among the Sino-Tibetan images produced in China, the imperial gilt metal sculptures of the Ming Dynasty Yongle period (1403-1424) are famed for their superb workmanship and gracefully natural appearance. Made by the imperial workshops of China, these images were intended for ceremonial use at the court, as well as for gifts to the high monks of Tibet.

This figure represents the Namasangiti form of Manjushri, Bodhisattva of Limitless Wisdom, associated with a Tantric text of the same name (*Manjushri Namasangiti*). This has been one of the most popular texts in Tantric Buddhism from ancient India to the present day Tibet. It speaks of the many different forms of Manjushri, his manifestations, his mandalas, and his limitless activities. It teaches the practices and meditations whereby ordinary beings can eventually attain a status equal to that of Manjushri.

Manjushri Namasangiti has four arms and is seated with his legs crossed in the *vajra* meditation posture. He wears a crown of five leaves representing the five wisdoms, and is adorned with jewels representing his unlimited virtues.[1] His upper right hand wields the flaming sword of wisdom to sever the bonds of ignorance. His upper left hand, poised in the gesture of philosophical explanation *(vitarka mudra),* must once have held an *utpala* flower supporting the text of Perfect Wisdom (*Prajnaparamita*). His lower hand carries a bow, and the right hand once held an arrow, now missing. The bow represents Manjushri's powerful wisdom, and the arrow the means by which he projects the power of his wisdom to destroy the many forms of ignorance wherever they appear.[2]

72
Manjushri Namasangiti
Gilt copper
China, Ming Dynasty, Yongle reign (1403-1424)
H: 22 cm; W: 14.5 cm
Tibet Museum, Lhasa
Published: *Tibet Museum Catalog*, pp. 86 and 89, no. 4

[1] Each of the Five Wisdoms (Sanskrit: *pancha jnana;* Tibetan: *ye shes lnga*) is associated primarily with one of the Five Buddhas and represents the purified and transformed nature of one of the Five Poisons:

1) Wisdom of ultimate reality (Sanskrit: *dharmadhatujnana*)—Vairochana—ignorance (*avidya*)
2) Mirror-like wisdom (*adarshajnana*)—Akshobhya—hatred (*patigha*)
3) Wisdom of equality (*samatajnana*)—Ratnasambhava—pride (*mana*)
4) Discriminative wisdom (*pratiyaveksanajnana*)—Amitabha—greed (*raga*)
5) Accomplishing wisdom (*krityanusthanajnana*)—Amoghasiddhi— envy (*irshya*)

[2] For similar figures, see Items 62 (acc. # P1994.8.6) and 236 (acc. # F1997.13.3) in the Collection of the Shelley and Donald Rubin Foundation. See also: Heather Karmay, *Early Sino-Tibetan Art* (Warminster, England: Aris and Phillips Ltd., 1975), fig. 54; Sheila C. Bills, "Bronze Sculptures of the Early Ming (1403-1450), Tibet in China, China in Tibet," *Arts of Asia* (September-October 1994): 73-87, pls.4-5; Ulrich von Schroeder, *Buddhist Sculptures in Tibet* (Hong Kong: Visual Dharma Publications, Ltd., 2001), vol. 2, no. 354 a-c.

Cittavishramana Avalokiteshvara (Avalokiteshvara Who Puts the Mind at Ease) was the tutelary deity of Phagpa Lama (1235-1280), the fifth patriarch of the Sakya order, whom Kublai Khan, first emperor of the Yuan Dynasty, appointed national preceptor (Chinese: *guoshi*) in 1260. This image of Avalokiteshvara, embroidered in the split satin stitch, is an intriguing stylistic hybrid, partly Chinese and partly Tibetan. The compassionate Bodhisattva sits on a crag in his mountain fastness, Potalaka (which gives its name to the Potala Palace), placed at the center of an eight-spoke Dharma wheel, embellished with garnets, pearls, and turquoise. Avalokiteshvara's princely, striped lower garment is Indian in style. He holds a string of prayer beads formed of real seed pearls and his other hand carries the lotus that rises up behind his shoulder. Hanging over the same shoulder is an antelope skin, more common to the Tibetan iconography of this Bodhisattva. However, on Avalokiteshvara's right is a Chinese-style stand, upon which sits a vase holding a willow branch (for sprinkling the elixir of life held in the vase), and a green parrot. The willow and parrot are standard elements in the Chinese iconography of Avalokiteshvara of the South Seas (known as Nanhai Guanyin in Chinese), a form in which the Bodhisattva sits on Mount Potalaka. Chinese Buddhists believe that Putuo Island, off the southeast coast of China, is Potalaka. The cloth-of-gold upon which the image is embroidered is clearly of Chinese origin and resembles fabrics woven in the 13th - 14th century (Yuan or early Ming Dynasties). The top and bottom mounting fabric is the same as the fabric used in the border mount of the protector Achala, an image that dates to the early 13th century (suggesting that Achala's mounting may have been renewed early in its career). The image has multiple dust covers, instead of a single one.

73
Mandala of Cittavishramana Avalokiteshvara
(Avalokiteshvara Who Puts the Mind at Ease)
Thangka, embroidered silk
Tibet, 14th century
H; 60 cm; L: 45.5 cm
Potala Palace Collection
Published: *Precious Deposits*, vol. 3, pp. 52-53, no. 22;
Xizang tangka, no. 118

169

This sculptural image of the Four-Armed Avalokiteshvara is the same form of the Bodhisattva seen in the silk tapestry (see no. 76); both were produced at the 18th century Qing Dynasty court. Although this form of Avalokiteshvara usually wears white robes and has a pristine white body, this wooden figure has been given a coating of brilliant cinnabar red lacquer, a typically Chinese way of preserving wood. His face is painted with gold. The central pair of hands is pressed together around the wish-granting jewel and the two raised hands once held a lotus and string of prayer beads.

The exquisite quality of this figure suggests that it was probably made as a gift from Qing Dynasty Emperor Qianlong (reigned 1736-1795) to a Dalai Lama.

74
Four-Armed Avalokiteshvara
Wood with lacquer, cold gold, gilt copper, and jewels
China, Qing Dynasty, Qianlong reign (1736-1795)
H: 50.5 cm; D: 37.5 cm
Potala Palace Collection
Published: *Treasures from Snow Mountains*, p. 99, no. 30

Sometime around 1758, Emperor Qianlong (reigned 1736-1795) had several textile images of Shadakshari Avalokiteshvara (Avalokiteshvara of the Six Syllables) made in the southern Chinese city of Suzhou, very likely to honor the as yet undiscovered Eighth Dalai Lama. The biography of Rolpay Dorje, the Third Zhangjia Khutukhtu and the Qing National Preceptor (1719-1786), describes the lavish gifts he carried, among them images of Avalokiteshvara, when he went to Lhasa at Qianlong's command to oversee the selection of the new incarnation. Rolpay Dorje extended his visit through 1760 so that he could visit monasteries all over central Tibet, apparently distributing copies of the Avalokiteshvara image along with their implicit message of Qing imperial support for the new Dalai Lama.

This *kesi* tapestry version, the largest of the known copies, survives today in the Potala Palace Collection, and is presumably the very gift Rolpay Dorje presented to the new incarnation. Two "file copies," a silk embroidery now in the National Palace Museum, Taiwan, and a second tapestry, whose present location is unknown, were placed in the imperial collection in the Forbidden City in Beijing. Both are listed in the 1793 supplement to the imperial Buddhist and Daoist art collection (*Bidian zhulin xubian*). A fourth copy, another identical silk embroidery, recently entered the collection of the Asian Art Museum in San Francisco, apparently recovered from a Tibetan monastery sometime after the Cultural Revolution. All four bear identically placed seals of Emperor Qianlong and his *Bidian zhulin* collection of sacred art.

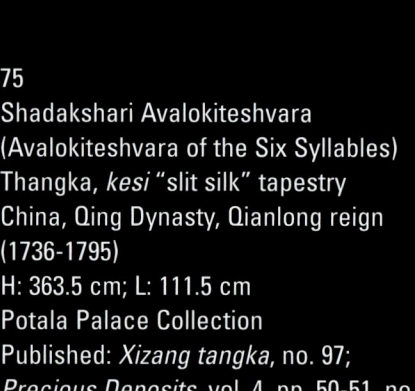

In all the surviving examples, the four-armed Avalokiteshvara sits on a luminous lotus as delicate lotus sprigs shower down around him. He is represented in a manner that repeats the composition of at least one late Ming Dynasty textile image of him. However the real subject of this group of images is not just Avalokiteshvara's elegantly realized body, but also the Six Syllable mantra, "Om Mani Padme Hum," that invokes him and is rendered in brilliant blue Sanskrit in the blossom-strewn space above.

The Tibetan inscription embroidered below Avalokiteshvara has a completely different function. It repeats an official prayer-poem often used in the Manchu imperial household in Beijing, one of four woven into bales of presentation scarves from as early as 1715 and well-known on Ming Dynasty blue-and-white ceramics (see no. 42). It reads:

May you be blessed with good fortune in the morning,
May you be blessed with good fortune at night,
May you be blessed with good fortune at noon,
May your days and nights always be blessed with good fortune,
May you ever be blessed with the good fortune of the Three Jewels!

75
Shadakshari Avalokiteshvara
(Avalokiteshvara of the Six Syllables)
Thangka, *kesi* "slit silk" tapestry
China, Qing Dynasty, Qianlong reign
(1736-1795)
H: 363.5 cm; L: 111.5 cm
Potala Palace Collection
Published: *Xizang tangka*, no. 97;
Precious Deposits, vol. 4, pp. 50-51, no. 20

Tibet: Treasures from the Roof of the World

76
Eleven-headed Avalokiteshvara
Gilt copper
Tibet 19th - 20th century
H: 109 cm
Norbulingka Collection
Published: *Treasures from Snow Mountains*,
pp. 104-105, no. 34

Avalokiteshvara, the Bodhisattva of Universal Compassion, often appears in his form as the white-bodied Sahasrabhuja Avalokiteshvara with eleven heads and one thousand arms and eyes. Here, his eleven heads are stacked in five tiers: the three lower tiers with three heads each and two upper tiers of single heads, the large head of Avalokiteshvara's wrathful form, Mahakala, and the crowning peaceful head of the Buddha Amitabha, Avalokiteshvara's spiritual father. His two major hands, pressed against his chest, hold the wish-granting jewel, which represents *bodhicitta* (the necessary attitude of a Bodhisattva). His two raised upper hands hold two more attributes: a lotus, representing purity, and a string of prayer beads. His middle hands carry a bow and arrow and the wheel of Dharma; his lower left hand holds a vase filled with the elixir of immortality and his lower right hand makes the gift-bestowing gesture. His other multiple hands, each incised with an all-seeing eye, radiate to form a halo around Avalokiteshvara's body. Avalokiteshvara is a peaceful deity, which is marked by his blue hair. However, Mahakala, his wrathful form, has flaming orange-red hair that stands on end and forms a diadem around his face and the head of Amitabha.

Sahasrabhuja Avalokiteshvara is one of many forms of Avalokiteshvara. There are, for example, one hundred and eight different forms of this Bodhisattva in the Monastery of the Kanak Stupa of Nepal. Each of the many forms arises as needed to teach and serve the needs of limitless beings with their different characteristics and dispositions. Likewise, thirty-eight of Sahasrabhuja Avalokiteshvara's thousand arms are described as holding various useful attributes, such as different types of flowers (*utpala*, *pundarika* and lotus) different jewels, a noose or snare, an alms bowl, sword, *vajra*, bell, sun, cudgel, wheel, and skull cup.

Some versions show Sahasrabhuja Avalokiteshvara with only eight hands holding attributes (rosary, disc, jewel, lotus, bow, and vase filled with the nectar of immortality, the wish-fulfilling jewel held between the first two hands). An antelope hide over his left shoulder symbolizes compassion. He has the *sambhogakaya* (bliss body) ornaments (earrings, necklaces, armlets, anklets, etc.). As in other versions, he has eleven heads.

The traditional history of Sahasrabhuja Avalokiteshvara is as follows. At the outset of his Bodhisattva career, he made his great Bodhisattva vow to Buddha Amitabha, saying that he would continually manifest in the three realms of *samsara* to bring about the liberation of each and every sentient being, without exception. Part of this vow was: "If my resolve to save all beings from *samsara* ever falters, may I fall apart and break into a thousand pieces." Receiving the blessings and powers of Amitabha, Avalokiteshvara developed the vast skills and methods to save limitless beings. These skills and methods were encompassed in the mantra of six syllables, "Om Mani Padme Hum." Armed with this mantra, Avalokiteshvara manifested in the hells, the *preta loka* (hungry ghost realm), among animals, humans, demigods, and gods. There was no being, no matter how depraved, hateful, greedy, proud, envious or ignorant who was not redeemed by Avalokiteshvara's compassion and wisdom. In this way the six migrations and three realms of *samsara* became empty.

Avalokiteshvara reported back to Amitabha, saying that he had fulfilled his great vow. Amitabha congratulated him on liberating countless beings, but suggested that he go back and make sure none was left. Doing this, Avalokiteshvara saw that in the brief time he was gone, *samsara* had filled up again with uncountable ignorant, vicious and miserable beings. In his shock and dismay, his Bodhisattva resolve (*bodhicitta*) faltered. He felt he could never succeed. With this, his body shattered into one thousand pieces.

Avalokiteshvara, now scattered on the ground in small pieces, was completely insensate, fainted dead away. Amitabha Buddha gathered up the pieces and said to him, "Do not be discouraged. You have accomplished great things. Even your shattering into one thousand pieces shows the great power of your vow. The Tathagatas of the three times and ten directions rejoice! I will reassemble you in a new form, with a thousand arms to give you the strength of a thousand universal emperors and a thousand eyes with the insight of the thousand Buddhas of the Golden Eon. Now you will indeed be limitless in your ability to encompass the welfare and liberation of all beings." Armed in this way, Avalokiteshvara proceeded to teach, train, and liberate beings much more effectively, dealing with each according the individual's needs and dispositions, and was never again daunted by the endless numbers of miserable beings.

77
Wrathful Head of an Eleven-headed Avalokiteshvara
Gilt copper
Tibet, 18th century
H: 24.5 cm
Tibet Museum, Lhasa
Published: *Treasures from Snow Mountains*, p. 101, no. 32

This wrathful Mahakala head was once part of a huge figure of the eleven-headed, thousand-armed Avalokiteshvara. His wrathful aspect is emphasized by his three bulging eyes (one in the middle of his forehead), flaming eyebrows, orange-red hair, fanged teeth, and diadem of five skulls. The small opening at the top of the chignon is designed to hold the missing topmost head of Amitabha, Avalokiteshvara's spiritual father.

Vajrapani is one of the great triad of Bodhisattvas (Tibetan: rigs gsum mgon po) of Tibet, together with Manjushri and Avalokiteshvara. Vajrapani embodies the secret power of all the Buddhas, as Manjushri embodies their wisdom and Avalokiteshvara their compassion.

Standing on a sun disk on a lotus throne with his right leg bent and left extended, the two-armed Vajrapani is surrounded by two concentric borders of Buddhas, Bodhisattvas, Lamas of the Taklung lineage,[1] and ferocious divinities. He stands upon the prostrate figures of a blue and a red worldly god, showing his ability to overcome the powers of deluded thoughts and harmful passions. He wields a *vajra* in his right hand, demonstrating his unconquerable compassion and limitless skill in saving living beings from the miseries of birth and death. In his left hand is the bell (*ghanta*), proclaiming his profound wisdom, which liberates from all illusions. He wears a five-Buddha crown rather than the more typical five-jewel crown. Like most wrathful deities, his hair is blazing orange and he has three bulging eyes, ferociously frowning eyebrows, and bared fangs. He wears only a tiger skin and snake ornaments, with many necklaces as well as armlets, anklets, and earrings.

By his left shoulder is an image of Vajrapani in union with his consort. There are six *garudas* above him and the nine planetary deities form a row at the very bottom. Typical of early Nepalese-style paintings, the background is overwhelmingly red, with one large central figure surrounded by a large number of small figures in niches.

[1] Taklung is one of the twelve major branches of the Kagyu order. The Taklung Monastery, 65 km. north of Lhasa, was founded in 1180 by Taklung Thangpa Chenpo, a.k.a. Tashipel, 1142-1210. This monastery flourished around the early 13th century and particularly patronized Nepalese artists. See: Jane Casey Singer and Philip Denwood, eds., *Tibetan Art: Towards a Definition of Style* (London: Lawrence King Publishing, 1997), p. 52.

78
The Guardian Vajrapani
Colors on cloth
Tibet, 13th century
H: 84 cm; L: 57 cm
Tibet Museum, Lhasa
Published: *Treasures from Snow Mountains*, p. 59, no. 8;
Tibet Museum Catalog, pp. 80-81

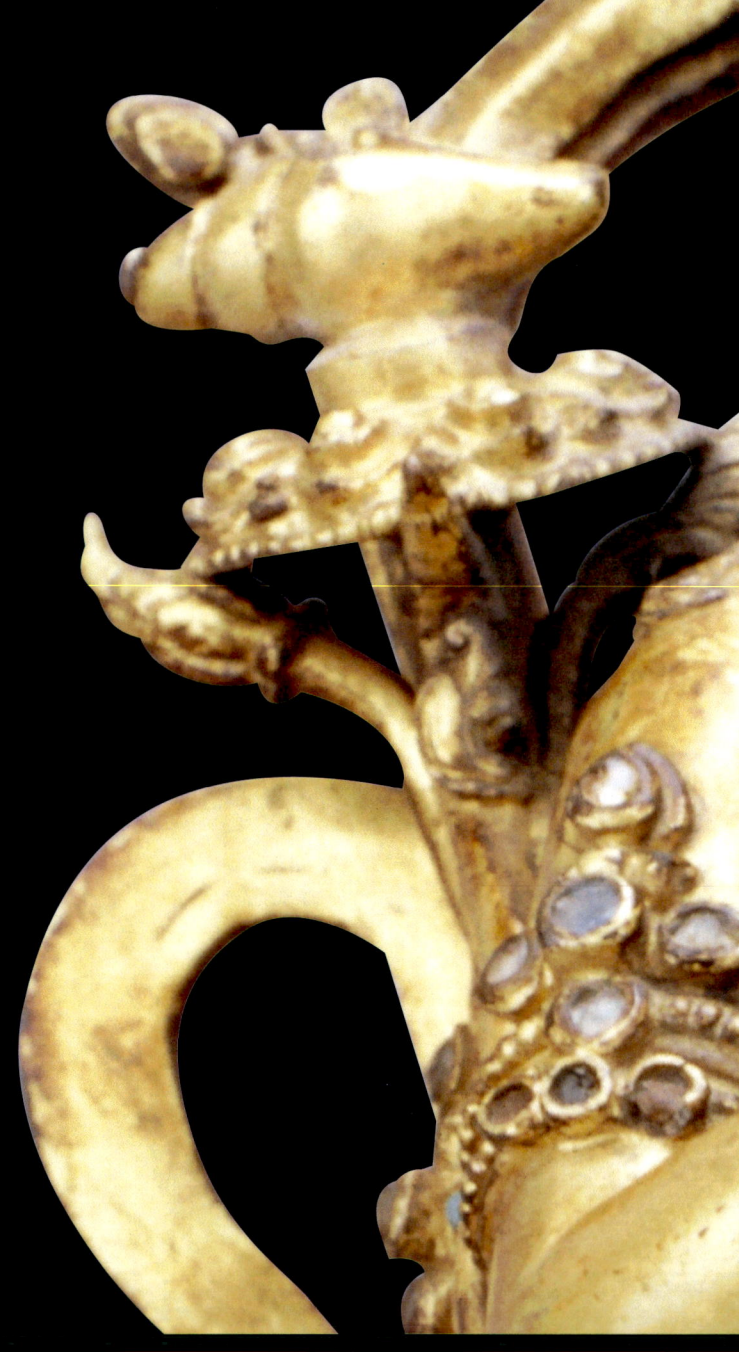

79
Unidentified Four-armed Goddess
Gilt copper
Tibet, 14th - 15th century
H: 29 cm; L: 23 cm; W: 16 cm
Tibet Museum, Lhasa
Published: *Precious Deposits*, vol. 3, pp. 56-57, no. 24; E. F. Lo Bue, *Tesori del Tibet: Oggetti d'arte dai Monasteri di Lhasa*, pp. 116-118, no. 76; Ulrich von Schroeder, *Buddhist Sculptures in Tibet*, vol. 2, p. 1040, pl. 260A.

Originally from the Red Palace inside the Potala, this unidentified goddess sits in meditation on a lotus throne placed on a lion pedestal. She has two pairs of hands. The bottom pair is held in the gesture of meditation. The top pair is in the gesture of preaching (*dharmachakra mudra*), while also holding two stalks of lotus blossoms, supporting a conch (left) and a vase of immortality (right) at shoulder level. The goddess is bedecked with jewels, mainly inlaid turquoise. Her head is enclosed within a cloverleaf halo and the wavy scarves behind her arms add a sense of movement.

In her elaborate ornament, jewel encrusted lower garment, and clover-shaped halo, this figure closely resembles a group of copper repoussé images from Densatil Monastery, a Kagyu establishment founded in the 12th century that was once located in central Tibet. During the 14th and 15th centuries, this region of Tibet was ruled by the Lang family, who generously patronized Densatil.

The goddess has three eyes and four arms, and is seated with one leg bent and the other pendant on the lotus throne. A small lotus springing from the pedestal supports the goddess's left leg, a style that harks back to the Pala sculptures of eastern India. The goddess carries a blue lotus (a flower shown in profile as opposed to the pink lotus, depicted in full bloom) in her upper left hand. Her major right hand grasps a *vajra*, while the left, resting gracefully on her left knee, carries a string of prayer beads. The statue is fire-gilded and turquoise and other precious gems ornament the goddess's jewelry, and the four petaled flowers on her striped lower garment. Her scarf forms a halo behind her head.

The style of the goddess and the sumptuous jewelry are consistent with sculptures attributed to Densatil Monastery (see no. 79).

80
Four-armed Goddess
Gilt copper and precious stones
Tibet, 14th - 15th century
H: 29 cm; W: 29 cm
Tibet Museum, Lhasa
Published: *Treasures from Snow Mountains*, p. 93, no. 26

81
White Tara
Thangka, appliquéd silk
Tibet, 18th century
H: 120 cm; L: 82 cm
Norbulingka collection
Published: *Xizang tangka*, no. 103; *Golden Treasures*, pp. 98-99

As in other piecework traditions, appliqué images in Tibet grew out of a desire to make use of leftover scraps of cloth. In Tibet, these were sometimes luxurious silks and well-worn court garments that originally came from China and elsewhere as tribute or gifts. Here, White Tara appears with her seven eyes: two regular eyes, one eye between the other two, two on the palms and two on the soles. According to the First Dalai Lama, who wrote a series of eloquent poems to White Tara, these last four allow her to see the four doors of liberation, thus allowing her to lead people to the blissful realm of liberation. Tara is seated on a freely rendered white lotus that emerges from a pond; she holds another white lotus in her left hand. White Tara is one of the three longevity deities, together with Amitayus and Ushnishavijaya, who appear top center and left. Sitasamvara *yab yum* ("father-mother") appears in the upper right. According to the traditional explanation, Tara is an emanation of Avalokiteshvara and she functions as one of the divinities who liberate beings from all that is fearful (the traditional list has Eight Great Fears: lions, elephants, poisonous snakes, government officials, thieves, fire, disease, untimely death (see no. 40).

At the bottom are two deities: the yellow wealth god on the left holds an ear of grain. The white form of the protector Achala, who holds a sword, is on the right. In front of Tara is the peaceful offering of the five senses: mirror for sight, cymbals for hearing, fruit for taste, conch holding yoghurt for smell, and a piece of a silk scarf for touch.

82
Green Tara
Gilt copper
Tibet, 15th century
H: 59 cm; L: 30 cm; W: 15 cm
Tibet Museum, Lhasa
Published: *Well-Selected*, p.80, no. 51; *Tibet Museum Catalog*, pp. 82-83, no. 2

Stately and serene, Green Tara sits with one leg bent and one leg pendant. Her right hand is lowered in the gift-bestowing gesture, and her left hand is held in the gesture of granting refuge. A popular deity in Tibet, Green Tara is a goddess of dynamic action. This is indicated by the right leg stretched forth, showing her ready to come to the aid of petitioners. Her right hand bestows the gift of accomplishing the stages on the path to enlightenment as well as the attainment of Buddhahood. Green Tara's left hand gesture indicates her ability to protect against all objects of dread, symbolized by the eight outer and inner causes of fear (Sanskrit: *ashtabhaya*; Tibetan: *'jigs pa brgyad*): lions/pride, elephants/ignorance, fire/anger, snakes/jealousy, thieves/wrong views, iron fetters/stinginess, rivers/desire). She is associated with Avalokiteshvara, the Bodhisattva of Universal Compassion. The early religious King Songtsen Gampo's Chinese and Nepalese queens were believed to be emanations of the White and Green Taras.

In this gilt copper image, Green Tara is supported by a lotus issuing from an elaborate throne, whose base is guarded by the Kings of the Four Directions. Behind her is an ornate halo bordered by curling flames, the main part sculpted with tendrils supporting small images of the twenty-one Taras, some of them now damaged. In her hands are two blue lotuses, shown in profile in contrast to the pink lotus, which is shown in full view. She wears an impressive crown bearing images of Buddhas (reminiscent of the crown seen in no. 51). Her elaborate jewelry is inlaid with turquoise and the inlay work on her belt is simple yet beautiful. Chased on her lower garment are symbols of treasures floating among clouds.

Rigdzin Chodrak (Rig 'dzin chos grags; Sanskrit: Vidyadhara Dharmakirti, 1595-1659) described Green Tara as follows:

> Just as Avalokiteshvara manifests the compassionate and skillful means of Buddha Amitabha, so Tara manifests his wisdom. In a previous eon, Noble Avalokiteshvara made a great vow in the presence of Buddha Amitabha: "I shall work continually for the benefit of sentient beings until *samsara* is emptied." Having made this pledge, he proceeded to encompass the welfare of sentient beings for innumerable eons, establishing them in the state of liberation. However, he perceived that despite his efforts the number of sentient beings remaining in *samsara* did not grow smaller. This caused him such great distress that tears flowed from his eyes. From these tears arose Tara and Bhrikuti (Khro gnyer cen).
>
> The Bhagavan Jetsun Tara proclaimed to the Noble Avalokiteshvara: "Wherever you go throughout the realms of existence, from whatever causes you fear or anxiety, from that I will protect you. Therefore have no more fear and be free of all dread." In this manner, Tara became the supreme friend and helper of the Noble Avalokiteshvara in his efforts to encompass the welfare of all living beings.

The Buddha Vairochana paid homage and offered the "Praise to the Twenty-one Taras in the Tantra known as The Manifest Arising of Tara" (Tibetan: *sgrol ma mngon 'byung gi rgyud*). Though she has one mental continuum, Tara has inconceivable manifestations with different configurations of body colors, faces, and arms.

83
Wrathful Goddess
Copper alloy
Tibet, 14th - 15th century
H: 67.5 cm
Tibet Museum, Lhasa
Published: *Tibet Museum Catalog*, p. 174, no. 2

This wrathful goddess is distinguished by her orange flame-like hair, eyebrows creased into a frown, bared fangs, and frightful expression. She wields the attributes of most wrathful goddesses and consorts of wrathful gods: the chopper in the right hand and skull bowl in the left. The skull bowl represents a vessel or crucible of enlightenment in which ordinary thoughts (symbolized by the brains in the skull) are transformed by the *vajra*-knife of wisdom into the omniscient and all-compassionate mind of enlightenment.

 The goddess stands on a type of lotus pedestal that is usually associated with attendant deities, and might once have been attached to a larger sculpture. The skin of a tiger forms her lower garment; the two paws waving in the back resemble the ends of scarves, and give a sense of movement to figure. Traces of cold gold remain from the original gilding.

Vajravarahi, the "*Vajra* Sow" is so named because of the sow's head which can be seen emerging behind the goddess' right ear. This dynamic and beautiful sculpture shows her dancing with her right leg bent and left foot trampling on the demon of ignorance. Her raised right hand clutches a chopper and her left hand supports a skull bowl. She is crowned and bejeweled, draped with a long garland of severed heads, and she wears a bone apron ornamented with a dancing skeleton. Her scarf forms a halo behind her, the ends of which are inlaid with lapis lazuli, turquoise, and red coral. Her human and sow faces are both painted with cold gold, a process where gold dust is mixed with glue. The matte surfaces contrasts with the rest of her body, which is finished in shiny mercury gilding.

The abbotesses of Samding Monastery near Lake Yamdrok are traditionally believed to be emanations of Vajravarahi.

84
Vajravarahi
Gilt copper
Tibet, 15th century
H: 41.5 cm; W: 2.3 cm
Potala Palace Collection
Published: *Treasures from Snow Mountains*, p. 92, no. 25; Ulrich von Schroeder, *Buddhist Sculptures in Tibet*, vol. 2, p. 1053, pl. 266D

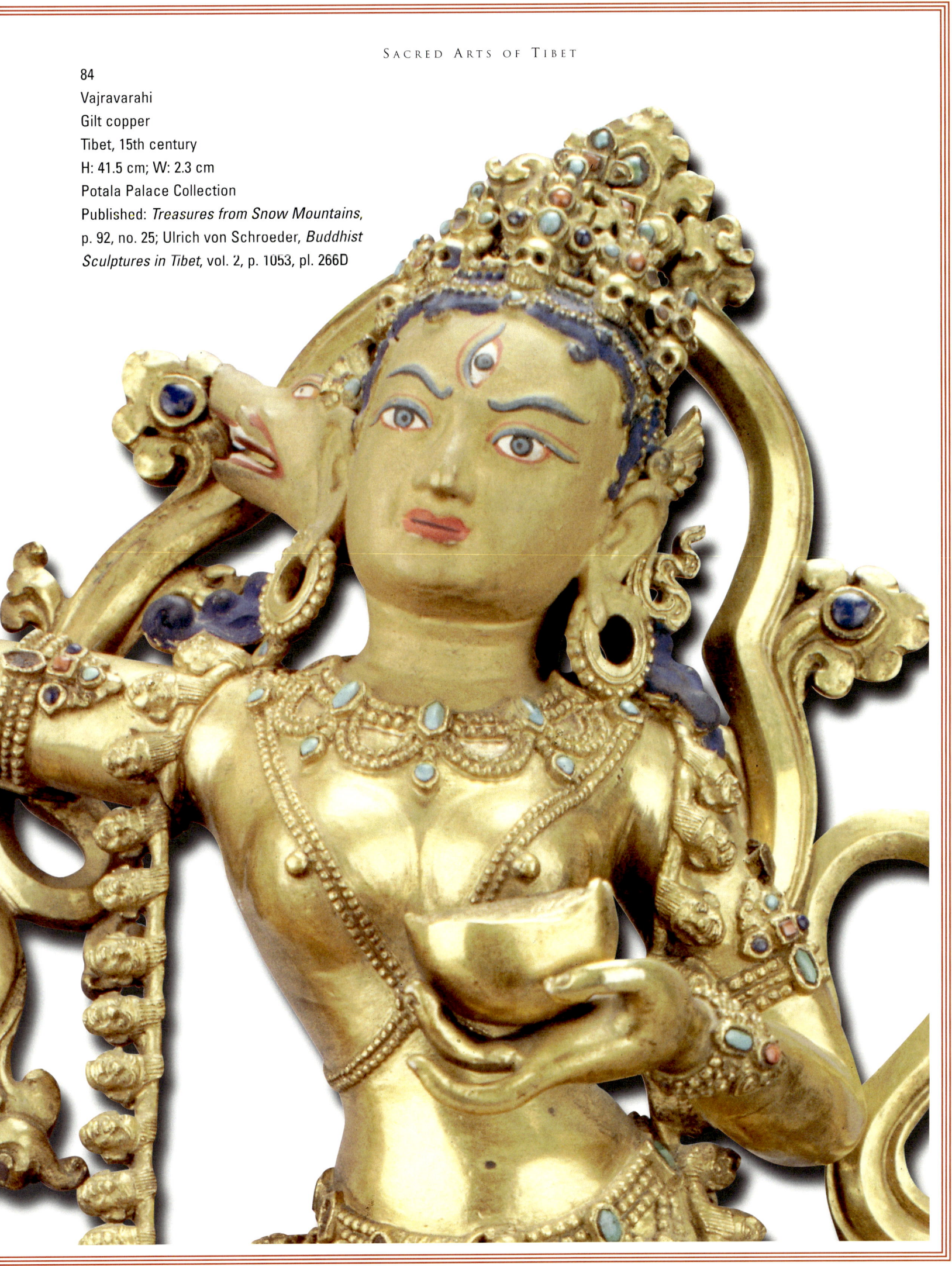

Tibet: Treasures from the Roof of the World

192

The central figure in this refined woven silk thangka, which was formerly kept in the Potala Palace, is the muscular, blue-bodied Achala Chandamaharoshana, a powerful protector, who is shown wielding a sword and kneeling in his characteristic posture with his left knee touching the sun disc on his lotus pedestal. As the story goes, the historical Buddha Shakyamuni invoked Achala when the demonic forces of war, famine, and plague threatened the world. When Achala placed his right knee on the ground, he destroyed Mara, who embodied the celestial demons. Then, switching to his left knee, Achala overcame the earthly demons, embodied in Vinayaka (the elephant-headed deity Ganesha, whom Achala converted and, at the Buddha's bidding, transformed into a deity of wealth).

85
Achala Chandamaharoshana
Thangka, *kesi* (slit silk tapestry)
Xixia (Tangut), early 13th century (before 1227)
H: 87 cm; L: 57 cm
Tibet Museum, Lhasa
Published: *Xizang tangka*, no. 102; *Well-Selected*, p. 102, no. 74; *Treasures from Snow Mountains*, pg. 58, no. 7; *Tibet Museum Catalog*, p. 66, no. 2

Achala's blue body contrasts brilliantly with the orange flames behind him. A snake-like dragon coils around his body. The snares he holds are twisted around his finger three times and are tipped with half-*vajras*. A small figure of the Buddha Akshobhya, Achala's spiritual father, sits in his crown. The complex floral scroll that winds around his flaming halo is an extraordinary feat of weaving. Another significant detail is the small pearls that form the *urnas* of the Five Buddhas in the top register, which have been threaded along the warp threads of this woven thangka, rather than being sewn on afterwards. This detail is shared by another early 13th century woven thangka of Vighnantaka, now in the Cleveland Museum of Art.[1]

The five Buddhas appear in a register at the top of the thangka. Just below, in the upper left, sits Kunga Nyingpo (1092-1158), recognizable by two white tufts of hair that shoot out from the sides of his bald pate, and, in upper right, his son, Drakpa Gyaltsen (1147-1216). Kunga Nyingpo was the first patriarch of the Sakya order, Drakpa Gyaltsen the third. In the bottom register, from left to right, are other deities: Mahakala (in his form as Gurgyi Gompo—Mahakala of the Tent), Avalokiteshvara, and the goddesses Green Tara, Ushnishavijaya, and Palden Lhamo. Above them are two female deities.

In Drakpa Gyaltsen's day, the Sakya order was affiliated religiously with the Xixia or Tangut royal house, whose realm occupied parts of what are now China's Gansu, Ningxia and Qinghai provinces. In 1227, the forces of Chinggis Khan destroyed the Tanguts, thereby ending the relationship with the Sakya. However, this Achala must have been completed before the death of Drakpa Gyaltsen in 1216. This fact can be determined from the inscription, which reads: "This is offered to the great, illustrious spiritual teacher, the venerable lord Drakpa Gyaltsen of Khon by his Khampa disciple Chang Tsundru Drakpa (Chang brtson 'grus grags)." The inscription at the top of the thangka is a series of five mantras (the universal mantra, *Om Ah Hum*; as well as the mantras of Avalokiteshvara, Achala, Tara, and Palden Lhamo).

[1] See James C.Y. Watt and Anne E. Wardwell, *When Silk Was Gold: Central Asian and Chinese Textiles* (New York: The Metropolitan Museum of Art in cooperation with the Cleveland Museum of Art, 1997), no. 24, pp. 90-4.

The four-armed Mahakala's body is covered with snake ornaments and he wears a tiger pelt as a lower garment and a crown of five skulls. A garland of decapitated heads wraps around his shoulders and falls sinuously over his body to form a semi-circle in front of his feet. Typical of wrathful deities, Mahakala has orange hair. His major hands are holding the chopper and skull cup. His other hands once held a sword of wisdom in the upper right and a trident-tipped *khatvanga* in the upper left. The trident-shape symbolizes the destruction of the three poisons, the three bodies of Buddha, and victory over the three realms of *samsara* (desire, form, and formlessness). His muscular body squashes the demon of ignorance, which lies on a bolster cushion that is placed on top of a lotus pedestal. The sides of the bolster are ornamented with scenes of the Eight Cemeteries, signifying that this Mahakala is worshipped as a Supreme Being (Tibetan: *yidam*). The Eight Cemeteries symbolize the entire world in a state of being transcended and are also seen in the outer rings of mandalas.

Mahakala has a small figure of Akshobhya seated at the top of his head, indicating that he belongs to Akshobhya's *vajra* family (one of the five Buddha families). He is a fully enlightened being who manifests in the form of a wrathful, protective deity in order to clear away all types of obstacles to enlightenment.

86
Four-armed Mahakala
Gilt copper
Tibet, 12th - 13th century
H: 43 cm
Tibet Museum, Lhasa
Published: *Well-Selected*, p. 80, no. 52-1; *Treasures from Snow Mountains*, p. 79, no. 18; *Tibet Museum Catalog*, p. 90, no. 4

87
Mahakala as Lord of the Tent (Tibetan: Gurgyi Gompo, Gur gyi mgon po; Sanskrit: Panjara Mahakala)
Thankga, colors on cotton
Tibet, early 17th century
H: 73.5 cm; L: 58.7 cm
Tibet Museum, Lhasa
Published: *Tibet Museum Catalog*, pp. 66-67, no. 3

In this brilliantly conceived thangka, Gurgyi Gompo—the great protector Mahakala in his role as Lord of the Tent—stands on top of a figure lying prostrate on a sun disc that is in turn supported by a lotus throne. The Lord of the Tent's bulky, dark blue form dominates the entire composition. His two hands hold a skull cup and curved chopper with a *vajra* handle (*driguk*), and across his chest he clutches a staff. Small black "messengers"—a man to the front, birds to the right, a dog to the left, an iron wolf (jackal) behind— emanate from his body. The *garuda* bird, who appears at the top of his brilliant, flaming aureole, is also his messenger.

Mahakala in this particular form as Lord of the Tent was very much favored by the Sakya order. In this painted representation, two groups of Sakya Lamas float on brilliantly colored, visionary clouds in the upper corners above Gurgyi Gompo. On the left are Kunga Nyingpo and his sons, Sonam Chemo, Drakpa Gyaltsen, and an unidentified person. On the right are Sakya Pandita, his nephew Phagpa Lama, and two others. In the landscape to the sides of Gurgyi Gompo, a black-hatted figure appears to be creating clouds from the palm of his hand. In the register immediately below the Lord of the Tent's pedestal are Ekajati (on the left), holding the flask of ambrosia (*amrta*) and wearing a white silk upper garment and a tiger skin, with her hair bound in a single lock; and the horrific Palden Lhamo (on the right), riding through a sea of blood. Five members of the great protector's eight-fold retinue, holding a sun disc, moon disc and other weapons, appear beneath this register.

Mahakala as Lord of the Tent held particular importance for Mongolian Buddhists, beginning with Kublai Khan's first Buddhist initiation at the hands of Phagpa Lama of the Sakya order in 1260. It is said that Phagpa Lama cast a famous gold image of the Lord of the Tent for Kublai Khan, which was designed as a battle standard to aid the Khan in his stalled military campaign against China. A surviving stone image of the Lord of the Tent, made in the Mongols' Chinese capital at Dadu and dated by its Tibetan inscription to 1292 (now in the Musée Guimet, Paris), suggests that Phagpa's golden image closely resembled the present thangka in form and attributes.[1] Phagpa's golden image reappeared in the early 17th century in Inner Mongolia in the hands of Ligdan Khan, leader of the Chahar Mongols. Upon his death in 1636, Ligdan Khan's family brought the image to the Manchus' capital at Mukden, where it was installed in a mandala-shaped monastic complex at the heart of the city. Finally, the Manchu Kangxi Emperor of the Qing Dynasty (reigned 1662-1722) brought the image to his Chinese-based capital at Beijing, where it was installed in the Pudu Monastery, just east of the imperial Forbidden City. It was apparently removed from that monastery during the Boxer Rebellion in 1900 and its present whereabouts are unknown.

[1] Heather Stoddard, "A Stone Sculpture of mGur mGon-po, Mahakala of the Tent, Dated 1292," *Oriental Art*, n.s., 31, no. 3 (Autumn 1985): 278-82.

88
Game board (*Salam Namshak*)
Thangka, colors on cotton
Tibet, early 20th century
L: 118 cm; W: 78.5 cm
Tibet Museum, Lhasa (originally from Norbulingka)
Published: *Well-Selected*, p. 109, no. 81;
Treasures from Snow Mountains, pp. 71-74, no. 14;
Tibet Museum Catalog, pp. 156 and 157

Known in Tibetan as *Salam Namshak* (exhibition of grounds and paths), this is one of the most popular games in Tibet and one of few games allowed in the monastery. It presents players with a map of the cosmos and the steps to enlightenment, inviting them vicariously to enter and participate. Each of the eighty-four squares of the board represents one of the many fearful underworlds, worldly planets, blissful heavens, and spiritual paths leading upward through the stages of salvation to the final state of enlightenment. The game is played with a dice incised with six letters: 1. *sa,* 2. *a,* 3. *ga,* 4. *da,* 5. *ra*, and 6. *ya.*

These six letters are also written within each of the eighty-four squares, indicating where the player who lands on that square is to go next. For example, if a player is on square seventeen (Planet of the Titans) and rolls a six (*ya*, this is the worst roll), he or she must proceed to square ten (realm of miserable *preta* ghosts). A roll of one (*sa*, the best roll) would send the player to twenty-three (the beginning of the Path to Nirvana).

The goal of the game is to reach Enlightenment, and play may continue for hours until every player has attained that goal. Progress through the squares is difficult, as a low roll (usually five, *ra*, or six, *ya*) may send a player back down to a lower level of the Path or even back to the underworld. In this way, the game teaches the structure of the cosmos and the path, and reinforces Buddhist ideas such as the impermanence and uncertainty of life, death, and transmigration, and the dangers of backsliding on the spiritual path.

The game is rooted in ancient Buddhist traditions. Sakya Pandita (1182-1251) was credited with giving the game its present form. He did this in order to entertain and educate his ailing mother.[1] Another tradition attributes the development of the game to Ngok Lekbei Sherab, who restored the Sangphu monastery in the 11th century. The elements of the game, however, go back all the way to ancient India and the teaching of the Buddha Shakyamuni (6th c. BCE).

Takser Rinpoche (Thubten Norbu), the elder brother of the present Dalai Lama, comments on this game in his book, *Tibet is My Country*: The first winner was rewarded with a prize of sweets. Sometimes such a game would last for hours, and occasionally it would get very noisy. Particularly fortunate or unfortunate throws were greeted with a chorus of congratulations or groans as the case might be.[2]

The game comes alive once the player begins to appreciate the meaning of each of the squares. Whether one is a Buddhist who believes in the reality of these many realms and possibilities of rebirth and spiritual development, or one is simply able to suspend disbelief and participate in a grand and complex fantasy, the *Salam Namshak* immerses the player in an ancient lore of venerable tradition and can prove a source of endless amusement.

[1] Mark Tatz and Jody Kent, Rebirth: *The Tibetan Game of Liberation* (New York: Anchor Books, 1977), p. 1.

[2] Thubten Norbu, *Tibet is My Country*, as told to Heinrich Harrer, Edward Fitzgerald, trans. (London: Hart-Davis, 1960), p. 93.

LIFE IN LHASA, THE HOLY CITY

TERESE TSE BARTHOLOMEW

The objects in this exhibition belong to the Dalai Lamas, and were once stored in the Potala (Figure 1), the winter palace, and in Norbulingka, the summer palace. Both of these palaces are located in Lhasa, the capital of Tibet. In order to understand these objects, it is helpful to know where they came from and for whom they were made, namely Lhasa, the Dalai Lamas, and the Tibetan nobility.

At twenty-nine degrees north of the equator, Lhasa has the same latitude as Gainesville, Florida. The main difference between these two cities is that Lhasa is situated at an altitude of twelve thousand feet above sea level. Lhasa enjoys a pleasant climate. The rainy season comes in summer, and the winter, though cold does not bring much snow. The daily temperature can fluctuate below zero at night to scorching highs during the day. In general, humidity is low in Lhasa, as in the rest of Tibet, and for this reason, art objects, especially ancient textiles, have often been preserved in pristine condition.

Lhasa, besides being the capital, is also Tibet's holiest city. Pilgrims from all over the country flock to visit the Jokhang, Tibet's most sacred temple, located in the heart of Lhasa. The pilgrims and locals can be seen every day circumambulating the temple. This road on which the Jokhang is located, known as the Barkhor, is also the main shopping center of Lhasa. Built by King Songtsen Gampo in the 7th century, Jokhang—also known as the "Tsuglag Khang"— houses the Jo Rinpoche, the most sacred image in all Tibet. This statue of the youthful Buddha Shakyamuni was included in the dowry of Princess Wencheng, who came from China to wed King Songtsen Gampo in the 7th century (see no. 2). It is said in Tibet that upon arriving in Lhasa, one should visit the Jokhang directly, and touch one's forehead to the knees of the Lord Buddha before the perspiration from the journey has dried on one's face.[1]

Seated on a high throne, the Jo Rinpoche is clothed in rich brocades, and his tall golden crown and shoulder cover are completely studded with jewels (Figure 2). His original face, covered by many layers of gold leaf through the centuries, is beyond recognition. Pilgrims and locals have given great quantities of their personal jewelry to this image, much of which can be seen on the silver pillars and on the gilt aureole behind the image, which is surmounted by the mythical bird Garuda. When Taktra was the Regent of Tibet, during the present Dalai Lama's minority, he purchased a beautiful eighteen-carat diamond from the high official named Tsarong Shapé, to be used as a centerpiece in a headdress that he offered to the Jo Rinpoche.[2] Numerous silver and gold butter lamps are lit throughout the day in front of the image, constantly replenished with butter from the pilgrims.

Figure 1
Potala Palace
Photo: Barry Waldman.

Opposite Page
Figure 2
Statue of Jo Rinpoche
inside the Jokhang, Lhasa
Photo: Tamara W. Hill

Lhasa sits in a broad valley, in the center of which are two rocky formations. The smaller one is Chagpori (Iron Hill), where the Medical College once stood, and the larger one is Marpori (Red Hill), which is dominated by the Potala, a massive white building with glittering gold roofs housing the mortal remains of past Dalai Lamas (Figure 3). 'Potala' is the Tibetan version of 'Potalaka,' the island abode of Avalokiteshvara, the Lord of Compassion. Its designation is especially appropriate because the Dalai Lamas are regarded as human manifestations of this compassionate god.

Because of Red Hill's strategic position, King Songtsen Gampo built his fortress there during the 7th century. A thousand years later, Desi Sangye Gyatso, the Regent of Tibet, began his construction of the Potala under the direction of the Fifth Dalai Lama. The Fifth Dalai Lama died before the palace was completed some twelve years later, but the Regent kept the death a secret for nine years, knowing very well that the laborers, hauling rocks and lumber free of charge, would stop work right away if they knew that their beloved leader was no longer living.

The Dalai Lamas, together with the Panchen Lamas in southern Tibet, are the leaders of the Gelug ('Virtuous Ones') Order, one of the four existing orders of Tibetan Buddhism. Founded by the reformer Tsong Khapa (1357-1419) in the late 14th century, this order, stressed scholarship, strict adherence to monastic rules, and celibacy. When a Dalai Lama dies, his assistants go all over Tibet to look for his rebirth, following clues left by the departed Lama himself, words of wisdom from the State Oracle, or visions seen by regents. The rebirth, a young boy, is chosen after a series of vigorous tests, including the ability to recognize his former possessions. "Dalai" is a Mongolian term meaning "ocean," and "Lama" is a Tibetan term for "spiritual master." The title thus indicates a spiritual master whose wisdom is as vast as the ocean.

Figure 3
Gold Roofs of the Potala
Photo: Peter C. Keller, Ph.D.

When the third Dalai Lama, Sonam Gyatso (1543-1588), went to Mongolia to convert the Mongols, he was given this honorific title by the Mongol leader Altan Khan (r. 1543-1582). He, in turn, retroactively applied this title to his two predecessors. During the reign of the Fifth Dalai Lama, the Mongols came to his aid in wars against local kings and other orders and made him the undisputed ruler of Tibet.

Against the deep blue Tibetan sky, the Potala Palace, with its blinding white walls is a magnificent example of 17th century Tibetan architecture. Successive Dalai Lamas lived in the central section of the Potala, which is painted crimson. The white section housed the administrative center of the Tibetan government. At least three authors have commented on the white-washing of the Potala and other houses in Lhasa which occurred annually in the months between September and December. The noblewoman Dorje Yudon Yuthok wrote that the whitewash was a soft chalk-like powder (*kara*) from north Tibet, and the proportion of the paint was one-third powder mixed with two-thirds water, stirred to the consistency of yogurt.[3] Spencer Chapman, (Private Secretary to Mr. B. J. Gould, Political Officer), who visited Lhasa in 1936, witnessed mixing of the paint mixture in a well beneath the Potala. A brigade of women then carried the whitewash in wooden or earthenware buckets and simply threw the paint onto the wall, both from below and from the roof above.[4] For the areas that could not be reached by the paint, men suspended from yak-hair ropes would finish the rest of the job, and also polish the gilt ornaments on the roof. Heinrich Harrer, who actually filmed the whole process, wrote that it took a hundred workers fourteen days to complete this task.⁵

Upon walking into the Potala, one is overwhelmed by its vast and rich furnishings. There are magnificent wall paintings everywhere, and every inch of the ceiling is covered with lengths of Chinese brocade, many of which date back to the Ming (1368-1644) and Qing (1644-1911) Dynasties, and some of which are uncut dragon robes. Chinese silk was, and still is, an important item of trade, and gift exchanges between Dalai Lamas and Chinese emperors always included bolts of this luxury fabric.

The audience halls are hung with textile awnings, and gold is the all pervasive color; it is found on the many gilt images, and especially on the floor to ceiling stupas containing the remains of the past Dalai Lamas. Ever since its completion in the early 17th century, the Potala has been a treasury for the possessions of the various Dalai Lamas. In fact, two of the four government treasuries of Tibet are located inside the Potala. Sir Charles Bell, the British Political Officer who befriended the thirteenth Dalai Lama (r.1876-1933), wrote about the Trede Treasury in the Potala, where revenues from the estates of the Dalai Lama and the government were stored along with money, butter, oranges from southern Tibet, and lumps of gold from Western Tibetan mines. Bell also mentioned the second treasury in the Potala, called "The Treasury of the Sons of Heaven," which housed gold, corals, and diamonds — a reserve treasury to meet the urgent needs of wars and calamities.⁶ In addition to the treasuries, there are at least two storehouses for textiles in the Potala. Gyeten Namgyal, the tailor who served both the thirteenth and fourteenth Dalai Lamas, was supplied with textiles for his work from the Namse Treasury in the upper reaches of the Potala. While he waited outside, officials had to remove their robes before entering there for fear of being accused of stealing. Namgyal noted another storage area, dug right into the mountain under the Red Palace, through which he had to light his way with torches.⁷

Figure 4
Stupa of Tupten Gyatso, the thirteenth Dalai Lama
Photo: *Gems of the Potala Palace*, p. 175.

The stupas containing the mummified bodies of past Dalai Lamas stand out as the most awe-inspiring monuments inside the Potala Palace. There are seven altogether, the ones belonging to the Fifth and Thirteenth Dalai Lamas being the most impressive. The nobleman Tsipon Shuguba remembered that when the thirteenth Dalai Lama died in December 1933 at the age of fifty-eight, slow mournful ritual drums sounded from the Potala and lamps were placed on the roof. Tibetans went into mourning by lowering prayer flags and other decorations from their homes; men unwound their hair, and women removed their jewelry and aprons.⁸ According to Gyeten Namgyal, who was among the eighty tailors selected to make brocade decorations for the memorial stupa, the preservation of the remains of the Dalai Lama and construction of his stupa took about a year. The mummification took place inside the Potala, where the body fluids were extracted with salt in a traditional manner. After the body was dried, it was covered in gold.⁹ The stupa of the thirteenth Dalai Lama was over forty-two feet high making it necessary to raise the roof of the Potala had to be raised (Figure 4). According to Heinrich Harrer over a ton of gold was used for gilding the surface of this memorial.¹⁰ Many officials donated their long earrings for decorating its exterior, and Gyeten Namgyal not only gave up his earring, he also made sure that it was the first to be placed in front of the stupa.¹¹ The noble ladies of Lhasa donated their jewelry for the tomb, and Rinchen Dolma Taring contributed a large turquoise and pieces of amber.¹²

The Potala is the winter residence of the Dalai Lamas. Although it is splendid and imposing externally, Heinrich Harrer found it "miserably dark and uncomfortable as a dwelling place."¹³ In the summer, the Dalai Lamas (at least the thirteenth and fourteenth) and their retinue moved to Norbulingka (Jewel Park), departing the Potala in a long procession along the two mile stretch between the two palaces. Norbulingka was begun by the seventh Dalai Lama in the 18th century, and finished by the thirteenth Dalai Lama. Its grounds, surrounded by a wall, are planted with willows and poplars. Within the grounds, a higher twelve-foot wall encloses the residence which consists of a number of small palaces and temples, and beautiful gardens planted with fruit trees and rare plants. While visiting Norbulingka, Sir Charles Bell saw at least ten types of flowers being cultivated, and also noticed many animals, including large and small dogs, deer, monkeys, porcupines, snow cock, pheasants, a leopard, and a Bengal tiger. All the animals, caged as well as free-roaming, were well cared for.[14] The thirteenth Dalai Lama definitely preferred his summer palace to the Potala. Stories circulated about his return to the Potala in autumn with much pomp and circumstance. As soon as the crowds were out of the way, he got into one of his three automobiles to be driven back to Norbulingka.[15] The fourteenth Dalai Lama found endless diversions at the Norbulingka. He enjoyed his walks in the beautiful gardens, feeding the fish, and watching the numerous animals. In addition to the ones mentioned above, there were camels, parrots, cranes, and even Canadian geese.[16] Jetsun Pema, younger sister of the fourteenth Dalai Lama, also loved the Norbulingka. She recalled her joy in watching the peacocks, and gathering walnuts on windy days, occasionally receiving bumps on her head as the nuts fell off the trees.[17]

The Nobility of Lhasa
The nobility of Tibet is made up of three groups. The first is a small group of people descended from the early kings. Another small group, originally from the peasant class, were ennobled because of their relationships to the Dalai and Panchen Lamas. The third and last group, which is also the largest, was comprised of officials who rose in rank by merit, having been given title and land in return for government service. All these nobles exercised great influence and power. They shared the higher government posts with the monk officials. Many nobles owned large tracts of land as did the monasteries, and had overseers in charge of their estates, supplying them annually with grains, butter, and wool. Many of the noble families employed their own traders, sending them off to India, Mongolia and China on trading missions, thus becoming even richer. Some of the main items of Tibetan export were wool, salt, borax, yak tail (used in India for making fly whisks and in the West for Santa Claus beards), musk, and medicinal herbs. They were traded for Chinese tea and silk, gold and silver, precious gems (diamonds, rubies, pearls, and sapphires), semi-precious stones (turquoise, coral, and amber), cotton and woolen goods, sugar, tobacco, hardware, machinery, and luxury goods.

In Lhasa were many private schools where children were taught to read and write, to do some arithmetic, and to memorize prayers. For those pursuing careers as officials, two schools had been established: one for the training of monks, and another for the training of lay people. Young monks were trained for an official career in a special school inside the Potala, while lay people attended school in the Finance Office, where they learned accounting and correspondence. The thirteenth Dalai Lama, under the influence of Sir Charles Bell, had sent four young Tibetans to be educated in London. An English school was started in Gyantse, in southern Tibet, and was attended by thirty aristocratic boys; it was soon disbanded after a few years due to objections from the conservative faction.[18] In 1922, when she was thirteen years old, Rinchen Dolma Taring, a member of the Tsarong family, became the first girl to be sent off to Darjeeling in India, to attend an American Methodist boarding school. Other noble families soon began to send their own children to missionary schools in India. The present Dalai Lama's youngest sister was educated in Catholic schools in Kalimpong and Darjeeling.

While noble sons studied to become officials, daughters, after finishing their schooling, learned how to run a household. Dorje Yudon Yuthok helped her mother keep track of the household accounts and kept records of various transactions, which included the goods received from various estates, those which were sent from their own estate to another, goods purchased for storage, and materials that went out on loan.[19] Heinrich Harrer noticed that every trifling object was locked and double-locked in Lhasa households and that the lady of each house always carried a large bunch of keys with her.[20]

Visitors to Tibet often commented on the beautiful jewelry worn by the nobility. Tibetans love jewelry, especially turquoise and coral. Despite this fondness, they would not hesitate to donate their jewelry to religious images and monuments (such as the mortuary stupas of high Lamas) as such donations were considered pious acts.

Tibetan jewelry differs from region to region and varies according to the status of its wearer. Tibetans followed the Chinese ranking system for government officials, establishing their own corresponding dress and jewelry codes. While there were nine ranks in China, there were only eight in Tibet. The Prime Minister, an officer of the first rank, wore a pearl on his headdress; the four ministers of the Kashag, being of the second rank, wore rubies.[21] Although most Tibetan men wore earrings, officials wore odd pairs, the left earring being three inches long, and made of gold, turquoise, and pearl. For practical reasons, the pointy element on the bottom of the earring was made of glass, imitating the color of turquoise, so it would not cost much to replace if it broke (see no. 89). According to Heinrich Harrer, each man was obliged to present to his wife only those jewels that accorded with his rank, and a promotion in rank was accompanied by a corresponding promotion in jewelry! Having wealth alone did not give a person the right to wear expensive jewels.[22]

Around 1929, the thirteenth Dalai Lama observed that the fascination with jewelry was driving many families into debt and hardship. In order to move around in high circles, many wives of the poorer officials had to borrow money to buy elaborate costumes and ornaments.[23] The thirteenth Dalai Lama not only forbade these women to borrow money, he essentially decreed that women were not to keep or wear an abundance of precious and expensive ornaments. The Dalai Lama decreed that such items as the pearl headdress (*mutig patruk,* see no. 96), could only be worn by women from families of the fourth rank or above. He issued regulations limiting the jewelry of fourth rank women to five hundred *dotse* in worth, and two hundred and fifty *dotse* for that of lower-ranking women.[24] He further established the *patruk* (see nos. 97 & 98) as the primary ornament for women below the fourth rank. Considering that the ordinary *patruk* was already studded with turquoise and corals, and that six *dotse* could purchase an ounce of gold in those days, the stern mandates did not seem too harsh. For a few years, the women of Lhasa tried to comply with the decree, but the craze for elaborate jewelry revived soon after the Dalai Lama's death in 1933.

The *patruk* mentioned above is the triangular headdress worn by the ladies of Lhasa. In 1939, prior to her arrival in Lhasa, several of these pearl and coral headdresses (*mutig patruk*) were presented to the Gyalyum Chenmo, mother of the present Dalai Lama. She found them too heavy and did not wear them, preferring her own jewelry from Amdo. Reting Rinpoche, the Regent, thought it appropriate that the mother of a Dalai Lama should distinguish herself, and supported Gyalyum Chenmo's wearing of her own traditional clothes.[25] Ladies throughout Tibet wore various forms of head gear. In the Sakya and Gyantse areas they donned bow-shaped headdresses which extended a foot from each side of the head, and severely limiting the wearer's movements. This type of headdress, strung with strands of pearls, and studded with corals and turquoise, weighs about twenty-five pounds. When Jamyang Sakya, a girl from Kham (eastern Tibet) who married Jigdal Rinpoche of Sakya, wore such a headdress for the first time, the act of balancing it gave her a stiff neck.[26]

Wife of Tsarong wearing pearl Headdress (top:back view, bottom front view) Tibet, 1937
Photo: Theos Bernard
The Theos Bernard Collection, Gift of the Eleanor Murray Estate.
Phoebe A. Hearst Museum of Anthropology, University of California Berkeley (R XVII-17, T-38-pict)

One of the most important personal adornments of Tibet is the *gau*, the amulet box (see nos. 35, 36, 95, 100 & 101). This beautiful ornament, a receptacle for small painted or cast images, printed prayers and charms, and other relics, is traditionally worn by both men and women for protection. The appearance and decoration of *gaus* differed over time, according to shifting fashion trends and the personal tastes of their owners. Those made for noble ladies in the 1930s were studded with gems such as diamonds and sapphires. Noblemen wore smaller *gaus* in their braided hair: one on the very top, and a slightly larger one behind.

In addition to fantastic jewelry and headdresses, Tibetan nobility wore robes (*chuba*) of fancy brocades which were woven in China, Russia, and Japan. On special occasions, such as the second day of the New Year (The King's New Year), some nobles wore the royal *gyaluché* costume (see nos. 92 & 93) together with elaborate ornaments (see no. 94).[27] For

women, the item of clothing that is uniquely Tibetan, is the striped apron (*pangden*) of heavy silk or light weight wool dyed in the seven colors of the rainbow. Noble ladies — who designed their own jewelry — also designed their aprons and had them fabricated by their household weavers. Each color stripe varied in measurement, and the three lengths of cloth that comprised the apron were sewn together so that the color lines did not meet. Wearing both the headdress (*patruk*) and the apron for the first time, signaled a young woman's coming of age. Up until 1959, special coming of age ceremonies took place when a girl reached the age of sixteen. Dorje Yudon Yuthok felt proud and grown up when it was her turn to wear these adult fineries. Being tall for her age, she was only fourteen when the ceremony took place.[28]

The above accounts are taken from books written by foreigners who traveled to Tibet before the 1950s, and by Tibetans after the 1950s, describe a world that is no more. This exhibition of objects belonging to the Dalai Lamas and the nobility of Tibet, offers a glimpse into the past, and hopes for a better future.

LIFE IN LHASA, THE HOLY CITY

Pilgrim wearing Amulet Box (*Gau*) in Barkor Market
Photo: Peter C. Keller, Ph.D.

Tibetan men traditionally wear a 'kimono' style *chuba*, with left lapel wrapped over right, buttoned under the armpit. The robe is belted at the waist, and is worn over an inner shirt (usually white) with the collar showing. The material used denotes a man's rank. This *chuba*, which once belonged to a nobleman, is made of material used for making the dragon robes of the Chinese court. Such robes were without pockets; instead, the wide belt was used for attaching various useful objects like pen cases (stuck diagonally in its folds), prayer beads, eating implements, and wallets. Following the Manchu custom of the Qing Dynasty court, Tibetan noblemen used eating sets containing a knife and a pair of chopsticks, hung behind their backs on the right, while their wallets were attached to the left.

Tibetan officials wear a single long earring on their left ears. It was usually gold and turquoise; the pointed bottom pendant, however, is turquoise colored glass. The summer hat is decorated with red tassels, and the jewel on top indicates the status of the wearer. A Tibetan official of the first rank wore a pearl, second rank a ruby, third a coral, and fourth a turquoise.

89
Garments for a Nobleman
Tibet, 19th - 20th century
Robe: L: 158 cm; L (sleeve): 77 cm
Cap: H: 11.5 cm; W: 33 cm
Ear ornament: L: 14 cm
Boots: H: 41 cm; L: 27.5 cm
Cover for knife: L: 31 cm
Tibet Museum, Lhasa
Published: *Treasures from Snow Mountains*, p. 172, no. 84

90
Cloak for a Dalai Lama
Silk
Tibet, 19th century
L: 155 cm
Potala Palace Collection
Published: *Treasures from Snow Mountains*, p. 171, no. 83

Sumptuous Russian and Chinese brocades are used to make this elaborate cloak, which is further ornamented by otter fur and jewels. The Russian brocade shows a flamboyant design of white daisies against a gold background. A four-clawed dragon in frontal view, dramatic against a dark background, covers half of the back. The collar and lapels are especially impressive, lined with otter fur and ornamented with gems and pearls, with silk cords demarcating the area into rectangular fields.

Such cloaks are worn by high Lamas and abbots of important monasteries. A photo of the Twelfth Situ Tulku, taken in 1971, shows him wearing a cloak of a similar style.[1] The statue of the Thirteenth Dalai Lama, opposite his memorial stupa, also shows him wearing a similar cloak.

[1] Compiled by Nik Douglas and Meryl White, *Karmapa the Black Hat Lama of Tibet* (London: Luzac & Company Ltd., 1976), p.160.

LIFE IN LHASA, THE HOLY CITY

TIBET: TREASURES FROM THE ROOF OF THE WORLD

Of Chinese origin, the peacock robe is loose fitting with a round neck, side vents, and buttons in front. Peacock feathers are light and warm and make a sumptuous winter robe. The feathers are laid horizontally onto a blue-cloth support and sewn on individually. In China, such robes were worn by members of the aristocracy or by the very rich. The fact that the peacock robe is lined with yellow silk (the imperial color of the Qing Dynasty), indicates that it was a gift from one of the Qing emperors of China.

The peacock has an added significance in Tibetan Buddhism. It is the mount of Vairochana, one of the five Buddhas. In Indian mythology, the peacock feeds on snakes and poisonous plants while staying alive and beautiful. Thus the peacock can be compared to the Bodhisattvas (those on the path to Buddhahood), who transmute the poisons of worldly passions into the enlightened qualities of body, speech, and mind.[1]

91
Robe
Peacock feathers and silk
China, Qing Dynasty, early 20th century
L: 107 cm; W: 50 cm; L (sleeve). 54.2 cm
Tibet Museum, Lhasa

[1] Robert A. F. Thurman and David Weldon, *Sacred Symbols, The Ritual Art of Tibet* (New York: Sotheby's, Rossi & Rossi, 1999), no. 32.

Made of thick brocade woven with a dragon pattern, both of these short jackets have long sleeves made up of a collage of various strips of brocade. The collars and sleeve ends are lined with fur, with a fancy border of silk cord in a key fret pattern.

These two jackets are part of the *gyaluché* (royal dress) costume worn by officials during ceremonial occasions, such as the "King's New Year." The King's New Year was celebrated on the second day of the Tibetan New Year, when officials wore costumes re-creating those of the royal princes of ancient Tibet. This type of jacket was worn together with a black, pleated, long satin skirt, and a voluminous rainbow-colored shawl wrapped across the chest, under the right arm, and over the left shoulder. An official, presenting himself before the Dalai Lama in the Great Audience Hall of the Potala Palace, would remove this shawl and use it as a rug for prostrations, symbolizing the obeisance of the prince to his sovereign. Other accessories are the wide sashes for the waist, whose tasseled ends hang over the pleated black skirt, a white hat shaped like a cockle shell[1], worn over the topknot, and a charm box. A special set of gold and turquoise ornaments is worn at shoulder level; one is shaped like a whelk shell and the other is a flat rosette. Photographs of Tibetan noblemen wearing similar jackets can be seen in *Tibet, The Lost Civilisation*.[2]

---

[1] Spencer Chapman, *Lhasa: The Holy City* (London: Readers Union Ltd., 1940), p. 219.

[2] Simon Normanton, *Tibet, The Lost Civilisation* (London: Penguin Group, 1988), p.121. See also: Valrae Reynolds, "From a Lost World: Tibetan Costumes and Textiles," *Orientations* (March 1981): pp. 6-22; *From the Sacred Realm, Treasures of Tibetan Art from the Newark Museum* (Munich, London, New York: Prestel Verlag, 1999), p. 84.

92
Ceremonial Jacket with Dragon Patterns
Brocaded silk
Tibet, 17th -19th century
L: 192 cm; W: 58 cm
Tibet Museum, Lhasa
Published: *Tibet Museum Catalog*, pp. 214-215, no. 4

93
Ceremonial Jacket with Dragon Patterns
Brocaded silk
Tibet, 18th - 19th century
L: 194 cm; W: 58 cm
Tibet Museum, Lhasa
Published: *Tibet Museum Catalog*, pp. 214-215, no. 5

94
Ornaments for a Nobleman
Silver, gold and turquoise
Tibet, 19th century
Chest ornaments: H: 7 cm
Ear ornaments: H: 16.5 cm; L: 64 cm
Rosary: L: 100 cm
Potala Palace Collection
Published: *Treasures from Snow Mountains*, p. 165, no. 77

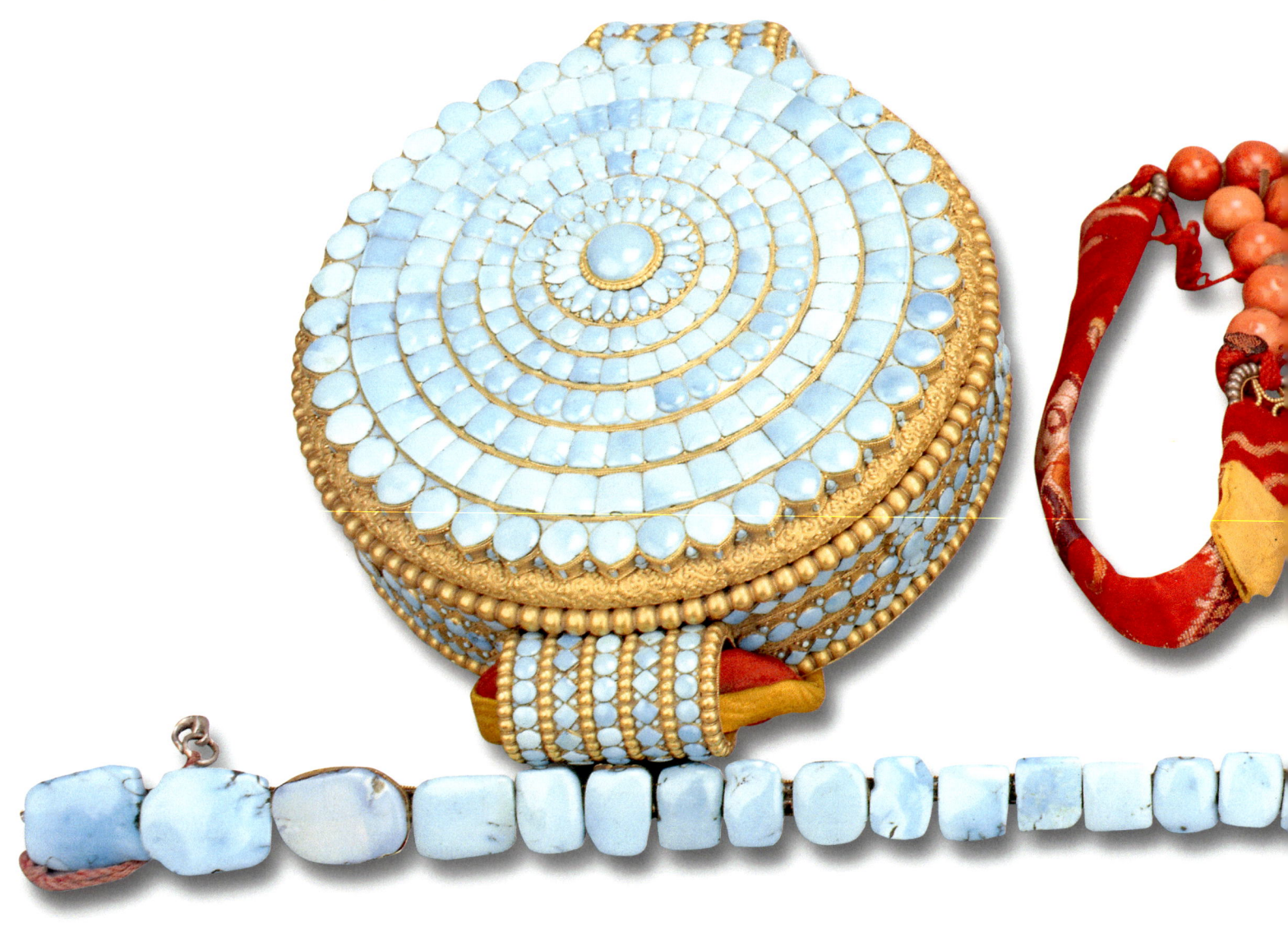

Life in Lhasa, The Holy City

The set of ornaments consists of a coral necklace, a strand of turquoise, a large gold and turquoise amulet box, and two smaller turquoise ornaments. On formal occasions, especially during the New Year celebration period, Tibetan noblemen wore such elaborate regalia together with the *gyaluché* costume (the "garment of royalty," a complex assemblage representing the costume of the ancient Tibetan). Spencer Chapman, who went to Lhasa in 1936-1937 as secretary to Mr. B. J. Gould (head of the British Mission to Tibet), described this garment and the accompanying jewelry:

> The junior officials wore a most attractive dress called geluche [*gyaluché*]. This consists of a short jacket of very thick brocade with long sleeves made up of several transverse strips of different coloured material. On each shoulder, set towards the front, were turquoise and gold ornaments, one shaped like a whelk shell and the other a flat rosette. In former times these were suspended from the top of the head and worn as earrings.[1]

The "whelk shell" described by Chapman is the smaller of the two ornaments bearing the *kyung* bird (a symbol of protection) on top, and the "flat rosette" is the ornament attached with a *vajra*. Notice the quality of the turquoise pieces; they are the type Tibetans prefer, mostly without flaws and black inclusions.

[1] Spencer Chapman, *Lhasa: the Holy City* (London: Readers Union Ltd., 1940), pl. 219.

The basic costume for the women of Tibet is a sleeveless floor-length garment known as a *chuba*, which is worn with a long-sleeved blouse. For the noble class, the *chuba* is often made from Chinese brocade. This versatile garment is wide and the excess is folded towards the back.

Married women wear a striped apron made from three lengths of narrow native woolen material, which is woven on a back strap loom. The patterns of the three lengths of cloth do not match, even though they come from the same bolt, resulting in an interesting effect. Triangular brocades decorate the top corners of the apron. Incorporating gold threads, these brocades came from China as well as Russia.

The noblewomen of Lhasa wear a triangular headdress (*patruk*) over their ornate hairdo, and elaborate ear ornaments with triple medallions inlaid with turquoise. Ladies of the fourth rank and above were allowed to wear a pearl *patruk*, while those of the fourth rank and lower wore coral and turquoise. All women wore a *gau* for protection as well as decoration. The *gaus* belonging to the nobility were often of gold, studded with turquoise, and coral, and, in 20th century examples, rubies, emeralds, and diamonds. The *gau* was accompanied by an elaborate necklace, strung with coral, pearls and *zi* beads (enhanced agate beads). A lady could wear numerous necklaces and also on the left shoulder, a flat band consisting of numerous strings of seed pearls.

95
Dress for a Noblewoman
Tibet, 19th - 20th century
Sleeveless dress: L: 143cm
Blouse: L: 53 cm; L (sleeve): 66cm
Overcoat: L: 130 cm
Apron: L: 74 cm; W: 58cm
Pearl necklace: L: 47 cm; W: 32.5 cm
Multi box: L: 30.5 cm; W: 11.5 cm
Ear ornament: L: 16cm; W: 5 cm
Boots: H: 38 cm; W: 23 cm
Tibet Museum, Lhasa
Published: *Treasures from Snow Mountains,* p. 173, no. 85

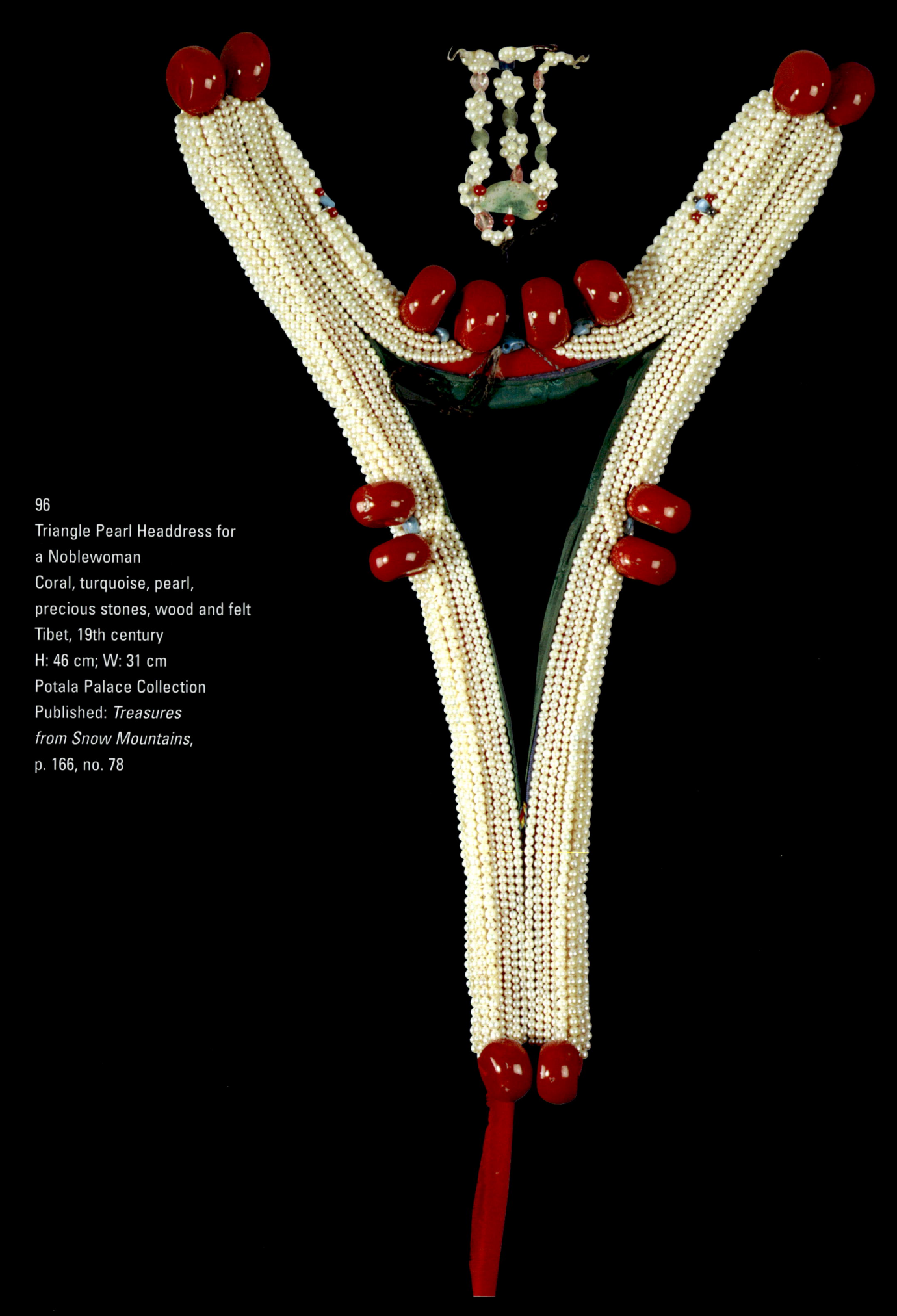

96
Triangle Pearl Headdress for a Noblewoman
Coral, turquoise, pearl, precious stones, wood and felt
Tibet, 19th century
H: 46 cm; W: 31 cm
Potala Palace Collection
Published: *Treasures from Snow Mountains*, p. 166, no. 78

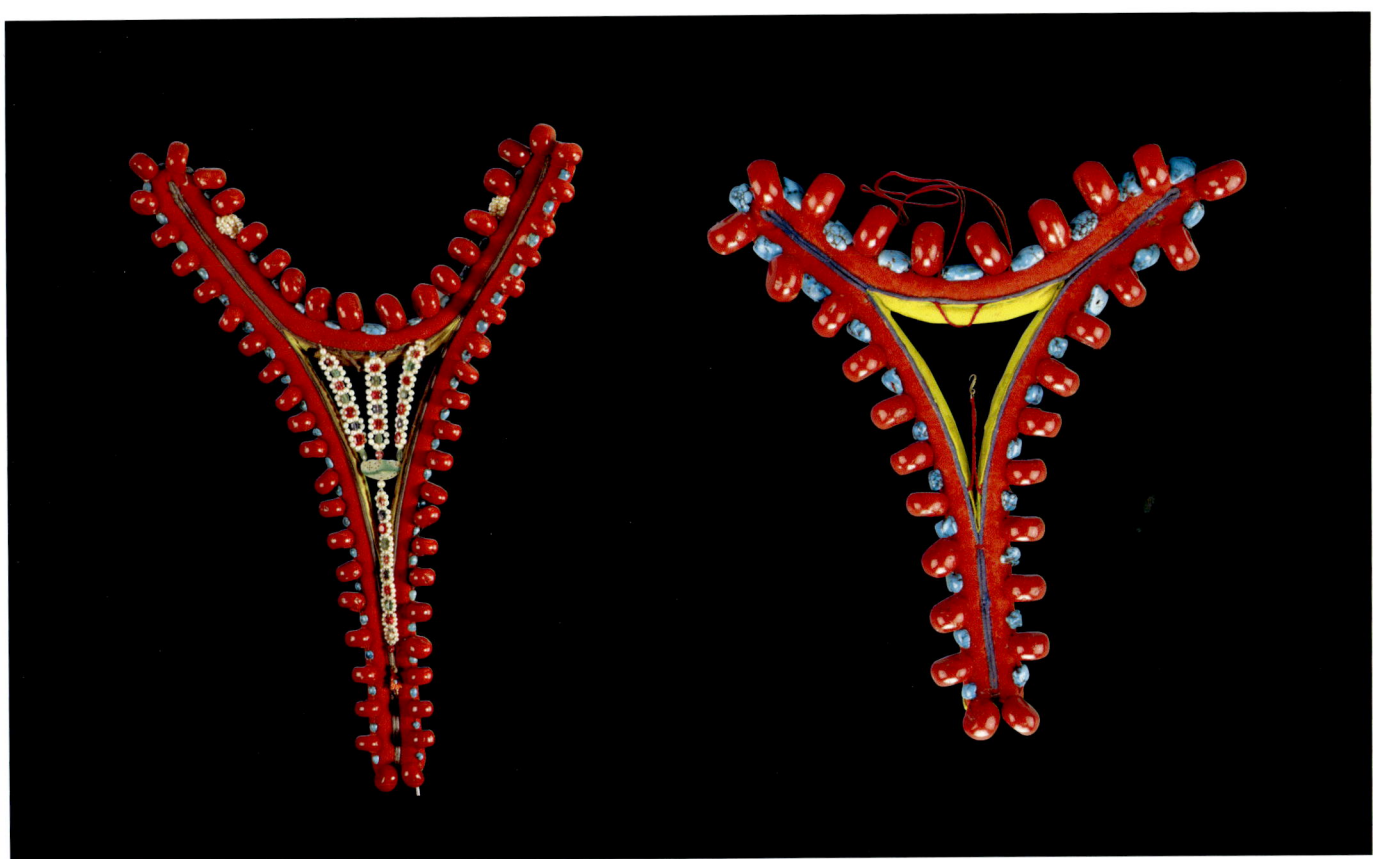

97
Triangular Coral Headdress
Coral, turquoise, pearl, precious stones, wood and felt
Tibet, 19th century
L: 53 cm; W: 34 cm
Potala Palace Collection
Published: *Treasures from Snow Mountains*, p. 167, no. 79; *Tibet Museum Catalog*, pp. 130-131, no. 2

98
Triangular Coral Headdress
Coral, wood, felt, turquoise and gems
Tibet, 18th century
L: 53 cm; W: 34 cm
Tibet Museum, Lhasa
Published: *Golden Treasures*, p. 320

Jewelry denotes a woman's status, wealth, and the region where she comes from. These impressive triangular headdresses, known as *patruk* (pronounced *patu*) are worn by the ladies of Lhasa. The framework is made of wood or some flexible material such as rattan or bamboo, and then padded with felt and silk and sewn with coral, turquoise, and pearls. While the red corals hail from the Mediterranean, the pearls are imported from India and from Basra in Iraq. The pieces of jadeite (originating in Burma) were worked in China. Placed upon their large hairdos, the headdresses are worn with the two points upward.

In Lhasa, ladies of the Fourth Rank or higher (the First Rank being the highest) wear the pearl headdress or *mutig patruk*, while those of the Fourth Rank or lower wear the coral headdress. Wives of rich merchants could also wear the coral headdress. Noble ladies possessed at least three headdresses or more, and like women elsewhere, they loved to possess jewelry and tried to outdo each other in their finery during social functions.

Gyalyum Chenmo, mother of the Dalai Lama, before reaching Lhasa in 1939, was presented with such headdresses of pearls and coral.[1] She found them too heavy and did not wear them, preferring her own jewelry from Amdo.

[1] Diki Tsering, *Dalai Lama, My Son*, edited and introduced by Khedroob Thondup, (New York: Viking Arkana, 2000), p. 104.

TIBET: TREASURES FROM THE ROOF OF THE WORLD

99
Pearl Crown
Tibet, 18th century
H: 19 cm; D: 24.5 cm
Tibet Museum, Lhasa
Published: *Tibet Museum Catalog,* p.130, no. 1; *Golden Treasures,* p. 321; *Precious Deposits,* vol. 5, p. 171, no. 101

Strung with thousands of tiny pearls, this beehive-shaped crown is a magnificent work of art. Interspersed with turquoise and gold beads, it is surmounted by a turquoise and gold ornament. Noblewomen of central and southern Tibet wore such crowns over their headdresses during festivals and important ceremonies. Similar examples can be found in Beijing and in the National Palace Museum, Taipei. The pearls, on a published example from Rehol, were strung with twisted paper.[1]

[1] National Palace Museum, *Monarchy and Its Buddhist Way: Tibetan-Buddhist Ritual Implements in the National Palace Museum* (Taipei: National Palace Museum, 1999), no. 36.

LIFE IN LHASA, THE HOLY CITY

TIBET: TREASURES FROM THE ROOF OF THE WORLD

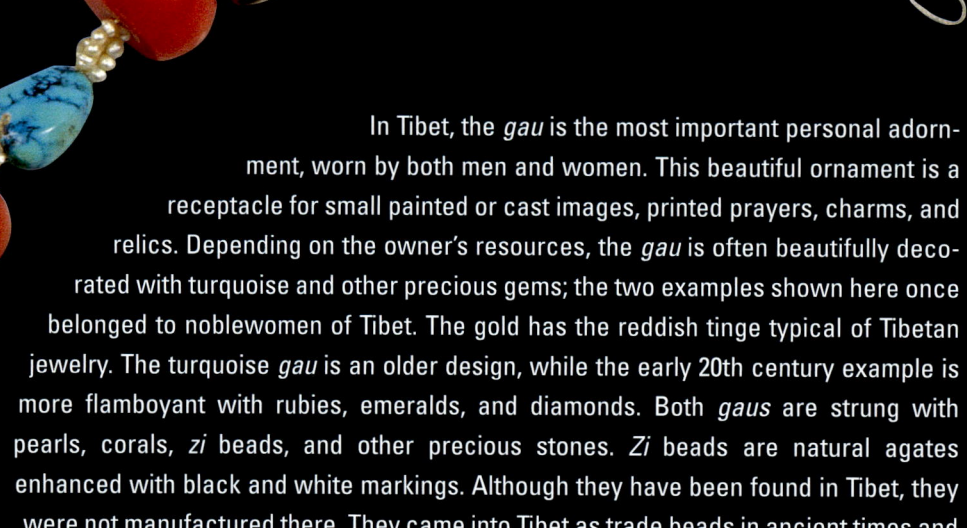

In Tibet, the *gau* is the most important personal adornment, worn by both men and women. This beautiful ornament is a receptacle for small painted or cast images, printed prayers, charms, and relics. Depending on the owner's resources, the *gau* is often beautifully decorated with turquoise and other precious gems; the two examples shown here once belonged to noblewomen of Tibet. The gold has the reddish tinge typical of Tibetan jewelry. The turquoise *gau* is an older design, while the early 20th century example is more flamboyant with rubies, emeralds, and diamonds. Both *gaus* are strung with pearls, corals, *zi* beads, and other precious stones. *Zi* beads are natural agates enhanced with black and white markings. Although they have been found in Tibet, they were not manufactured there. They came into Tibet as trade beads in ancient times and Tibetans consider them as powerful talismans against evil.

The noble ladies of Tibet loved to design their own jewelry. In *Seven Years in Tibet*, Heinrich Harrer described the daily activities of the noble ladies—how they spent hours making up their faces, restringing their necklaces, selecting new material for dresses, and thinking of how to outshine their friends at the next party.[1]

100
Necklace and Gold Chest Ornaments
Gold, turquoise, *zi* (*gzi*) beads, and coral
Tibet, 19th century
L: 49 cm
Tibet Museum, Lhasa
Published: *Treasures from Snow Mountains*, p. 170, no. 82;
Tibet Museum Catalog, pp. 212-213, no. 5

LIFE IN LHASA, THE HOLY CITY

101
Necklace with Amulet Box (*gau*)
Gold, sliver, turquoise, and coral
Tibet, 1930s
L: 34.8 cm; W: 15 cm
Potala Palace Collection
Published: *Treasures from Snow Mountains*,
p. 168, no. 80

¹Heinrich Harrer, *Seven Years in Tibet*, translated by Richard Graves. (London: R. Hart-Davis, 1953), p. 159.

225

102
Penholders
Wood inlaid with gilt copper
Tibet, 17th - 18th century
L: 37 cm; W: 4 cm
Tibet Museum, Lhasa
Published: *Treasures from Snow Mountains*,
p. 208, no. 118

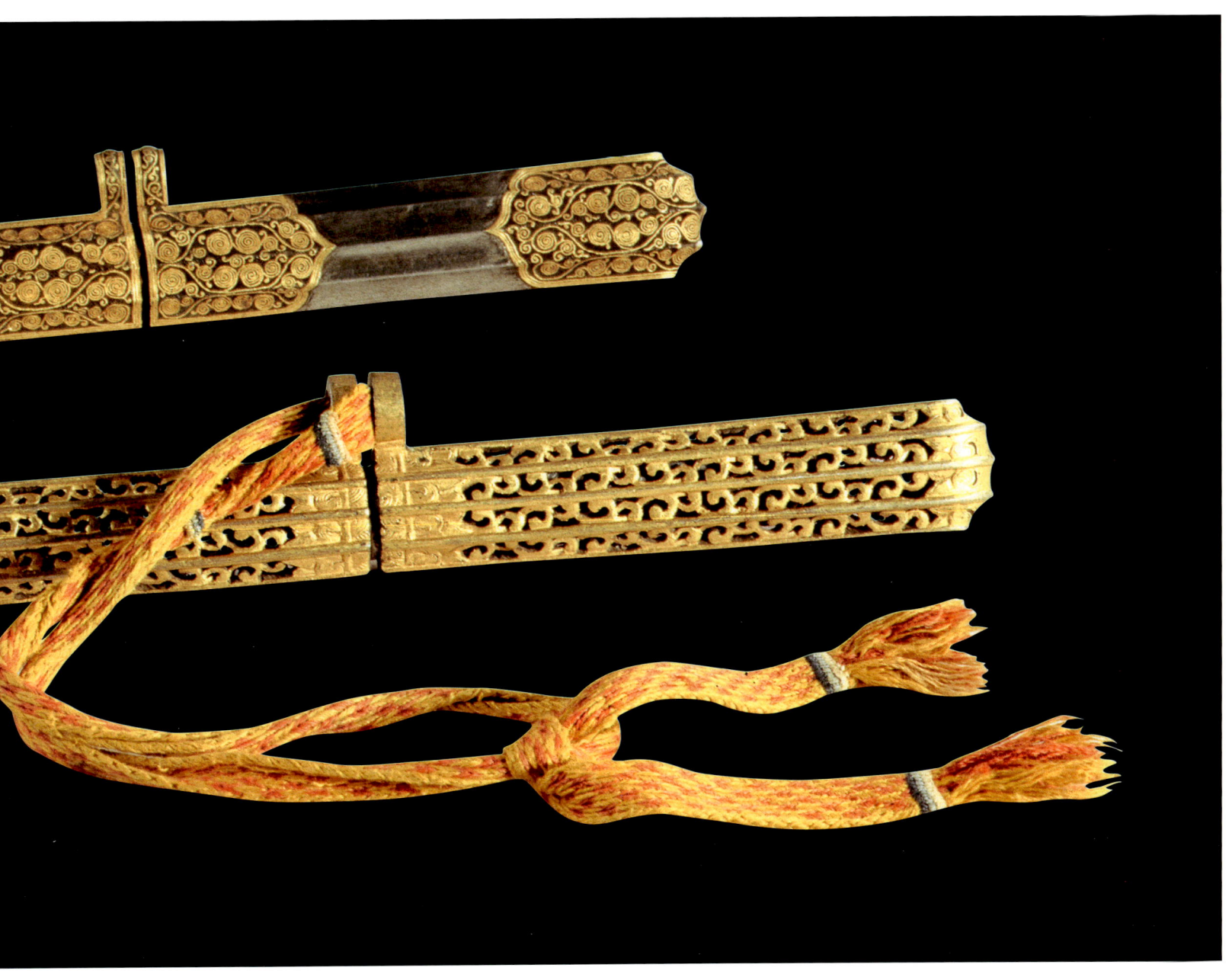

Although Tibetan pens are simply fashioned from bamboo or wood, their containers are beautifully worked in metal. These penholders consist of two sections, the body for holding the pens and the lids to keep them in place. Fitted tightly together, two rings are soldered to the joint, so that they can be strung with a cord and secured to a belt. Penholders can be made completely of metal or of wood ornamented with metal. Iron, copper, and silver are commonly used for penholders, with iron being the popular choice. The decorations are done in a variety of metal techniques such as gilding, chasing, damascened work, engraving, and openwork. These examples, made for the nobility, are beautifully gilded.

Penholders are carried by anyone who can write, be they commoners, scribes, noblemen, or monks. They are a mark of status, signifying that the owners are men of learning.

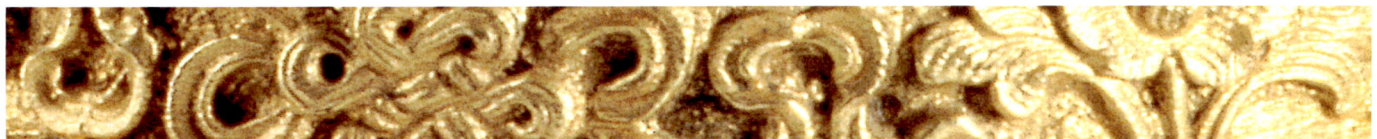

103
Inkpot
Silver, partially gilt
Tibet, 18th century
H: 15 cm; D: 7.5 cm
Tibet Museum, Lhasa
Published: *Well Selected*, no. 148; *Treasures from Snow Mountains*, p. 210, no. 120; *Precious Deposits*, vol.5, pp. 32-33, no. 6

Originally from the Norbulingka, this inkpot has a typical Tibetan shape: flat lid surmounted by a lotus bud-like terminal, bulbous body with a flat top, narrow waist, and circular foot. The lotus bud is chased with leaves, the bottom of the lid and top of the pot are ornamented with the Eight Buddhist Symbols connected with scarves and bound by two pearl borders, while a band of meanders decorates the base. All these decorations are gilded.

The inkpot is structured in such a way that when it is tipped over, the ink will not leak even when the pot is full. There are two iron balls inside the bottle, which keep the ink flowing when shaken. Tibetan ink is made from hide glue and soot. When school children practiced calligraphy they used a watered-down version.

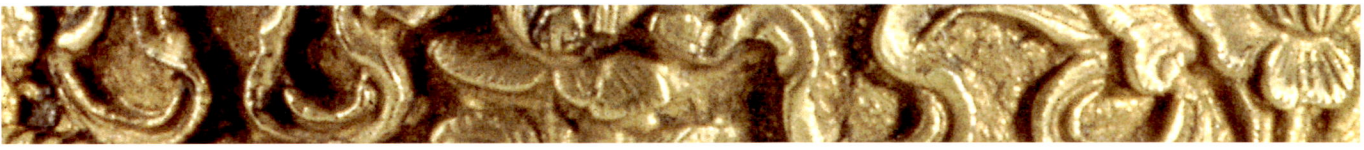

TIBET: TREASURES FROM THE ROOF OF THE WORLD

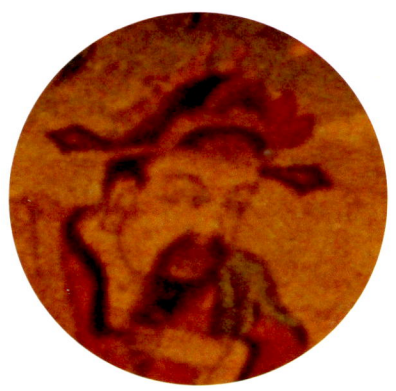

104
Stationery Box
Painted wood
Tibet, early 20th century
H: 5 cm; L: 34 cm; W: 6 cm
Tibet Museum, Lhasa
Published: *Well-Selected*, no. 150; *Treasures from Snow Mountains*, p. 209, no. 119; *Precious Deposits*, vol.5, p. 109, no. 52, pp. 140-141, no. 76, p. 164, no. 94, p. 166, no. 97; *Tibet Museum Catalog*, pp. 102-103, no. 2

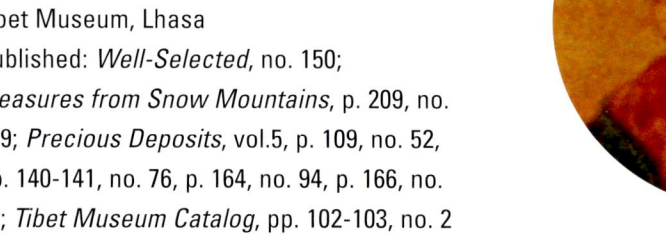

LIFE IN LHASA, THE HOLY CITY

While pens can be carried in penholders stuck in one's belt, in noble homes they are stored in wooden stationery boxes similar to this example, which belonged to the Norbulingka. The top and the sides are painted with scenes from Tibetan life and other auspicious motifs. Some of the subjects depicted are: the theme of the elephant, monkey, rabbit, and bird (a symbol of universal brotherhood); a noble household; an ascetic meditating in his grass shelter; farmers plowing; people traveling; merchants arriving with goods; and monks debating in a monastery.

In describing her home, Rinchen Dolma Taring remembered that in the shrine room a side table held her father's silver inkpot and lacquered pen case.[1]

[1] Rinchen Dolma Taring, *Daughter of Tibet* (London & Southampton: The Camelot Press Ltd., 1970), p. 3.

The message board (Tibetan: *samdra*) is an ingenious device for saving precious handmade paper. The two painted covers enclose double-sided blank boards used for sending formal messages between officials or noble households. Prior to writing with a bamboo or wooden pen, the boards are greased with butter, and then coated with a fine layer of ash or white chalk. The boards are then stacked together and the raised borders protect the message from being scratched. They are then placed in an elegant case and carried by a servant to the recipient who, after wiping off the first message, repeats the process and inscribes a reply.

This fairly large set was used by officials. The top, bottom, and sides are lacquered red, and decorated with gold traceries. The four reserves depict Chinese immortals and their attendants in a landscape, painted by a Tibetan hand.

Two Tibetan noble women have written about the use of *samdra* in their autobiographies. In *Daughter of Tibet*, Rinchen Dolma Taring recorded her experience when she worked for Tsarong, the one-time Commander-in-Chief of the Tibetan army.[1] When letters came to Tsarong from the Thirteenth Dalai Lama, they were written on similar tablets about nine inches by two, painted black and dusted with white chalk powder. Her job was to copy the letters immediately, as the tablets had to be returned right away. Jamyang Sakya, in *Princess in the Land of Snows*, wrote that when the Prince of Sakya asked her uncle for her hand, he wrote the message in a *samdra*, bound together with a decorated band of leather and silk, and sealed and wrapped in a white silk scarf.[2]

---

[1] Rinchen Dolma Taring, *Daughter of Tibet* (London: Wisdom Publications, 1986), p. 74.

[2] Jamyang Sakya and Julie Emery, *Princess in the Land of Snows: The Life of Jamyang Sakya in Tibet* (Boston & Shaftesbury: Shambhala, 1990), pp. 79-80.

105
Set of Writing Boards
Wood, painted and gilded
Tibet, late 19th early 20th century
L: 50.5 cm; W: 12 cm
Tibet Museum, Lhasa
Published: *Treasures from Snow Mountains*, p. 209, no. 119

Used to secure the front doors of the White Palace, within the Potala, this iron lock is an object of historical interest as well as artistic merit. This is the largest lock known to date from Tibet. The workmanship is exquisite, consisting of chased four-claw dragons and leafy tendrils inlaid with gold. The key is also chased and gilded, and the top end has a hole that can be strung with a cord. Before the application of gold, the iron ground was scratched, so that the precious metal could adhere better. There are basically two types of Tibetan locks, those that release by pushing in the key vertically and those where the key is inserted horizontally. This example is the horizontal type.

When Diki Tsering, the mother of the present Dalai Lama, visited the Potala for the first time, she noticed the huge iron locks on the wooden entrance doors on all sides of the Potala.[1] As everywhere else in the world Tibetans used locks to secure their homes and their belongings. The lady of the house was identified by the large ring of keys dangling from her belt.

The lock works on the barbed-spring principle, just like a barb that moves forward easily but resists backward movement. The springs spread out when the lock is secured, thus preventing removal until the key is inserted to compress the springs, and the lock opens.

This type of lock is commonly used in countries throughout the Middle East to China, where such locks were already in use during the Tang Dynasty. It may have been introduced to Tibet in the 7th century when the Chinese Princess Wencheng married King Songtsen Gampo.

[1] Diki Tsering, *Dalai Lama, My Son*, edited and introduced by Khedroob Thondup (New York, Viking Arkana), p. 110.

106
Lock from the Potala Palace
Iron and gold
Tibet, 17th century
H: 16.5 cm; L: 60 cm
Potala Palace Collection
Published: *Treasures from Snow Mountains*, p. 212, no. 122;
Precious Deposits, vol. 5, pp. 130-133, no. 68

107
Surgical Instruments
Iron
Tibet, ca. 17th century
Box: H: 27.5 cm; W: 22.5 cm
Longest one: 25 cm
Shortest one: 9 cm
Tibet Museum, Lhasa
Published: *Well-Selected*, no. 151; *Precious Deposits*, vol. 4, pp. 234-236, no. 105; *Tibet Museum Catalog*, p. 106, no. 4

Life in Lhasa, The Holy City

These finely crafted instruments, originally from a set of ninety, are ornamented with silver and gold. They are used for external therapies, such as incision, excision, scraping, and extraction. External therapy is one of the four kinds of remedies in traditional Tibetan medicine, the others being conduct, diet, and internal medication.[1] Among the instruments are tools for probing and scraping, for making incisions, and for excision. There are forceps of interesting shapes for extracting foreign bodies from deep wounds, one of them in the shape of a lion's mouth. There are also lancets for bloodletting, a spatula, and scrapers for removing hemorrhoids.

Inlaid in some of these instruments is the name "Dar." This suggests that these were the instruments of Janggo Dargye (Byang ngos Dar rgyas), court physician and personal physician to the Fifth Dalai Lama. Judging from the quality of these instruments, there is a real possibility that this could be true. The Fifth Dalai Lama was certainly interested in medicine. In 1662, Janggo Dargye requested that the Fifth Dalai Lama have woodcuts carved for a new xylographic version of the 16th century edition of the *Four Tantras*, an ancient medical text of uncertain origin, considered the fundamental treatise on medicine in Tibet. Sangye Gyamtso (1653-1705), the Regent of Tibet at that time, wrote the *Blue Beryl Treatise* in 1687-1688, a commentary to the *Four Tantras*. At the same time, he designed extraordinary illustrations to accompany his commentary. Instruments similar to these can be found among the illustrations in the *Blue Beryl Treatise*.[2]

[1] Yuri Parfionovitch, Gyurme Dorje and Fernand Meyer, eds., *Tibetan Medical Paintings, Illustrations to the Blue Beryl Treatise of Sangye Gyamtso (1653-1705)* (New York: Harry N. Abrams, Inc., 1992), vol. 1, pl. 34.

[2] Ibid, vol. 1, p. 84.

Just as Americans care about their automobiles and their furnishings, Tibetans pay close attention to their horses and horse trappings. Horses provide the major means of transportation in Tibet and their saddles reflect the wealth and status of their owners. This saddle, for a Dalai Lama, is a masterpiece in gilt copper repoussé technique. The top register of decoration on the pommel shows a *kirtimukha* (face of glory) (a monster mask for warding off evil). Two dragons confronting the Eight Buddhist Symbols (combined into one image) occupy the second section. The third register shows the three flaming jewels, representing the Buddha, his teachings, and the Buddhist community. All these designs are surrounded by curling tendrils and are further enhanced with turquoise.

The padding on the seat is made of sumptuous non-Chinese brocade and the stirrups follow the traditional design of two confronting dragons whose mouths meet to form an opening for the stirrup strap.

108
Saddle for a Dalai Lama
Gilt copper and turquoise
Tibet, 18th - 19th century
Overall: H: 50 cm
Overall: L: 60 cm
Tibet Museum, Lhasa
Published: *Tibet Museum Catalog*, p. 137; *Precious Deposits*, vol. 5, pp. 90-91, no. 37

Life in Lhasa, The Holy City

TIBET: TREASURES FROM THE ROOF OF THE WORLD

109
Stem Cup
Jade, gold, and semi-precious stones
China and Tibet, 18th century
H: 12 cm; D (mouth): 13.5 cm; D (foot): 4 cm
Tibet Museum, Lhasa
Published: *Treasures from Snow Mountains*, p. 190, no. 100; *Tibet Museum Catalog*, pp. 202-203, no. 2

Tibetans drink numerous cups of buttered tea every day. While the majority of Tibetans use wooden cups turned on a lathe, noblemen and high monks drink from cups made of precious materials. Fine cups of jade and porcelain are provided with elaborately made lids and stands. The earlier of these two jade cups (no. 109) is nephrite from Hetian (Khotan), in present-day Xinjiang province. Its profile with a flared mouth rim and deep belly is typical of the Qianlong period of the Qing Dynasty (1736-1795). On the other hand, the foot covered in gold shows Tibetan workmanship. Flaring lotus petals support the base of the cup, inlaid with precious stones. Two rows of beading ornament the top and bottom of the foot. This piece has its own wooden container with gilt copper decoration.

The second example (no. 110) is a cup made from jadeite, a precious stone from Burma, but carved in China. Both the lid and stand are finely worked in Tibetan gold, which has a reddish tinge, and are further embellished with pearls, turquoise, diamonds, and other precious stones. The addition of diamonds and other stones indicates a 20th century date. The top knot is red coral.

In describing her father's room in *Daughter of Tibet*, Rinchen Dolma Taring mentioned her father's jade cup with a silver stand and lid on his elaborately carved lacquered table. Three smaller lacquered tables in the same room always held "at least one cup with a silver stand and lid, so that tea could be served immediately to visitors."[1] When Chogyam Trungpa (the founder of a large meditation center in Boulder, Colorado) visited Akong Tulku at the Drolma Lhakhang, he was served tea in a jade cup on a gold and silver stand and rice was offered to him in a jade bowl, while his monks ate their food in dishes made of Chinese porcelain.[2]

[1] Rinchen Dolma Taring, *Daughter of Tibet* (London & Southampton, 1970), p. 3.
[2] Chogyam Trungpa, *Born in Tibet* (New York: Penguin Books, Inc., 1972), p. 82.

110
Jade Cup with Gold Lid and Cup Stand
Jadeite, gold, turquoise, pearls, precious stones, and coral
China and Tibet, 18th - 20th century
Cup: H: 19.8 cm; D (mouth): 11 cm; D (foot): 4 cm
Cup Stand: D (mouth): 14 cm; D (base): 7 cm
Tibet Museum, Lhasa
Published: *Treasures from Snow Mountains*, p. 194, no. 104; *Tibet Museum Catalog*, p.196, no. 1

Life in Lhasa, The Holy City

Made to hold a Ming Dynasty porcelain stem cup, this openwork gilt copper case is a consummate work of art and demonstrates the care Tibetans lavished on fine Chinese porcelain. To protect these fragile vessels, Tibetans made cases of wood, leather, and other materials, such as this example in gilt copper.

Writhing dragons, their claws clasping jewels, decorate the lid, body, and foot of the cup case. They are shown against leafy tendrils rendered in openwork. Boldly worked meanders ornament the side of the lid and the mouth rim, while square lugs on opposite sides engraved with coin motifs are designed to hold a strap.

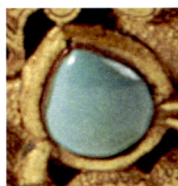

111
Cup Case
Gilt copper and turquoise
Tibet, 14th - 17th century
H: 15 cm; D (mouth): 18 cm; D (base): 6 cm
Tibet Museum, Lhasa
Published: *Treasures from Snow Mountains*, p. 189, no. 99; *Tibet Museum Catalog*, p. 128, no. 2

112
Teapot
Gold inlaid with turquoise
Tibet, 20th century
H: 26 cm; D (mouth): 14 cm; D (base): 12 cm
Tibet Museum, Lhasa
Published: *Well Selected*, p. 117; *Tibet Museum Catalog*,
p. 194, no. 3; *Treasures from Snow Mountains*, p. 198, no. 108

This magnificent gold teapot for serving milk tea (*suja*) originally came from the Norbulingka. It has a lotus lid chained to the dragon handle and a spout formed by the mouth of a *makara*, a crocodile-like mythical beast of Indian origin that is associated with water. Over two hundred pieces of turquoise ornament this gold teapot. Besides being a precious metal for showing off one's wealth, gold is believed to have the ability to detect poison.

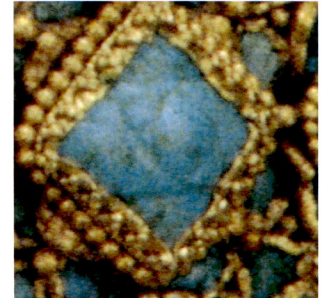

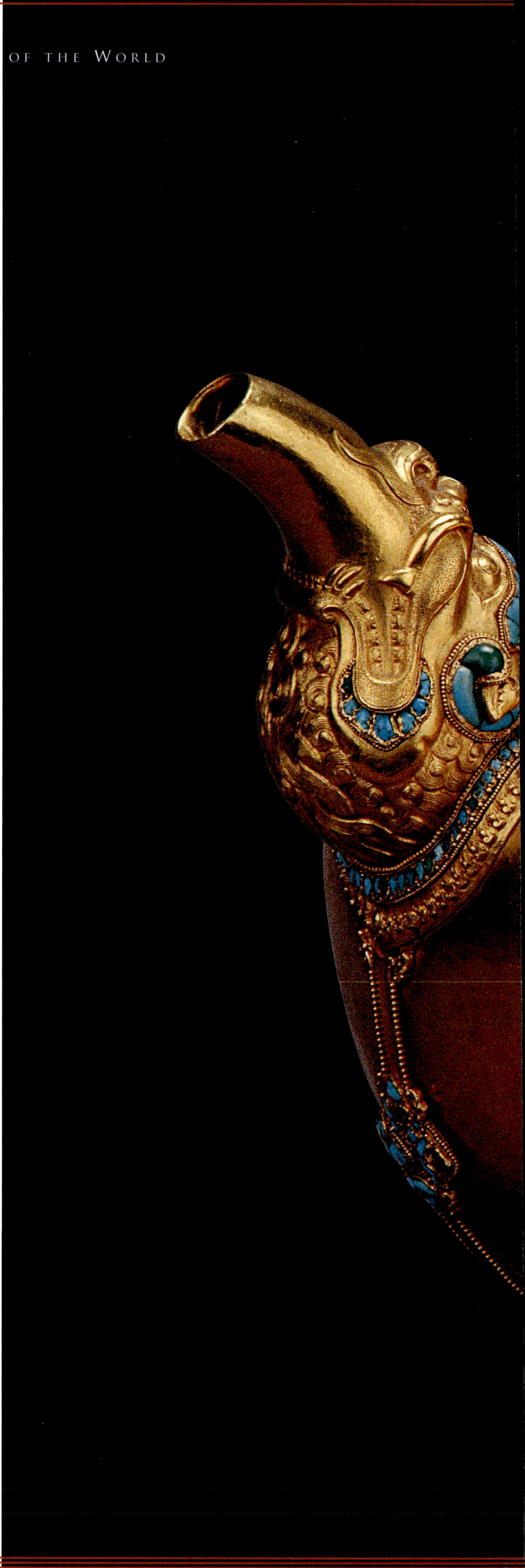

Life in Lhasa, The Holy City

Food containers in Tibet are commonly made of wood banded by metal. Here, the wooden prototype has been reproduced in gold inlaid with turquoise. The vertical and horizontal bands serve only a decorative function, and are beautifully chased and inlaid with turquoise. The exquisitely worked lid is surmounted by a lotus knob, which rests on a lotus base. Such an object would have been used only by the noble class or by very high monks.

113
Food Container
Gold inlaid with turquoise
Tibet, 19th century
H: 35 cm; D (mouth): 18 cm; D (base): 21 cm
Tibet Museum, Lhasa
Published: *Treasures from Snow Mountains*, p. 193, no. 103; *Tibet Museum Catalog*, p. 194, no. 2

LIFE IN LHASA, THE HOLY CITY

Opposite Page
114
Pitcher
Gilded silver
Qing Dynasty, 1644-1912
H: 48 cm; D (mouth): 12 cm; D (base): 12 cm
Tibet Museum, Lhasa
Published: *Treasures from Snow Mountains*, p. 195, no. 105; *Tibet Museum Catalog*, p. 204, no. 1

These two vessels are based on a Tibetan metal-hoop like wooden prototype, which is used for serving beverages. The top portions of both resemble monks' caps. Porcelains incorporating this design were already produced by Ming Dynasty potters (see no. 42). This porcelain pitcher from the Kangxi period is covered with a three-color glaze, in emulation of the *sancai* (three-color) glaze used in China during the Tang (618-906) and Liao (907-1125) Dynasties. During the Qing Dynasty, emperors often resurrected ancient Chinese glazes. They also typically sent Tibetan rulers gifts that imitated Tibetan vessel shapes.

The partially gilt silver vessel was also made in China, but is later in date (late Qing Dynasty, 19th - early 20th century). Although the spout follows Tibetan convention in having the shape of a *makara* (a crocodilian creature), the handle differs from Tibetan examples, which usually take the form of a dragon.

115
Pitcher
Pottery with polychrome glaze
China, Qing Dynasty, Kangxi Period (1662-1722)
H: 42.4 cm; D (mouth): 12.5 cm
Tibet Museum, Lhasa
Published: *Treasures from Snow Mountains*, p. 197, no. 107; *Tibet Museum Catalog*, pp. 204-205, no. 3

TIBET: TREASURES FROM THE ROOF OF THE WORLD

116
Basin with Phoenix
Gold and turquoise
China, Qing Dynasty, 18th century
D: 36 cm; D (foot): 18.8 cm
Tibet Museum, Lhasa
Published: *Golden Treasures*, p. 292

Gifts from the emperors of China were often lavish and of the best workmanship, an ongoing effort to inspire awe in their recipients. These two golden vessels were gifts to the Dalai Lama and were crafted in the imperial workshops in the Forbidden City in Beijing. The plate shows an auspicious motif of two dragons frolicking among clouds, contending for the flaming pearl. The sides are in the shape of chrysanthemum petals, conveying a wish for longevity, while the scalloped edge is finely decorated with floral designs.
    The basin bears a mythical phoenix spreading its wings and the Eight Auspicious Symbols. Along the rim are over fifty turquoises and other semi-precious stones. This basin was used for serving food—beef, mutton, or deep-fried pastries—to the Dalai Lamas. Dragons and phoenixes are the most important mythical animals of China and are part of the standard decorative repertoire for imperial objects.

117
Plate with Double Dragon Designs
Gold
China, Qing Dynasty (1644-1911)
H: 3 cm; D (brim): 25.5 cm; D (base): 18 cm
Potala Palace Collection
Published: *Treasures from Snow Mountains*, p. 200, no. 110

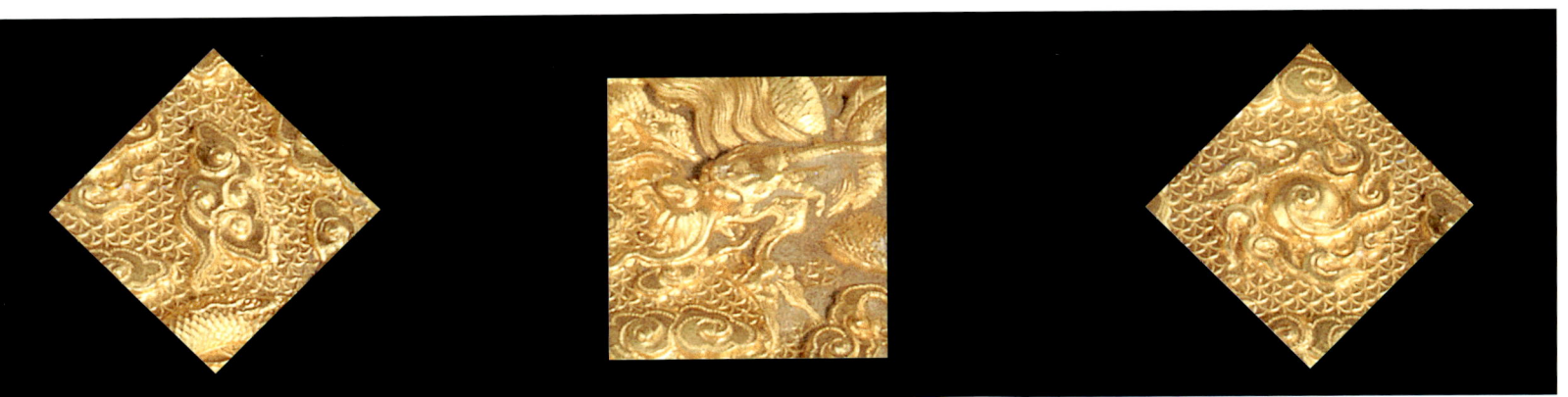

Endnotes

Chapter 1: Tibet: Its Land and History

1. Giuseppe Tucci, *To Lhasa and Beyond* (Roma: Istituto Poligrafico Dello Stato, 1956), p.14.

2. Tarthang Tulku, et al., *Ancient Tibet* (Berkeley: Dharma Publishing, 1986), pp. 70-73.

3. Ibid, p. 54ff.

4. R. A. Stein, *Tibetan Civilization* (Stanford: Stanford University Press, 1972), p. 248.

5. Ibid, p. 15-22.

6. Li Huaizhi, et al., *Tibet* (Shanghai: Shanghai People's Publishing House, 1981), p. 49.

7. Thubten Jigme Norbu and Colin M. Turnbull, *Tibet* (New York: Simon and Schuster, 1968), pp. 28-29. See also: John Powers, . *Introduction to Tibetan Buddhism* (New York: Snow Lion, 1995), pp. 122-123.

8. Tarthang Tulku, et al., *Ancient Tibet*, p. 91.

9. John Powers, *Introduction to Tibetan Buddhism*, pp. 126-127.

10. Gos Lo tsa wa ba gZon nu dPal (1392-1481). *Deb-ther sngon po,* trans. by George N. Roerich as *The Blue Annals* (Delhi: Motilal Banarsidass, 1979), p. 219. See also: Powers, p. 127.

11. David Snellgrove and Hugh Richardson, *A Cultural History of Tibet* (Boulder: Prajna Press, 1980), p. 74.

12. Tarthang Tulku, et al., *Ancient Tibet* , p. 209.

13. H.H. Tenzin Gyatso, the XIV Dalai Lama of Tibet, *The Opening of the Wisdom-Eye*, (Bangkok: Social Science Association Press of Thailand, 2511, 1968), pp. 3-4.

14. Valrae Reynolds, *From the Sacred Realm* (New York: The Newark Museum, 1999), p.26.

15. Nyingma traditions hold these *terma* texts to be teachings given by Padmasambhava, and then concealed in various forms to be revealed in later times by *tertons* (treasure revealers) who were Padmasambhava's disciples assigned to take rebirth for that purpose. See: Guiseppe Tucci, *The Religions of Tibet,* trans. by Geoffrey Samuel (Berkeley: University of California Press, 1988), p. 38-39.

16. Helmut Hoffmann, *The Religions of Tibet,* trans. by Edward Fitzgerald (New York: Macmillan Company, 1961), pp. 135-139.

17. Ibid, pp. 166-167.

18. H.H. Tenzin Gyatso, the XIV Dalai Lama of Tibet, *The Opening of the Wisdom-Eye*

19. Tsering Shakya, *The Dragon in the Land of Snows* (New York: Columbia University Press, 1999), pp. 2-6.

20. Li Huaizhi, et al., *Tibet*, pp. 14 ff. See also: Tsering Shakya, *The Dragon in the Land of Snows*, pp. 314-347. See also: Shakabpa, Tsepon W. D., *Tibet: A Political History* (New Haven: Yale University Press, 1967); and John F. Avedon, *In Exile from the Land of Snows* (New York: Vintage, 1979), pp. 221-319.

Chapter 3: Sacred Arts of Tibet

1. Pratapaditya Pal, *Himalayas, An Aesthetic Adventure* (Chicago: The Art Institute of Chicago in association with the University of California Press and Mapin Publishing), 2003, Catalog nos. 176-177.

2. Sumner Carnahan with Lama Kunga Rinpoche, *In the Presence of My Enemies, Memoirs of Tibetan Nobleman Tsipon Shuguba* (Santa Fe: Clear Light Publishers, 1995), p.136.

3. Gyeten Namgyal as recounted to Kim Yeshi, "A Tailor's Tale," in *Cho Yang, The Voice of Tibetan Religion & Culture*, 1994, No. 6, p. 28-63

4. Ian Alsop, "Repoussé in Nepal," *Orientations* (July 1986), pp. 14 – 27.

5. Heinrich Harrer, *Seven Years in Tibet* (New York, E. P. Dutto and Company, Inc., 1954), p. 215.

6. U.C. Ibid, p. 255.

7. See catalog essay, "Life in Lhasa, the Holy City," Figure 2; *Precious Deposits*, vol. 1, pls. 60, 77.

Chapter 3: Diplomatic Gifts

1. Christopher Beckwith, *The Tibetan Empire in Central Asia: A History of the Struggle for Great Power Among Tibetans, Turks, Arabs and Chinese During the Early Middle Ages* (Princeton: Princeton University Press, 1987), p. 24. Beckwith cites Liu Xu, *Jiu Tangshu* (Old History of the Tang), (Beijing, 1975 edition), 3:52.

2. Ibid, pp. 25-26, citing Sima Guang, *Zizhi tongjian* (Beijing, 1956 edition), 199: 6269-6270.

3. See, for example, *Zhongguo shiku: Dunhuang Mogao ku* (Tokyo: Heibonsha Ltd., 1988), vol. 4, pl. 91.

4. See *Chugoku sekkutsu: Ansei Yurinkutsu* (Tokyo: Heibonsha Ltd., 1990), pls. 143, 153.

5. See Heather Stoddard, "A Stone Sculpture of mGur mGon-po, Mahakala of the Tent, Dated 1292," *Oriental Art* n.s., 31, no. 3 (Autumn 1985): 278-82, for a Yuan-Dynasty image of Gurgyi Gompo dated 1292

ENDNOTES

6. See Anning Jing, "The Portraits of Khubilai Khan and Chabi by Anige (1245-1306), a Nepali Artist at the Yuan Court," *Artibus Asiae* 54, no. 1-2 (1994): 49-86.

7. For a detailed study of Yongle's sea expeditions, see *Louise Levathes, When China Ruled the Seas: The Treasure Fleet of the Dragon Throne, 1405-1433* (New York and Oxford: Oxford University Press, 1994).

8. The entire 54 foot-long hand scroll is reproduced in *Precious Deposits* (Beijing: Morning Glory Publishers, 2000), vol. 3, no. 48, pp. 94-137. For much more on this plenary mass and its ramifications, see H. E. Richardson, "The Karma-pa Sect. A Historical Note," *Journal of the Royal Asiatic Society* (October 1958), 139-164; (April, 1959), 1-17; and Patricia Berger, "Miracles in Nanjing: The Fifth Karmapa's Journey to the Chinese Capital," in Marsha Weidner, ed., *Cultural Transactions in Later Chinese Buddhism* (Honolulu: University of Hawaii Press, 2001), 145-169.

9. See Heather Karmay, *Early Sino-Tibetan Art* (Warminister, England, Phillip Aris, 1974) for complete historical sources.

10. See David Farquhar, "Emperor as Bodhisattva in the Governance of the Ch'ing Empire," *Harvard Journal of Asiatic Studies* (1975): 5-35, for the first detailed study of this period of Qing-Tibetan relations. See also Patricia Berger, *Empire of Emptiness: Buddhist Art and Political Authority in Qing China* (Honolulu: University of Hawaii Press, 2003).

11. *Donghua quanlu,* Shunzhi X, 13.

12. For a complete study of the temples at Chengde and their function in Qing diplomacy, see Anne Chayet, *Les temples de Jehol et leurs modèles tibétains* (Paris: Editions Recherche sur les Civilisations, synthèse no 19, 1984). See also Terese Tse Bartholomew, "Thangkas for the Qianlong Emperor's Seventieth Birthday," in Marsha Weidner, ed., *Cultural Transactions*, pp. 170-188; and Patricia Berger, *Empire of Emptiness*, especially pp. 14-23, 180-2.

Chapter 4: Life in Lhasa: The Holy City

1. Rato Khyongla Nawang Losang, *My Life and Lives, The Story of a Tibetan Incarnation* (New York, E.P. Dutton), 1977, p.43.

2. Dundul Namgyal Tsarong, *In the Service of His Country, The Biography of Dasang Damdul Tsarong, Commander General of Tibet* (Ithaca: Snow Lion Publications, 2000), p.109.

3. Dorje Yudon Yuthok, *House of the Turquoise Roof* (Ithaca: Snow Lions Publications, 1990), pp. 61-62.

4. F. Spencer Chapman, *Lhasa, The Holy City* (London: Readers Union Ltd. by arrangement with Chatto & Windus, 1940), p. 176.

5. Heinrich Harrer, *Seven Years in Tibet* (New York, E. P. Dutton and Company, Inc., 1954), pp.266-67.

6. Sir Charles Bell, *Portrait of a Dalai Lama, The Life and Times of the Great Thirteenth* (London, Wisdom Publication, 1987) First published in 1946 by Wm. Collins, London, p.186.

7. Gyeten Namgyal as recounted to Kim Yeshi, "A Tailor's Tale," in *Choyang, The Voice of Tibetan Religion & Culture*, No. 6, 1994, p.42.

8. Sumner Carnahan with Lama Kunga Rinpoche, *In the Presence of My Enemies, Memoirs of Tibetan Nobleman Tsipon Shuguba* (Santa Fe, Clear Light Publishers, 1995), pp. 65-66; Gyeten Namgyal as recounted to Kin Yeshi, "A Tailor's Tale," p. 35.

9. Gyeten Namgyal as recounted to Kim Yeshi, "A Tailor's Tale," p. 36.

10. Heinrich Harrer, p. 227.

11. Gyeten Namgyal as recounted to Kim Yeshi, "A Tailor's Tale," p. 36.

12. Rinchen Dolma Taring, *Daughter of Tibet* (London: John Murray, 1970), p. 114-115.

13. Heinrich Harrer, p.186.

14. Sir Charles Bell, pp. 266-267.

15. Heinrich Harrer, p.187.

16. Tenzin Gyatso, the Fourteenth Dalai Lama of Tibet, *Freedom in Exile* (New York: Harper Collins, 1991), p. 36.

17. Jetsun Pema, *Tibet My Story* (Boston: Element Books Inc., 1998), pp. 9-10.

18. Dundul Namgyal Tsarong, *In the Service of His Country*, p. 62.

19. Dorje Yudon Yuthok, *House of the Turquoise Roof*, p. 59.

20. Heinrich Harrer, p.159.

21. John Clarke, *Tibet: Caught in Time* (Reading: Garnet Publishing Limited, 1997), p. 113.

22. Heinrich Harrer, p. 142.

23. Rinchen Dolma Taring, *Daughter of Tibet,* p. 114.

24. Dorje Yudon Yuthok, *House of the Turquoise Roof,* p. 189.

25. Diki Tsering (Edited and Introduced by Khedroob Thondup), *Dalai Lama, My Son* (New York: Viking Arkana, 2000), p.104.

26. Jamyang Sakya & Julie Emery, *Princess in the Land of Snows: The Life of Jamyang Sakya in Tibet* (Boston & Shaftesbury: Shambhala, 1990), p.102.

27. Hugh Richardson, *Ceremonies of the Lhasa Year* (London: Serindia Publications, 1993), pp. 14-17.

28. Dorje Yudon Yuthok, *House of the Turquoise Roof*, p.196.

Bibliography

Abbreviations:

Collection of Historical Archives of Tibet
Compiled by The Archives of the Tibet Autonomous Region, A *Collection of Historical Archives of Tibet* (Beijing: Cultural Relics Publishing House, 1995).

Gems of the Potala
Liu Hongxiao, *Gems of the Potala* (Beijing: China Nationality Art Photograph Publishing House, 1999).

Golden Treasures
National Museum of History and Tibet Museum, eds., *Jinse Baocang (Golden Treasures)* (Beijing: Tibetan Press, 2001)

Potala Catalog
Tibetan Administrative Office of the Potala, *The Potala: Holy Palace in the Snow Land* (Beijing: China Travel and Tourism Press, 1996).

Precious Deposits
Zla-ba-tshe-ring, et al., *Precious Deposits* (Beijing: Morning Glory Publishers, 2000).

Well-Selected
The Management Committee of Cultural Relics of the Tibetan Autonomous Region, ed., *Xicang Wenwu Jingcui, A Well-Selected Collection of Tibetan Cultural Relics* (Beijing: The Forbidden City Publishing House of the Palace Museum, 1992).

Tibet Museum Catalog
Tibet Museum, ed., *Tibet Museum* (Beijing: Encyclopedia of China Publishing House, 2001).

Treasures from Snow Mountains
Shanghai Museum, *Treasures from Snow Mountains: Gems of Tibetan Cultural Relics* (Shanghai: Shanghai Books and Paintings Publisher, 2001). Wenwu 9, 1985

Xizang tangka
Cultural Relics Committee of the Tibetan Autonomous Region, ed., *Xicang Tangka* (*Tibetan Thangkas*) (Beijing: Wenwu chubanshe, 1985).

Suggested Reading

Alsop, Ian, "Repoussé in Nepal" *Orientations* (July 1986).

Avedon, John F., *In Exile from the Land of Snows* (New York: Vintage, 1979).

Bartholomew, Terese Tse, "Thangkas for the Qianlong Emperor's Seventieth Birthday," in Marsha Weidner, ed., *Cultural Transactions in Later Chinese Buddhism* (Honolulu: University of Hawai'i Press, 2001).

Beckwith, Christopher, *The Tibetan Empire in Central Asia: A History of the Struggle for Great Power Among Tibetans, Turks, Arabs and Chinese During the Early Middle Ages* (Princeton: Princeton University Press, 1987).

Bell, Sir Charles, *Portrait of a Dalai Lama, The Life and Times of the Great Thirteenth* (London: Wisdom Publication, 1987). First published in London: Wm. Collins, 1946.

Berger, Patricia, "Miracles in Nanjing: The Fifth Karmapa's Journey to the Chinese Capital," in Marsha Weidner, ed., *Cultural Transactions in Later Chinese Buddhism* (Honolulu: University of Hawai'i Press, 2001).

Berger, Patricia, *Empire of Emptiness: Buddhist Art and Political Authority in Qing China* (Honolulu: University of Hawai'i Press, 2003).

Bernard, Theos, *Penthouse of the Gods* (New York & London: Charles Scribner's Sons, 1939).

Bills, Sheila C.,"Bronze Sculptures of the Early Ming (1403-1450), Tibet in China, China in Tibet," *Arts of Asia* (September-October 1994).

Bills, Sheila C., "Sino-Tibetan Sculpture: The Tibetan Legacy," *Marg*, Vol. XLVII, no. 4, 1996.

Carnahan, Sumner, with Lama Kunga Rinpoche, *In the Presence of My Enemies, Memoirs of Tibetan Nobleman Tsipon Shuguba* (Santa Fe: Clear Light Publishers, 1995).

Chapman, Spencer, *Lhasa: the Holy City* (London: Readers Union Ltd., 1940).

Chayet, Anne, *Les temples de Jehol et leurs modèles tibétains* (Paris: Editions Recherche sur les Civilisations, synthese n 19, 1984).

Chogyam Trungpa, *Born in Tibet* (New York: Penguin Books, Inc., 1972).

Clarke, John, *Tibet: Caught in Time* (Reading: Garnet Publishing Limited. 1997).

Dagyab, Loden Sherap, *Tibetan Religious Art* (Wiesbaden: Otto Harrassowitz, 1977).

Dawa Norbu, Tibet, *The Road Ahead* (London: Rider, 1998).

Diki Tsering, *Dalai Lama, My Son*, edited and introduced by Khedroob Thondup (New York: Viking Arkana, 2000).

Farquhar, David, "Emperor as Bodhisattva in the Governance of the Ch'ing Empire," *Harvard Journal of Asiatic Studies* (1975), pp. 5-35.

Gos Lo tsa wa ba gZon nu dPal (1392-1481), *Deb-ther sngon po*, Trans. By George N. Roerich as *The Blue Annals* (Delhi: Motilal Banarsidass, 1979).

Gyeten Namgyal as recounted to Kim Yeshi, "A Tailor's Tale," in *Cho Yang, The Voice of Tibetan Religion & Culture*, 1994, No. 6., pp. 28-63.

BIBLIOGRAPHY

Harrer, Heinrich, *Seven Years in Tibet*, translated by Richard Graves. (London: R. Hart-Davis, 1953).

Heller, *Tibetan Art: Tracing the Development of Spiritual Ideals and Art in Tibet, 600-2000 A.D.* (Milan: Jaca Book, 1999).

Hoffmann, Helmut, *The Religions of Tibet*, Trans. By Edward Fitzgerald (New York: Macmillan Company, 1961).

Hungkar Dorje, ed., *Kailash: A Journal of Himalayan Studies*, vol. III, no. 4 (1975)

Hungkar Dorje, ed., *Tangkas in Golog: The Tangka Album of Lung-ngon Monastery* (Qinghai: Golok Lung-ngon Monastery, 2001).

Huntington, Susan L. and John C., *Leaves from the Bodhi Tree: The Art of Pala India (8th-12th centuries) and Its International Legacy* (Dayton, Seattle and London, 1990).

Jackson, David P., and Janice A. Jackson, *Tibetan Thangka Painting: Methods and Materials* (London: Serindia publications, 1988).

Jamyang Sakya and Emery, Julie, *Princess in the Land of Snows: The Life of Jamyang Sakya in Tibet* (Boston & Shaftesbury: Shambhala, 1990).

Jetsun Pema, *Tibet My Story* (Boston: Element Books Inc., 1998).

Jing, Anning, "The Portraits of Khubilai Khan and Chabi by Anige (1245-1306), a Nepali Artist at the Yuan Court," *Artibus Asiae* 54, no. 1-2 (1994).

Karmay, Heather, *Early Sino-Tibetan Art* (Warminster, England: Aris and Phillips Ltd., 1975).

Levathes, Louise, *When China Ruled the Seas: The Treasure Fleet of the Dragon Throne, 1405-1433* (New York and Oxford: Oxford University Press, 1994).

Li Huaizhi, et al. *Tibet* (Shanghai: Shanghai People's Publishing house, 1981).

Malandra, Geri H., "The Mahabodhi Temple," in Janice Leoshko, ed., *Bodhgaya, The Site of Enlightenment* (Bombay: Marg Publications, 1988).

National Palace Museum, *Monarchy and Its Buddhist Way: Tibetan-Buddhist Ritual Implements in the National Palace Museum* (Taipei: National Palace Museum, 1999).

Normanton, Simon, *Tibet, The Lost Civilisation* (London: Penguin Group, 1988).

Pal, Pratapaditya, *Nepal, Where the Gods Are Young* (New York: The Asia Society, 1975).

Pal, Pratapaditya, *Indian Sculpture* (Los Angeles: Los Angeles County Museum of Art,1986).

Pal, Pratapaditya, *Art of the Himalayas: Treasures from Nepal and Tibet* (New York: Hudson Hills Press in association with The American Federation of Arts, 1991).

Pal, Pratapaditya, *Himalayas, An Aesthetic Adventure* (Chicago: The Art Institute of Chicago in association with the University of California Press and Mapin Publishing, 2003).

Parfionovitch, Yuri, Gyurme Dorje and Fernand Meyer, eds., *Tibetan Medical Paintings, Illustrations to the Blue Beryl Treatise of Sangye Gyamtso (1653-1705)* (New York: Harry N. Abrams, Inc., 1992).

Powers, John, *Introduction to Tibetan Buddhism* (New York: Snow Lion, 1995).

Rato Khyongla Nawang Losang, *My Life and Lives, The Story of a Tibetan Incarnation* (New York: E. P. Dutton, 1977).

Reynolds, Valrae, "From a Lost World: Tibetan Costumes and Textiles," *Orientations* (March 1981).

Reynolds, Valrae, *From the Sacred Realm, Treasures of Tibetan Art from the Newark Museum* (New York: The Newark Museum, 1999).

Rhie, Marylin, and Robert Thurman, *Wisdom and Compassion: The Sacred Art of Tibet* (New York ; San Francisco: Asian Art Museum of San Francisco and Tibet House in association with Harry Abrams, 1991).

Rhie, Marylin, and Robert Thurman, *Worlds of Transformation: Tibetan Art of Wisdom and Compassion* (New York: Tibet House, New York in association with The Shelley and Donald Rubin Foundation, 1999).

Richardson, Hugh E., "The Karma-pa Sect. A Historical Note," *Journal of the Royal Asiatic Society* (October 1958).

Richardson, Hugh, *Ceremonies of the Lhasa Year* (London: Serindia Publications, 1993)

Sangay Tenzin, Khempo and Gomchen Oleshey, "The Nyingma Icons. A Collection of line drawings of 94 deities and divinities of Tibet," translated by Keith Dowman in *Kailash: A Journal of Himalayan Studies*, vol. III, no.4 (1975)

Schroeder, Ulrich von, *Buddhist Sculptures in Tibet* (Hong Kong: Visual Dharma Publications, Ltd., 2001).

Schroeder, Ulrich von, *Indo-Tibetan Bronzes* (Hong Kong, 1981).

Shakabpa, Tsepon W. D., *Tibet: A Political History* (New Haven: Yale University Press, 1967).

Singer, Jane Casey, "Bodhgaya and Tibet," in Janice Leoshko, ed., *Bodhgaya, The Site of Enlightenment* (Bombay: Marg Publications, 1988).

Singer, Jane Casey and Philip Denwood, eds., *Tibetan Art: Towards a Definition of Style* (London: Lawrence King Publishing, 1997).

Snellgrove, David and Hugh Richardson, *A Cultural History of Tibet* (Boulder: Prajna Press, 1980).